POWER STRUGGLE

WHY ROLLING BLACKOUTS CONTINUE

ISAAC MALGAS

First published by Isaac Malgas, 2024

ISBN: 978-0-7961-3004-4 (print)

ISBN: 978-0-7961-3005-1 (e-book)

Cover design and typesetting by Gregg Davies Media

www.greggdavies.com

A luta continua; vitória é certa

DEDICATION

To those who have toiled and sacrificed for a sustainable African power sector

DISCLAIMER

This book is produced for educational and informational purposes. The opinions and views expressed are solely the author's and do not necessarily reflect the opinions and beliefs of affiliates.

While great care has been taken to accurately provide the contents and contexts in this book, the author assumes no responsibility or liability for any errors or omissions. The information contained herein does not constitute professional advice and no legal liability is accepted by the publisher or the author.

November 2023

PREFACE

POWER STRUGGLE – WHY ROLLING BLACKOUTS CONTINUE

Three major struggles frame South Africa's recent history. The **first**, a protracted political struggle for freedom, which in 1994 ushered in an era of democracy. Notwithstanding the country's relatively peaceful transition and the achievement of political freedom, it soon became clear that the political transition on its own would not bring about the promised improved living conditions for most South Africans.

The **second** struggle was consequently for economic freedom, as citizens realized that their hopes for better lives for themselves and their descendants required an opening of the economy to allow more people to share in the national prosperity of the country. While the economic policies enacted by the new government were aimed at uplifting the lives of the poor and marginalized, these policies largely failed to deliver the promised economic freedom to many ordinary South Africans.

In this context, the **third** important struggle emerges. A large part of the country's post liberation era has been marked with increasing bouts of rolling blackouts, and during this time period intermittent electricity power outages have become a regular way of life for ordinary South Africans. Insufficient electricity has resulted in decreased investment, low economic growth, increased unemployment, and waning productive capacity. The embedded hopes and aspirations of the first two struggles, has become dependent on South Africa overcoming this third struggle – the struggle to keep the lights on.

This book deals with the third struggle. It explores the factors that undermine the ethos promised by the first two struggles. It examines the challenges associated with ensuring sufficient electrical energy on the African continent in general, and specifically in South Africa. Moreover, it describes the factors that have contributed to the problems of insufficient electricity generation. Finally, it offers solutions for how policies, institutional frameworks and broader power sector reforms can be approached to resolve the problems of inadequate generation.

FOREWORD

POWER STRUGGLE

I was somewhat diffident when asked to write the foreword to this book, worried about the optics of a prologue penned by the brother of the author. As I gave the idea further thought it became clear that I was, to some extent, both a plausible and legitimate choice. At the time when I was asked, I was already performing a language edit and initial proofreading, which made me one of a small group of people who had already read the manuscript more than once. Moreover, my background working on climate change and environmental issues within civil society organisations had provided me with a slightly-more-than-general understanding of the country's energy sector.

That background had also, however, fostered in me a peremptory sense of what should be done versus what was actually being done regarding South Africa's energy mix. In my idealistic vision, back then, all fossil-fuel generated electricity must immediately be done away with and replaced with 'people's power,' in the form of decentralised renewable energy systems. My brother, an engineer working for Eskom, set out to convince me that it wasn't that simple. And so, many a post-lunch discussion on Sunday afternoons—some more heated than others—were dedicated to unpacking why it's not so simple. To that extent, I'd like to think I have a small share—however humble—in bringing this book into being.

As the title of the book implies, it deals with loadshedding, the rolling blackouts that has been experienced in South Africa over the last several years, seeking to provide a comprehensive account of why Eskom is unable to supply the electricity the country needs. In doing so, it will reveal that the story of South Africa's electricity supply industry is one of complexity, challenge, and, unfortunately, controversy. It is a sometimes-technocratic narrative, replete with bureaucracy and institutional dynamics, interwoven with threads of history, policy and economics. It is a journey through the national corridors of power and the influence of international multilateral organisations, tracing the arc of South Africa's electrification from its roots in the repressive Apartheid regime to the hopeful early flickering of democracy and the promise of equality, freedom and prosperity for all. At its heart lies Eskom, fuelling the growth of mining, manufacturing, and urbanization, its power lines crisscrossing the landscape like veins of progress. Yet, as the winds of change swept across South Africa, so too did the need for transformation within its electricity sector.

Energy reform is a key topic and point of departure for the range of issues discussed in this book. It describes the blueprints of electricity industry reorganization, aimed at changing national utilities from vertically integrated monopolies to competitive markets, which would deliver electricity at the lowest price. While this blueprint has worked well elsewhere in the world, no utilities in African countries have successfully undergone this transformation. To postcolonial

African governments, it would seem, privatisation of utilities and other state-owned enterprises (SOEs) is seen as akin to loss of sovereignty. In the idiom of the text, it is "viewed as being against the political interest of leaders in government since divestiture could undermine the government's ability to use public corporations as instruments of employment creation and patronage". To that end, political and social goals are often pursued at the expense of the commercial and performance goals of SOEs in question. The result is a hybrid market, in which the national utility remains dominant in the electricity market alongside a number of small private sector players, an arrangement which calls for the development of complex processes when it comes to energy planning, procurement of new generation capacity and regulation of the sector, to name but a few.

Another key element in the story is the environment, and the factors relevant to South Africa's coal-heavy energy mix as the country sought to respond to climate change and the imperative to decarbonise. Here we see the failure to harmonize energy policies across sectors and across different policy documents, inconsistencies between its climate change commitments and its integrated resource plans, the strategy and budget of its utility at odds with its renewable energy procurement programme. Also explored through the narrative are more nuanced issues pertaining to the global climate change response, such as the expectation that developing countries would make significant sacrifices toward the energy transition even though their share of historic emission is miniscule. Most salient is the discussion on the "just energy transition". The text probes the origin of the concept, which is initially represented as a tension between labour and environmental movements, going on to unpack four essential components to the justice—procedural, restorative, distributive and participatory—to which the word "just" refers. The relevant chapter proceeds to critically appraise the Just Energy Transition process as it has unfolded in South Africa, noting the need for clear "characterisation and understanding of local conditions" in developing country contexts, and that "any transition plans must be adapted to meet the basic needs of vulnerable citizens and communities".

Most pointedly, however, this book takes a deep dive into the multifarious ways in which things were going (and continue to go) wrong at Eskom, and how it went from a utility of global stature to one that is barely able to keep the lights on. Unlike other forerunners to this work, this book is not a tell-all. It does, however, reveal some telling facts, the vast majority of which is sourced from the public domain, drawn from media articles and annual reports.

At the operational level, it tells of corruption in procurement processes, of dishonest coal suppliers, often in collusion with Eskom officials, delivering sub-par quality coal or coal contaminated with rubble or metals which caused damage to plant equipment and materials handling systems. It tells of rail infrastructure vandalised by an organised network of coal and mining transport mafias. It tells of incidents of fraud involving truck drivers and Eskom weigh-bridge operators, in which Eskom was invoiced for coal that was never delivered. It tells of outright acts of sabotage—damage to plant equipment—and theft of spares amounting to R 1.3 billion.

At the management level, it tells of duplicity and political interference, of ruling party members serving as chairmen or holding seats on the board. It tells of ineptness in the retention of skills on the part of Eskom's human resources department, of employees with years of experience replaced by untrained graduates, so that "while employee numbers remained relatively stable, the number of cumulative years of related experience in key functions dropped precipitously, as followed the levels of performance". It tells of an indifference in monetary reward incentives for good or poor performance, of the promotion of numerous Eskom employees involved in corrupt business dealings while the honest employees replaced by the corrupt ones were suspended on full pay for many weeks, where an appointment to certain positions were "likened to a poisoned chalice that left a curse on the future careers of those who drank from it". Indeed, it would appear that at least two Group Chief Executive Officers had literally been poisoned.

And yet, despite these challenges, there is cause for optimism. That such a comprehensive array of insights has been gathered together in one volume demonstrates that the technical failure as well as the moral and ethical decay at Eskom is an observed and measured phenomenon, even if the ethical depravity cannot be said to be fully understood. We know what the problems are, and through this work of scholarship, we are better equipped for tackling them.

I thus commend this book to readers from all walks of life. While it is an indispensable resource to professionals in the fields of energy, environment and even public administration, it is likely to be of deep relevance to any individual with an interest in the bigger picture.

Sincerely
Lester Malgas

TABLE OF CONTENTS

PART I - INTRODUCTION

PART II - POWER SECTOR REFORM

PART III - STATE OWNED ENTERPRISES

PART IV - INDEPENDENT POWER PRODUCERS

PART V - ELECTRICITY PLANNING

PART VI - SYNTHESIS AND CONCLUSION UNDERSTANDING INSUFFICIENT GENERATION

PART I

INTRODUCTION

CHAPTER 1

POWER SECTORS IN AFRICA – A DIAGNOSIS

Power sector reforms, undertaken across developing regions over the past three decades and driven by the need to improve sector performance and attract new investment, has resulted in a largely unexpected outcome. Rather than a new market model characterized by competitive wholesale and retail electricity markets, what presently predominates is a *hybrid* market. Here state-owned generators and independent power producers co-exist. These hybrid markets present a host of challenges, including the need to create alternative policy, regulatory and institutional frameworks. Unless addressed, these challenges may impede further investment.

While African countries with well-functioning power sectors do exist, most power sectors in Sub-Saharan Africa have insufficient electrical generation capacity, thus being unable to cater to all its residential, commercial, and industrial needs. Compared to other developing regions, the power sectors of most African countries are relatively undeveloped and characterised by insufficient generation capacity, high costs, poor reliability and service quality, and low access rates. South Africa has been able to buck this trend of insufficient capacity for many decades in the twentieth century. However, the policy, regulatory, and institutional frameworks that have hampered effective functioning of most other African power sectors, caught up with South Africa after the country's transition to democratic rule in 1994. These outcomes only became fully apparent a decade later. By then, however, the damage was done.

Characterising African Power Sectors – a Developing Country Diagnosis

Generally, Africa has low levels of installed generation capacity when compared with other developing regions globally. With growth rates in capacity additions lagging the rest of the developing world during the last four decades, the gap between Africa and the rest of the developing world has continually widened.

Given the low levels of installed electricity generation, electricity access rates amongst many African countries are comparably low. Based on data from the International Energy Agency, the electrification rate in Africa is on average at least two times lower than the average rate of developing regions. Furthermore, electrification rates for rural areas are three times less than the average for all developing countries. Since 1990, the East Asia, Latin America, and Middle East developing regions have all increased their access rates[1]. By contrast, due to population growth and household formation exceeding new connections, overall access levels in Sub-Saharan Africa have been in decline. While most regions saw declines in electricity access during the COVID-19 pandemic, the decline in Africa has been more pronounced[2]. The United Nations Sustainable Development Goal of achieving universal access to clean, affordable energy (SDG-7) is unlikely to be achieved in Sub-Saharan Africa as the available finance to reach this goal by 2030 remains only a fraction of what is required[3].

Low access levels may in part be attributed to affordability of power. The average residential power tariff in Sub-Saharan Africa is roughly double the average of other developing regions[4]. Electricity is therefore more expensive in Africa. This is due to several factors. National power systems are typically small. Hence, African power sectors do not benefit from the economies of scale that bulk generation offers. Excluding Nigeria and South Africa, no Sub-Saharan African country has an installed capacity greater than 6 000 megawatts (MW)[5]. Countries not endowed with sufficient primary energy resources face even higher power costs as expensive fossil fuels are imported. Large network losses in inefficient power systems exacerbate the problem. Finally, low population densities raise the cost of extending electricity networks.

Actual costs are even higher for African consumers when, due to poor reliability of the power systems, the cost of back-up generation is factored into the equation. In Kenya, Nigeria, Tanzania and Uganda, the majority of large companies depend on their own sources of back-up generation because power networks are unreliable, further pushing up the price of power. In 2019, a report by the International Finance Corporation showed that fossil fuelled back-up generators provided 9 percent of the electricity consumed in sub-Saharan Africa. The region that consumed the second highest percentage of electricity from back-up generators was South-East Asia at 2 percent. In West

Africa alone, owing largely to the contribution from Nigeria as much as 40 percent of the annual electricity consumed was from back-up generators. Electricity costs from self-generation in Nigeria exceed that spent on electricity from the national grid[6].

Power shortages have also led governments to contract short-term emergency power from private power companies. Although such projects may be up-and-running within a matter of months, they remain comparatively expensive. Notwithstanding the costly option of rental power to make up for electricity shortages, power outages are still endemic to Africa.

As far back as 2007, the World Bank reported that the average number of monthly outages for Sub-Saharan Africa is more than three times the average of Eastern Europe and Central Asia, and Latin America and the Caribbean[7]. This gap between Sub-Saharan Africa and its developing country counterparts has been steadily widening since. According to more recent surveys conducted in 2022, the average number of power outages for a typical month continues to be high in Africa. Benin, Burundi, Central African Republic, the Democratic Republic of the Congo, The Gambia, Niger, and Nigeria all experience at least weekly power outages[8].

Inadequate electricity capacity comes at a huge cost to firms that operate in these countries. In Kenya, Mali, Nigeria, and Senegal, roughly two-thirds of companies own back-up generators to make up for the shortfall in electricity supply. In South Africa, at least a third of companies own a back-up generator – with this number rising rapidly. A 2018 study by the *Center for Global Development* reported that from a survey of 3 000 companies in 37 Sub-Saharan African countries, more than 25 percent of businesses lost double-digit sales due to power interruptions—with many companies averaging sales losses as high as 30 percent. At the extreme, some individual firms reported sales losses of over 70 percent. Not only does back-up generation have direct and indirect costs that accrue to firms, but these costs also accrue to national economies. It increases the national costs of production and decreases country competitiveness[9].

A key reason for capacity shortages is insufficient investment in generation infrastructure. Many utilities are unable to finance investment off their balance sheets as tariffs barely cover operating and maintenance costs. Large transmission and distribution losses are incurred due to load centres being far from generation—and coupled with electricity theft, translate into revenue losses for utilities. Poor billing and collection rates have similarly impacted on investment and have led to inadequate maintenance of existing facilities.

Official development assistance has been inadequate to plug the financing gaps. Although private sector investment has helped to alleviate capacity shortages over the past three decades, this has been insufficient. In Africa, private investment lags that of other developing countries. A number of obstacles remain.

Power Sectors in Disarray - Diagnosing the Problems and Administering the Cure

In addressing the dire situation in many African states, reforms were embarked on to improve the functioning of power sectors, and more specifically state-owned utilities—in part by attracting increased investment into the sector. Acutely aware of the need to change and gear policies to recover from sector malaise, governments often—

with the assistance of external consultants—implemented strategies to enhance performance. This was generally prompted by development finance institutions, the principal lenders to African power sectors. In the early 1990s, the World Bank and other multilateral and bilateral financial institutions recommended specific new policies to improve sector performance. These policies were specified in a World Bank policy document, *The World Bank's Role in the Electric Power Sector: Policies for Effective Institutional, Regulatory, and Financial Reform*. The objectives of these policies were to: promote increased financial and technical efficiency in utility operations; to reduce the financial and administrative burdens that utilities impose on the state; to reduce the level of debt assumed by government from the power sector; and to reduce the cost of electricity by subjecting the generation and distribution sub-sectors to competitive market forces[10].

Development finance institutions were supportive of programmes to establish transparent regulatory processes and legal frameworks that would support power sector restructuring. It was believed that such frameworks would instil investor confidence and facilitate competition among suppliers by establishing, among other things, institutional structures to define government's role more clearly as policy maker, instead of power producer. In the same vein, utilities were called upon to corporatize and operate on commercial principles in order to create autonomous entities that manage their own budgets, procurement, as well as staff benefits. Corporatisation and commercialisation were marked as the first steps to address sector inefficiencies and prepare for private sector participation.

Private participation was initially prescribed at the generation level through Independent Power Producers (IPPs). Private investment in generation was aimed at reducing the cost of power through competition in the sector. Mindful of the fact that investors would seek assurances for market risk, these projects would be on a Build-Own-Operate (BOO) or Build-Own-Operate-Transfer (BOOT) basis with Power Purchase Agreements (PPAs) to assure electricity sales revenues to IPP investors and lenders. Thereafter it was intended that competition would exist between generators in an electricity market, to bid and sell power on to customers through a transmission company or directly to large consumers.

Despite many African countries initially embarking on the reform prescriptions, little reform has actually taken place. Although some of the reform steps were implemented in countries that assumed restructuring policies, most power sectors remain vertically and horizontally integrated—with IPPs operating at the fringes in the Generation sector. Despite exceptions such as Côte d'Ivoire, Morocco, and Tanzania (depending on hydrological conditions), where more than 50 percent of power is produced by IPPs, nowhere on the African continent have the entire suite of power sector reforms, including wholesale competition between electricity generators, been implemented.

In many countries state-owned utilities have resumed responsibility for additional capacity expansions, instead of the private sector as initially planned. In some cases, challenges in attracting private investment have left many governments and power sectors abandoning the road to reform. In other cases, the initial drivers for reform have eased, thereby lending support for increased state investment in generation infrastructure.

Difficulties in implementing the entire suite of power sector reform steps up to and including competition at the generation and the distribution levels have left African power sectors in an intermediate state. What has emerged is an *alternative model*: power sectors are *between* the old vertically integrated, state-owned structure and the intended competitive market structure.

The Challenges of Hybrid Markets

The *alternative model* has its own significant challenges in attracting timely generation investment, as is demonstrated in this book. In the face of fragmented and stalled reforms, new investments have occurred largely in the form of IPPs, resulting in *hybrid markets*. State-owned utilities and IPPs now co-exist in the sector. And although IPPs represent an important new source of investment, problems of insufficient capacity still persist. To date, experience in Africa and elsewhere has shown that hybrid markets face their own set of challenges and paradoxes in securing adequate generation investments. Despite hybrid markets presenting an opportunity for private sector investment, unattractive conditions and negative experiences in some countries have led to diminished private sector involvement.

Regardless of reforms aimed at improving economic performance—such as cost recoverable tariffs—most experiences have shown that these initiatives have proven difficult to implement and maintain in African power sectors. Over the long-term, steep increases in fuel costs and high inflation have undermined efforts to contain costs and facilitate mutually beneficial investments for power off-takers and investors. Despite the need for flexibility in such unstable economic environments, long-term Power Purchase Agreements generally lock in fixed charges for up to thirty years.

Power Sector Planning in Hybrid Markets

Power sector planning is complex. It involves critical linkages between power sector data collection agencies, planning agencies, fuel suppliers, utilities, various interest groups and stakeholder institutions, regulatory agencies, licensing agencies, developers, insurers, and environmental agencies, amongst others. Where reforms have been initiated, planning and contracting has moved from the state-owned utility to the Ministry of Energy or a related agency set up to administer these functions—in many cases, without due consideration for devising robust planning processes or adequate skill to staff these departments. Consequently, planning has often failed to encompass the complexities involved in contracting new capacity. This has led to extensive delays in developing new generation projects and made generation capacity shortages inevitable.

In many cases SOEs undermine private investment by dragging their heels in engaging and contracting private power. In theory, they are important stakeholders to the agreements signed by IPPs. SOEs act as off-takers of power and therefore must agree to the terms of the Power Purchase Agreements. In practice, they often contest the higher charges that new investments bring compared to their own plants where capital has been depreciated or where tariffs do not reflect the true cost of power. In many countries 'IPP' goes hand-in-hand with increased costs; consumers often support the state-owned utility in lobbying to build new plants, expand their power base, and protect their turf.

In Africa, there has been little evidence of transparent criteria for the allocation of new-build opportunities amongst state-owned utilities and IPPs. Procurement policies are often inadequate, while contracting frameworks often lack certainty and transparency resulting in lengthy, confusing negotiations, and allowing opportunity for corruption. Weak regulatory and governance frameworks erode the credibility of investment and contracting decisions: clear linkages between planning and the timely initiation of competitive tender processes is often non-existent.

This book examines the new challenges that arise in hybrid power markets in Africa and other developing countries. Citing the detailed experiences in South Africa, it evaluates how policy, regulatory, and institutional arrangements might respond to such markets and addresses how specific challenges may be overcome to enhance the performance of the power sector.

Understanding Stalled Power Sector Reforms

Power sector reforms were formulated in part to address the problems of insufficient electricity capacity. In Africa, however, reforms have not unfolded as planned. Instead, what has transpired as a result of initial reform efforts is a hybrid market in the Generation sector—made up of the incumbent state-owned utility and IPPs.

The predicament illuminated here is that despite private investment coming into the sector to alleviate the problems of power shortages, a new hybrid market creates its own challenges, which require specific policy, regulatory, planning, institutional and contracting measures.

This book explores the salient features of hybrid markets and how they come into being. It helps to comprehend the functioning of hybrid electricity markets. It describes how the emergence of hybrid markets creates new challenges to attracting investment into generation capacity in Africa. Furthermore, this book demonstrates how policy, regulatory, and institutional frameworks have inadequately responded to the special challenges of hybrid markets.

Are hybrid electricity generation markets indeed an end-state, or a prolonged plateau of stalled power sector reforms? To answer this question, further issues linked to generation investment must be examined: Who assumes responsibility for planning in hybrid markets, and is planning flexible and dynamic enough for changing market conditions? Have transparent and equitable criteria been developed to allocate new opportunities for generation investment to SOEs and IPPs in a fair manner? Are planning processes explicitly linked to a timely initiation of International Competitive Bids? How are unsolicited bids treated or accommodated in the framework? Have explicit and efficient tender, bid and procurement mechanisms been put in place? Do legal and regulatory frameworks create clear and sustainable off-taker contracting arrangements between SOEs and IPPs? Have suitable governance arrangements been developed to ensure that electricity market frameworks operate transparently and clearly? Do hybrid market arrangements create sufficient certainty for potential investors, thereby facilitating new private investment? How could policy, regulatory and institutional frameworks better respond to the challenges of hybrid markets?

This book is an exploration of the nature of hybrids markets and how they are influenced by their varied country contexts. While the book attempts to offer some solutions to the problems of insufficient electricity generation, it also raises many questions about hybrid markets. The book further explores how hybrid markets address decarbonisation objectives, and how lapses in planning contribute to the problem of insufficient electricity generation.

At the end of this book, we will return to these questions and attempt to provide responses to the questions posed here in this introductory chapter.

CHAPTER 2

THE SOUTH AFRICAN POWER SECTOR – PAST AND PRESENT

This chapter provides a brief history of the South African power sector, with specific reference to the electricity generation sub-sector. It details the establishment of the forerunner to the current national utility, Eskom, and provides details of key events in its one-hundred-year history. Presented in this chapter is how national and industrial policies shaped the power utility in the 20th century and how policy ambiguity in the 21st century contributed to its fall from grace. With acknowledgements to the Eskom Library department, the Eskom Heritage repository[11] provided much of the information to compile the content for this chapter, which focusses on the utility's rise to radiance, and its subsequent decent from distinction.

The Birth of an African Energy Giant

In the early part of the twentieth century, as the South African gold-mining industry recovered the after-effects of the Anglo-Boer war (fought between October 1899 and May 1902), electricity requirements for mines were on the increase. During this time, the Victoria Falls and Transvaal Power Company (VFTPC) Limited owned four thermal plants in Johannesburg to provide the bulk electricity supply to mostly gold mines. As further gold prospecting continued and more gold deposits were found, the augmented scope of mining projects signalled a need for more centralised electricity supply arrangements to secure adequate capacity for mining exploitation and expansion. Advocates for electrification of railway lines (for mineral exports) also added to the notion that centrally organised power generation would be better suited for long-term national economic expansion—as electricity demand was increasing due to the growth in mining and the expected growth in rail transportation.

By 1910, the Transvaal government recognized the importance of centralised and coordinated electricity supply and enacted laws that would limit the future powers of private generators and eventually permit state expropriation of power generation assets. The desire for a centrally controlled electricity supply industry led to the passing of the Electricity Act of 1922 and paved the way for the establishment of the Electricity Supply Commission (ESCOM). The main purpose of the Commission was to provide an abundant source of cheap electrical power. One of the main authors of the Electricity Act of 1922, Dr Hendrik Johannes van der Bijl, would accept the reins as the Commission's first chairman and pioneer the Union of South Africa into an era of unprecedented industrialisation.

Established as a public company in March 1923, the ownership structure of ESCOM was dominated by a desire for efficient central control of power generation for the country's industrial development. From that time, ESCOM would finance and own new power generation facilities to supplement the 160 MW of the Victoria Falls and Transvaal Power Company Limited.

While the Electricity Act of 1922 imbued ESCOM with the legal powers to raise finance, build, and own power generating plants, it was recognised that the organisation did not yet have the skills to efficiently operate these plants. While the nascent Electricity Supply Commission had ambitious plans to centralise control of the country's power generation assets, its ambitions were initially bridled with certain constraints, most notably its relative inexperience in operating power stations. Acknowledging this initial weakness, the construction and operation of newer power stations was left for the Victoria Falls and Transvaal Power Company Limited to fulfil.

Van der Bijl realized that ESCOM's provision of reliable, cheap power was dependent on achieving low capital costs for the development of power generating plants—and then, efficient operations, which at that point in time only Victoria Falls and Transvaal Power Company Limited could provide. Over the longer term, however, van der Bijl was unyielding in his view that private ownership would not sustainably translate into the lowest cost electricity for consumers.

Despite the prudence and the slow start, as early as 1925, ESCOM steadily increased its geographic reach and obtained approval to supply power in areas outside Johannesburg, including Cape Town, Witbank, Sabie, and Central Natal. A year later, ESCOM commissioned two coal-fired power stations, Colenso and Witbank, and two years thereafter, the Congella and Salt River coal-fired power stations were operational.

By 1932, significant discoveries of gold deposits coupled with a steep increase in the gold price, resulted in a huge demand for additional power generation. The following year, under van der Bijl's direction—and wasting no time to achieve its long-term ambitions of achieving low capital costs for the development of new power plants—ESCOM floated publicly traded loans that were oversubscribed. This enabled the Commission to fund future generation power stations, as well as grid expansions.

Between 1934 and 1935, ESCOM expanded the capacity of Salt River Power Station in Cape Town when the plant's electricity generation capacity increased to 90 MW. Projections for future national electricity demand continued as mining and non-mining industries continued to bloom. In 1938, development work started on the Vaal Power Station—financed and owned by ESCOM but constructed and operated by the Victoria Falls and Transvaal Power Company Limited.

In 1939, in spite of the looming Second World War, the supply from the Congella Power Station to the city of Durban increased. As the war efforts increased, the need for combat supplies interrupted the expansion of the Congella Power Station when factories in Britain prioritised supplying war equipment, rather than providing parts for power plants under construction in Southern Africa. During the war period, fuel, equipment, and material shortages, resulted in several delays to large power generation construction and maintenance projects. Britain commandeered essential equipment for the war, and therefore factories could not ship parts to South Africa.

As war efforts increased, maritime shipping on certain routes also became a risky undertaking. In 1943, German submarines torpedoed ships sinking essential equipment that was due for use at the Congella Power Station. The equipment and parts supply situation put severe strain on ESCOM's supply network. Smaller generators from ISCOR (the South African Iron and Steel Industrial Corporation), municipalities, and from the Rand Water Board, assisted ESCOM to secure the required additional generation capacity. Despite construction delays, ESCOM eventually completed the Congella power station at the end of the war in 1946.

Post-war economic activity spurred increased demand for electricity and the growth in demand required ESCOM to plan for new electricity generation plants. In 1946, ESCOM approved plans to build the Hex River plant in Worcester in the Cape Province, and approvals were also obtained to buy smaller plants in the Eastern Cape. By 1948, ESCOM's finances were sufficiently favourable to bring about the long-anticipated expropriation of the Victoria Falls and Transvaal Power Company Limited. In the preceding twenty-five years, the Commission had learnt more about raising debt for power generation projects, and by this time it also had ample experience as a power generation operating utility.

In June 1948, ESCOM signed an agreement to purchase the Victoria Falls and Transvaal Power Company Limited, including its Generation, Transmission, and Distribution assets. Sadly, van der Bijl died later that same year, and he was succeeded by Albert Jacobs who had worked as the commission's chief engineer and technical officer.

By 1950, ESCOM acquired the Kimberley Central Power Station from De Beers and supplied most areas in the Norther Cape. Throughout the

1950s, ESCOM's generation fleet expanded significantly. Improvements in pressure vessel technology and pulverised fuel technology allowed for the design and construction of larger boilers for ESCOM plants. By the mid-1950s, ESCOM's generation capacity reached 2 000 MW and by the end of that decade, it exceeded 3 300 MW. This growth was remarkable for ESCOM and beneficial for the region. It took advantage of the post-war global economic boom.

In the 1960s, technological innovation, the need for increased power, and the prospect of benefiting from economies of scale further advanced new plant designs. In 1961, the first unit of Komati Power Station was built. By this time, ESCOM was building units of 100 MW each. When the last unit of Komati Power Station was commissioned in 1964, the 1 000 MW plant was the largest in the ESCOM fleet. In 1963, Ingagane Power Station was commissioned near Newcastle in Natal. The plant consisted of five 100 MW coal-fired units, signalling ESCOM's continued intent to build larger power stations with higher capacity generator sets. Additional power generation facilities developed in the 1960s were the Camden, Grootvlei, and Hendrina Power Stations. Commissioned towards the end of the decade, the units at these power stations consisted of 200 MW generators. As the Commission became captivated by the economies of scale that larger units offered, it clearly signalled ESCOM's early appetite for increasingly larger plants.

Towards Full Integration

By the mid-1960s, South Africa became increasingly aware of the need for regional integration and the opportunities that regional integration offers. Once again, the government amended The Electricity Act to permit ESCOM to increase its reach internationally—and to link and supply neighbours, Lesotho, Mozambique, and Swaziland. The favourable reduction in the cost of electricity not only resulted in ESCOM exporting power to neighbouring countries but made it uneconomical for municipalities to continue investing in their own generation power plants. Municipalities were economically better off to abandon their own plans for developing baseload plants and instead purchase power from ESCOM. Consequently, by the end of the 1960s, municipalities ceased applications to develop their own baseload power stations.

In 1966, as the Commission was seeking alternatives for coal-fired power generation in order to diversify supply-side options in its interconnected national grid, work started on the development of a hydro power station on the Hendrik Verwoerd dam (now called the Gariep dam). At the same time, discussions were also ongoing for the establishment of a hydro-electric plant that would shore up the water from the Zambezi in the north of Mozambique. By 1968, ESCOM signed agreements with the Portuguese government (which at the time still ruled Mozambique as a colony) to purchase power from the planned Cahora Bassa hydro-electric scheme.

In keeping with its plans to seek alternatives for coal-fired power generation, that same year ESCOM bought the Duynefontein farm outside Cape Town, which would later serve as the site for the Commission's first nuclear power station. Internationally there was a great deal of interest in commercial nuclear power generation as nuclear construction projects were underway in North America, Europe, and the far East.

Transmission technology also advanced, permitting ESCOM to transmit power at higher voltages. Enabled by transmission projects that allowed greater interconnections, by 1972 ESCOM was operating a nationally integrated electricity supply system. Full integration of the power sector meant that ESCOM could optimise the operation of its plants on a networked transmission grid—benefiting from cheaper stations situated close to coal resources that operated under a baseload regime and using more expensive coastal plants for peaking and emergency generation. By then, ESCOM had demonstrated that operating a fleet of large generating plants in an interconnected national grid was the optimal way to minimise electricity costs.

Global Energy Crises, Domestic Energy Security, and National Electricity Demand Growth

In 1970 alone, electricity sales increased by 10.7 percent and ESCOM realised that it would require substantial capital to expand its power generation capacity. The Electricity Act was subsequently amended to allow ESCOM to raise tariffs in a way that would permit sufficient revenue for future expansion projects. In the 1970s, capital was in short supply globally— capital markets were affected by the repercussions of the 1973 oil embargo, which contributed to the end of the post-war economic expansion. In South Africa, higher bond interest rates and economic isolation due to Apartheid policies made it difficult to raise sufficient capital internationally to realise the expansion of the ESCOM generation fleet.

Throughout the early 1970s, however, notwithstanding a global recession sparked by international energy shortages, domestic electricity demand growth continued—and ESCOM started to develop larger plants supported by more modern technology. ESCOM used reheat boiler technology in its fleet for the first time at Arnot Power Station and this feature allowed for greater plant efficiencies. Since the excess rejected thermal loads released into the Vaal Dam became too much for conventional wet cooling towers, improved technology also paved the way for dry cooling at the last two units of Grootvlei Power Station.

During this era of technological innovation and advancement, ESCOM developed respectable expertise to explore and use modern technologies to further exploit potential plant efficiencies, benefit from economies of scale, and adapt plant designs and operations to environmental considerations. While the 350 MW Arnot units were considered large at the time, ESCOM engineers realised that even larger new plants were needed—not only to keep up with increased electricity demand, but also to make up for lost generation from decommissioning older plants of the Victoria Falls and Transvaal Power Company Limited. ESCOM would have to add approximately 1 000 MW of new capacity each year during the decade of the 1970s.

The decision to build Kriel Power Station in the Eastern Transvaal (now called Mpumalanga province), resulted in the six 500 MW units becoming the largest coal-fired plant in the ESCOM fleet when the plant reached commercial operations. The 'six-pack' arrangement, as it became known, would go on to become the standard for developing new coal-fired generation units at ESCOM power stations for the next 50 years. The Matla and Duvha Power Stations, situated in the

Mpumalanga province, would follow the Kriel benchmark, each with their six 600 MW units.

As western states were feeling the effects of the global oil embargo in the early 1970s and developed commercial nuclear power stations in response to their domestic energy security risks, the Commission also decided to build the Koeberg Power Station in the Cape Province, near the city of Cape Town.

The Investment Implications of Electricity Demand Growth

Despite producing affordable power during the 1960s and establishing a reliable network of generators and transmission infrastructure, the 1970s would however, see public sentiment change towards the Electricity Supply Commission. While ESCOM wanted to manage the risk of the country running out of electricity and steer the domestic energy sector through the global energy crisis of the 1970s, the inclusion of future capacity provisions in the electricity tariff meant that consumers were paying significantly more for electricity.

South Africa registered sharp increases in electricity prices between 1971 and 1977 by an annual average of 27 percent per annum. This was to shore up capital reserves for future generation expansion. The general public perception was that the company had become too independent and that it lacked formalised and agreed rules for understanding and guiding its investment decisions, as well as moderating the impact thereof.

During this period, ESCOM also experienced significant environmental challenges with its emissions due to ineffective electrostatic precipitators at its newly commissioned Duvha Power Station. This contributed to high ash emissions from the plant—a problem that persisted until 1984. The situation further shifted public sentiment as communities in close proximity to these plants gained public sympathy against an unchecked behemoth, which apparently had become too big for its boots.

Consumers considered a move of the company's Johannesburg head office from its humble beginnings in Braamfontein to upmarket Sandton, as lavish and wasteful. This further swayed public opinion against ESCOM. The public believed that ESCOM was not strictly fulfilling its not-for-profit mandate. To make things worse, in December 1975, a fault in the transmission system resulted in a grid collapse, where most of the country was without power for at least a day. As a result, on the instruction of the Minister of Economic Affairs, the Board of Trade and Industry stepped in to investigate the way ESCOM operated.

ESCOM cooperated with the Board of Trade and Industry and subsequently overhauled its accounting systems. Nevertheless, the capacity expansion provision in the electricity tariff (a significant contributor to the prevailing public resentment toward the Commission at the time) was retained despite the accusations that ESCOM was unreasonable when insisting on large generation reserve margins.

As economic sanctions were mounting against South Africa, energy security and independence remained a national priority as the after-effects of the global energy crisis was still foregrounded in national energy policies. The government therefore continued to support all strategic reserves, especially energy reserves, and particularly electrical power generation reserve margins. Against a backdrop of increasing electricity demand, the unreliable electricity supply from Cahora Bassa (due to civil war in Mozambique) and reservations that Koeberg Nuclear Power Station would not be developed due to potential trade restrictions, fuelled support for decisions to order more coal-fired power plants. Due to a significant drought in 1983 (affecting auxiliary cooling at thermal plants), low availability factors amongst ESCOM generation plants, plus incidences of unserved demand, also reinforced the belief that new large-scale generation investment was indeed needed. ESCOM therefore approved the investment decisions for the Lethabo, Tutuka, Matimba, and Kendal coal-fired power stations.

Despite the investigation from the Board of Trade and Industry, public sentiment towards the Commission continued to be a problem for ESCOM. In 1983, ESCOM power stations were operating at an average availability of 72 percent and interruptions in supply were commonplace. In the mid-1980s there were also significant lapses in corporate and fiscal governance and ESCOM lost 'hundreds of millions of rands' in secret deals as state plunder was a routine occurrence in the public sector. Corruption was the order of the day, as National Party and other operatives set up elaborate schemes to defraud government institutions of financial and other resources. In one single sophisticated overseas nuclear fuel transaction involving ESCOM accountant Gert Rademeyer, the Commission reportedly lost R 67 million. Therefore, in 1983, the government appointed the de Villiers Commission of Inquiry, to investigate matters that impacted on plant performance, planning, and investment costs.

Governance and Oversight – and Stranded Generation Assets

From the recommendations of the de Villiers Commission of Inquiry emanated two important and significant changes to the way that ESCOM was managed. The first change was the establishment of an independent board, the Electricity Council, which would provide oversight on the operational management of the company. The second change was constraining the annual amounts that ESCOM could include in the tariff for future capital expansions.

Although the construction of the Koeberg, Lethabo, Matimba, and Kendal plants would continue in the 1980s, during their construction concerns over excess capacity emerged. Economic sanctions against the Apartheid regime resulted in reduced domestic growth, economic contraction of certain industrial and manufacturing export sectors, and lower growth in electricity sales. The Lethabo, Matimba, and Kendal plants would add nearly 12 000 MW of coal-fired generation to the national grid. As their construction continued in the 1980s, towards the time of their completion, it became clear that ESCOM would be stranded with significant excess generation capacity due to the slump in national electricity consumption.

The National Party government's insistence in advancing Apartheid policies met with increasing economic isolation when in August 1985 Prime Minister, Pieter Willem Botha (in his Rubicon speech), announced that his government will not allow the world to dictate the terms of its policies. The global economic isolation and ensuing economic sanctions resulted in poor economic growth and low demand for electricity—difficulties for ESCOM and South Africa. The result was an over-investment in generation infrastructure. This led to generation assets that were constructed, but for which there was insufficient electricity sales to recoup capital costs. The stranded generation assets therefore required higher electricity tariffs, which put a further damper on sales.

When Life Gives you Power Stations ...

Once again in 1987, the government amended the Electricity Act when ESCOM was dual branded as the Electricity Supply Commission (ESCOM in English) and Elektrisiteits Voorsienings Kommissie (EVKOM in native Afrikaans). With significant excess generation capacity, the utility started to chart a new course to accelerate the electrification of the country. By that time, only 40 percent of the country had access to electricity. The majority of the Black population was marginalised and enjoyed little or no access.

ESCOM set its focus on increasing sales to make up for the reduction in electricity demand. The utility initiated the 'Electricity for All' programme, and the endeavour gained traction as it contributed to increased sales amongst rural consumers, as well as urban Black citizens and businesses. To increase their overall electricity consumption, low price incentives also resulted in higher sales amongst energy intensive users (mostly in the aluminium and ferro-alloy industrial sectors). Large municipalities also benefited from lower costs, as ESCOM passed price reductions through to high-volume customers.

In spite of the programmes to increase sales, electricity supply capacity hugely exceeded demand. As the Majuba, Matimba, and Kendal Power Stations reached commercial operations in the 1990s, there was still not sufficient demand for electricity to use all the available power generation. ESCOM subsequently decided to mothball its most expensive older plants.

In 1994, as the African National Congress, the first democratically elected government of South Africa came to power, the government formally adopted the 'Electricity for All' programme as an essential energy policy objective. The government absorbed the electrification programme as part of the country's broader social policy objectives and the programme received financial contributions from the National Treasury since it was no longer solely a programme objective of the utility.

By this time, ESCOM had also committed as its mission statement, to provide *'the lowest cost electricity for growth and prosperity'*. This mission aligned well with the ambitions of the newly elected government, who had the electoral mandate to improve the country's investment climate, promote economic growth, reduce unemployment, and alleviate poverty.

In 1995, the Electricity Board was succeeded by the National Electricity Regulator (a forerunner to the National Energy Regulator of South Africa), which was granted broader powers to regulate the electricity supply sector. The same year also saw the establishment of the Southern African Power Pool. The power pool was set up as a common grid and market for electricity trading amongst Southern African Development Community (SADC) countries.

While the 'Electricity for All' programme was vastly successful in providing access to poorer Black citizens, regrettably the government's employment and broader economic policies were unsuccessful in creating sufficient employment and alleviating poverty—resulting in poor citizens being unable to afford the electricity to which they now had access. A confluence of factors gave rise to the financial woes of the utility. These included artificially low tariffs to incentivise sales among energy intensive users while tariffs were not reflecting *replacement* electricity generation costs; reduced tariffs for poorer South Africans; the inability of many poor customers to pay for electricity; and a growing culture of non-payment amongst some citizens. These cumulative effects contributed to a reduction in long-term sustainable revenues for the utility and insufficient savings for future generation investment and expansion.

In a milieu of excess generation capacity (including mothballed power plants) and where tariffs were not reflective of (or increasing towards) the sustainable long run marginal cost of electricity, future generation investment was not an immediate pressing concern for the utility, its customers, or the government.

Signalling the Power Sector Transition

In 1998, an Energy White Paper published by the government signalled a notable change in the South African energy sector. In an about-turn from the intrepid central planning vision of van der Bijl, the authors of the white paper equally courageously signalled that future investment in generation plants would come from the private sector, and not from ESCOM. Despite the government of South Africa publishing the Energy White Paper, it was clear that within the governing tripartite alliance, consisting of the African National Congress, the South African Communist Party, and the Congress of South African Trade Unions, there was no clear nor agreed consensus on the plan to privatise the country's energy landscape. Furthermore, in line with the

Commission's vision to provide the *'the lowest cost electricity for growth and prosperity'* tariffs were kept low. However, at the time standard electricity tariffs were simply too low to attract private investment in greenfield generation capacity.

At the time that the Energy White Paper was issued, senior managers and executives at ESCOM therefore expressed justified concerns about future investment in generation infrastructure, the sustainability of low tariffs, and the role of the utility in future power sector planning. Not only did South Africa need to make future investment decisions for new plants—plants required to come online in less than a decade (the duration considered reasonable for building another six-unit power station). The Energy White Paper also signalled the end of future greenfield generation investment by ESCOM. ESCOM cautioned government on the timing of the reforms cited in the White Paper, pointing out the unattractive tariffs for private sector investment, the uncertainty on the electricity market restructuring, and the brief time available to bring new generation plants online. The cautions from ESCOM went unheeded.

A Utility of Global Stature

With the older inefficient power stations mothballed and the 'distraction' of building new generation capacity quelled, the organisation was set to focus on operational efficiency. While the organisation had marginally improved on its energy availability factor during the 1980s, the utility required another bold vision to strive for in the 1990s. To this end, ESCOM committed itself an Energy Availability Factor target of 90 percent for its operating generating fleet.

By 1998, ESCOM had achieved an energy availability factor of 92.7 percent, becoming the world's undisputed lowest cost provider of electricity. This achievement brought the utility renowned status. In 2001, at the Financial Times' annual Global Energy Awards, it was furnished with the accolade of 'Global Energy Company of the Year'[12]. The award was for providing the world's lowest-cost electricity; making superior technological innovations; increasing transmission system reliability; and developing economical, efficient and safe methods for combustion of low-grade coal[13]. The achievement was the utility's most significant acknowledgement during its existence. Later that same year, with the Eskom Conversion Act 13 of 2001, the government decided to legally incorporate the organisation, and in 2002, ESCOM subsequently became a fully incorporated limited liability state-owned company. The Government of South Africa, represented by the Ministry of Public Enterprises, became the only shareholder. With the change in legal status, also came a change in name. The dual name of ESCOM/EVKOM (in two different languages) was replaced by a single name—Eskom, as it will be referred to hereafter.

Keeping the Lights On

While South Africa was still basking in the shine of the top global energy company award, senior officials within the utility were concerned about the rapid growth in electricity consumption without concrete plans to add new generation capacity. At the time, there was limited detailed planning performed within the company to match future demand with sufficient electricity generation supply. The policy uncertainty with respect to *who would be responsible for additional generation capacity expansion* remained. The Eskom fleet's impressive energy availability factor (at greater than 90 percent) slightly delayed the need for new generation capacity. At the very least, the improved operational performance provided headroom to buffer delays in the critical decision to develop new generation capacity.

By 2003, the government was finally realising the extent of the problems looming in the electricity supply industry. Even though the government left planning and effective contracting for new generation too late, senior Eskom officials believed that the worst could be averted. In 2003, the Eskom board took a decision to recommission the mothballed coal-fired plants—Komati, Grootvlei, and Camden Power Stations. The South African government also authorised Eskom to build two new coal-fired plants (the Medupi and Kusile Power Stations), as well as a pumped-storage hydro plant (the Ingula Power Station). To avert power shortages in the short-term, the Eskom board approved the development of the Ankerlig Power Station (in Atlantis near Cape Town) and Gourikwa Power Station (near Mossel Bay in the Western Cape province). In 2006, Eskom commenced with the construction of these diesel-fired peaking plants, using open-cycle gas turbine technology.

The Lights go Out

Despite construction having started on the Ankerlig and Gourikwa peaking plants, they would not be completed in time to avert the looming power shortages. By October 2007, rolling blackouts started as the transmission system operator could no longer match electricity supply and demand. The rolling blackouts occurred again early in 2008. In 2009, the commissioning of the Ankerlig and Gourikwa plants brought relief in the short term, but the longer-term impacts of the delayed investment decisions in generation infrastructure was still a significant concern.

Although the construction of the Medupi Power Station had commenced (and government had approved the development of the Kusile coal-fired plant and the Ingula Pumped Storage scheme), Eskom still projected that it would struggle to match generation supply with demand—at least until these new plants were scheduled to enter commercial operations. Furthermore, although Eskom had made the investment decision for these new plants, the utility had insufficient reserves on its balance sheet to fund them all. Insufficient company savings and low tariffs meant that Eskom was starting its capital expansion off a weak balance sheet and a feeble income statement.

By 2008, in addition to its poor balance sheet, the realities of the global economic recession meant that less capital could be raised through international bonds to fund Eskom's ambitious generation capacity expansion. In 2007 and 2008 therefore, South Africa also saw electricity tariff increases well above the rate of inflation—spurred by valid concerns over interest payments on loans taken to fund the new generation investments.

The generation reserve margin dropped to low single digits, far from the recommended 15 percent for the Eskom generation fleet. At the time, several operational coal-fired generation plants were operated with only critical maintenance executed to keep the lights on, as stadia and various facilities were being built for the hosting of Africa's first FIFA World Cup in 2010. In addition to ensuring that facilities were ready for the much-anticipated games, South Arica had to project the impression domestically and internationally that it was well prepared to host the beautiful game, even if it meant sweating its generation hardware at the expense of future performance.

The Fight to Complete New-Builds, Stay Afloat Financially, and Keep the Lights On

Due to concerns over significant tariff increases, insufficient generation capacity, and Eskom's proposal to limit power usage to its largest consumers (represented by the Energy Intensive Users Group), consumer industries delayed consumer plans for large new investments and expansion in power-user technologies that have high electricity consumption. By 2013, Eskom realised that the 'interim' strategy to forgo some maintenance in return for increased generation output was starting to hurt plant performance across the fleet.

Continued running of operational plants without the requisite scheduled maintenance would reduce their long-term longevity. Eskom undertook to establish a five-year generation maintenance strategy that would no longer postpone essential maintenance on key power plant components. With the older previously mothballed coal-fired plants back in the operating generation fleet, Eskom changed the fleet Energy Availability Factor target to 80 percent. Eskom envisaged that the older plants would not sustain high Energy Availability Factors, but the target revision for the coal fleet would allow the company to execute the much-needed maintenance. Similarly, Eskom projected that the commissioning of the first Medupi Power Station units would allow opportunities for older plants to execute the extensive maintenance that had been forwent in earlier years.

There were considerable delays at the Medupi, Kusile, and Ingula construction sites—primarily due to industrial action, poor contractor management, and recurring industrial safety accidents. Notwithstanding the commitment to perform critical plant maintenance, the low generation reserve margins made it difficult to perform the required critical maintenance and avert sporadic rolling blackouts. By 2015, continued delays in critical maintenance resulted in a steep escalation of breakdowns in the coal fleet. While Eskom devised short-term recovery strategies to enable extensive maintenance on unreliable units, they were met with the same constraints as the original strategies. With the limited available reserve margins, there were simply not enough opportunities to perform the required maintenance *and* keep the lights on.

Four years earlier (in 2011), the Minister of Energy, Dipuo Peters, had announced that her department would enter into power purchase contracts with renewable energy independent power producers (IPPs)[14]. While Eskom initially expressed support for the IPPs to provide power, it later withdrew this support in 2015, when due to affordability concerns its Group Chief Executive Officer stopped signing the Power Purchase Agreements (PPAs) for renewable energy IPPs in further procurement rounds[15]. Although signing the PPAs would not have necessarily averted immediate power shortages, it could have provided future relief and opportunities to perform the much-needed maintenance on the operational coal-fired fleet. Private generation capacity approvals would be delayed for at least four years (as illustrated later in Chapter 11) while the problems of insufficient generation capacity, inadequate maintenance, and increased loadshedding slowly intensified.

By 2015, substantial delays experienced in completing the first units of the newly constructed Medupi Power Station, did not help with stemming power shortages as anticipated. Although 2015 saw the first synchronisation of a generation unit at the Medupi Power Station, the new units were beset with technical design faults resulting in exceptionally low unit availability outcomes. To make matter worse, cash reserves to keep the new-build programme on track was dwindling, ratings agencies had downgraded Eskom's credit ratings (making it harder to raise capital), and unpaid municipal debt was on the increase. Subsequently, there were insufficient funds readily available to correct the defects and resolve the issues on the new plants.

By this time in 2015, loadshedding became a periodic occurrence that disrupted daily life for most South Africans. Local computer programmers developed innovative mobile phone applications – and it provided users' smartphones with push notifications on scheduled rolling blackouts in their respective geographic regions. While the mobile application brought little real comfort to customers whom the utility adversely impacted by unplanned power cuts, the novelty assisted consumers to anticipate and plan for the inevitable power outages. Geographic power outage schedules were synchronised with the programmed switching of the regional transmission and distribution system operators. *Loadshedding,* as rolling blackouts became known in South Africa, was presented in stages whereby each 1 000 MW tranche of unserved electricity demand was represented by an additional stage.

In 2016, Eskom recommitted itself to an energy available factor of 80 percent over the following five years until 2021, however, the traction required to achieve this target remained elusive. The following year (2017), Eskom pulled through by meeting a declining electricity demand. Incurring no public loadshedding during that year, the company announced that it had recovered adequate generation capacity.

Plans for Additional Electricity and more Power Plants

In 2016, South Africa also signed a Memorandum of Understanding for taking 2 500 MW of the planned 4 800 MW Inga hydro generation project on the Congo River in the Democratic Republic of the Congo. In support of African regional integration, this signing was to display that there was indeed a key anchor customer for the power generated from this project and assuage risk-averse investors and potential lenders to the hydro scheme.

Within the context of the newly adopted 2015 Paris Climate Agreement, non-carbon emitting projects were back on the table, even the politically risky Inga and Grand Inga Hydro projects, which had been on and off the cards for at least three decades. In keeping with domestic power generation technologies that supported a low-carbon energy future, the administration of former President Jacob Zuma initiated a programme to procure 9 600 MW of nuclear power generation to deal with future electricity demand. The government considered nuclear power to be a suitable replacement for ageing baseload coal-fired plants that would be due for decommissioning. However, two years later opposition groups successfully mounted a legal challenge to the nuclear procurement programme in the courts—and the programme was subsequently cancelled.

In 2018, as two additional Medupi units and the first Kusile unit were being synchronised to the national grid, it became clear that the introduction of Eskom's largest new coal-fired generators was not going to solve the problems of insufficient generation capacity in the short-term. The initial performance of the units continued to be underwhelming, and their operations were characterised by design-related faults and equipment performance failures.

Significant contractual problems between Eskom and Engineering Procurement and Construction companies ensued. The new units were not able to generate at their nameplate capacity, the boiler and turbine control systems were not compatible, and it would cost billions of rands more to resolve technical defects on the plants. This meant that the planned maintenance programmes for the ageing coal fleet would again be subordinate to keeping the lights on and reducing the incidences and durations of power shortages.

By 2019, Eskom remained unable to generate sufficient power to meet national demand. The existing fleet was exhibiting inferior performance, and so were the newly commissioned generation units at Medupi and Kusile. While Eskom had assured stakeholders a year earlier (when public loadshedding stopped from 2017 to 2018) that it would in all probability decommission older coal-fired stations earlier than anticipated due to expected overcapacity, 2019 saw a vast increase in rolling blackouts. For the first time, loadshedding had advanced and deepened to stage six, meaning that at least 6 000 MW of electricity demand could not be satisfied—to the chagrin of ordinary South Africans.

Deteriorating Financial and Generation Plant Performance

Increasing municipal debt, the higher cost of capital due to successive downgrades by major ratings agencies, as well as tariffs that were below the cost of providing the electricity, created a challenging fiscal environment for the utility to stay afloat financially. The government agreed to inject liquidity into operations, and company executives tried to find ways of realising savings within the company. Fuel purchases rapidly consumed government fiscal injections to Eskom when large quantities of diesel were procured to operate Eskom's open-cycle gas turbines—plants needed for limiting the frequency and duration of power outages.

Insufficient cash reserves also meant that Eskom could not always plan and execute the required maintenance to improve the operational performance of an ageing coal-fired fleet. Increasing prices for new coal contracts also exerted upward pressure of primary energy costs, thereby further reducing available finances for maintenance on the operational fleet. As Eskom desperately tried to contain primary energy and related operational costs, unionised workers at the utility expressed their dissatisfaction that the company targeted the wage bill as an area for future financial savings. When incoming Group Chief Executive Officer, Phakamani Hadebe offered Eskom staff a 0 percent wage increase, it triggered waves of labour strikes at multiple coal-fired plants. This resulted in increased incidences of rolling blackouts, as certain unionised workers embarked on illegal and unprotected industrial action.

In 2020, after Eskom recommitted to sign Power Purchase Agreements with renewable energy independent power producers, the Ministry of Minerals and Energy resumed the Renewable Energy Independent Power Producer Procurement Programme (REIPPPP). Despite the resumption of the REIPPPP, the numbers of days of rolling blackouts continued to increase from 54 days in 2020 to 75 days in 2021. By 2021, the reliability of Eskom's coal-fired power stations had continued their downward performance trajectory and based on the limited maintenance that Eskom performed, it was clear that the trend would continue.

With significant under-expenditure in scheduled maintenance on critical components and on capital refurbishments, the performances of certain plants were sharply deteriorating. The average age of coal-fired plants was more than 40 years old, with the oldest units being 60 years old. The concern was that if Eskom continued to sweat its generation assets in the manner that it had during the previous decade, it could completely wipe out the remaining economic operational lifespans of the thermal plants—and that there would be no economic assets left to maintain or refurbish.

To avert the worst plant and personnel safety incidents, where generation units faced degradation to the point where considerable damage from continued operation could occur, Eskom shut down the units. Similarly, where the utility could no longer guarantee safety standards, Eskom switched off those units—incurring rolling blackouts to enable performing the required maintenance.

Furthermore, the inability to meet minimum emissions standards also contributed to coal-fired units being unable to generate at their maximum outputs—all this while more stringent emission standards were looming. Instead of leaning toward the achievement of more stringent emissions limits, the coal-fired emissions were worsening. This also necessitated further reductions in electricity generation output.

During this period in 2020, many industrial electricity users bemoaned the fact that in the midst of rolling blackouts they were not permitted to build their own generation plants with capacities greater than one megawatt. They were obligated to apply to the Minister of Minerals and Energy for generating licences and follow the same costly, time-consuming, and cumbersome licencing process as did Eskom. In the hope that Eskom's performance would once again improve, the Minister would not accede to the requests to lift the cap from 1 MW, as requested by industry consumer stakeholders[16].

Eventually, in June 2021 South Africa's president, Cyril Ramaphosa, overruled the Minister of Minerals and Energy and increased the 1 MW limit to 100 MW[17]. Despite the country's president overriding the Minister of Minerals and Energy to allow smaller energy producers to supply excess power to the Eskom transmission system by increasing the licensing exemption threshold to 100 MW, this did not provide any short-term relief. Prospective generators stated that the administrative processes under the 100 MW exemption was as arduous as full licensing with the National Energy Regulator.

In July 2022, after the country had experienced (at the time) the worst continuous bout of stage six loadshedding (i.e., 6 000 MW of unserved electricity demand), the president announced sweeping reforms to power sector regulations, permitting Eskom to purchase power from authorised suppliers *by all reasonable means necessary.* But this announcement came too late to bring about any short-term improvements in the energy supply situation.

By November 2022, the utility had no more budgeted funds to buy diesel for operating its open cycle gas turbines. Eskom was able to reallocate funds from other areas in the business, to purchase the fuel for its peaking plants. The year 2022 went on record as the first time that the utility had more days of rolling blackouts, than days without power cuts.

By the time that the utility should have celebrated its centenary in March 2023, for the first time Eskom had also experienced approximately six months of continuous days of rolling power cuts. With the company's one hundredth birthday, there remained little to celebrate. Loadshedding would become a way of life for most South Africans—at least in the medium term. In September 2023, when Eskom published its 52-week system outlook, the annual forecast showed that for every single week there was an expectation that electricity demand would outstrip supply. This was the first time that Eskom's *planned* risk level and likely risk scenarios were all showing red—cautioning South Africans of ongoing rolling blackouts for at least another year.

◈ ◈ ◈

In summary, in large part due to Johannes van der Bijl, South Africa's Electricity Supply Commission started with a bold vision, a clear objective, and disciplined execution. The Electricity Commission experienced a sharp learning curve during its first twenty-five years until becoming a monopoly in 1948. During its tumultuous history it had become the mainstay of the South African economy. In the 1970s—at the time of its Golden Jubilee (~ 50 years) the Electricity Supply Commission lost public confidence and support. But by the time of its diamond Jubilee (~75 years), the utility regained that support by providing the world's lowest cost reliable electricity.

Yet, by the time it of its centenary, the utility found itself at its lowest point in its existence. Originally created to provide reliable and affordable electricity to spearhead South Africa's industrialisation, one hundred years later the company's performance was weighing down the economy—providing an electricity supply considered neither reliable, nor affordable.

Interlude: Book Outline for Examining the Problems of Insufficient Electricity Generation

Parts II, III, IV, and V of this book dissect the four proposed factors that contribute to the problem of insufficient generation capacity. Each of the four Parts starts with a general description of experiences of each of the main factors that contribute to insufficient generation in developing country power sectors. Thereafter, within each of the four Parts (II, III, IV, and V), the text provides details of specific experiences in the South African power sector. The general organisation of the text is as follows:

Part II: Power Sector Reforms

Firstly, power sector reforms in developing countries, especially in Africa, came about largely as a result of dissatisfaction among power sector stakeholders with the ineffective functioning of national utilities and their poor performances under state ownership. Mainly prompted by development finance institutions such as the International Bank for Reconstruction and Development, developing countries embarked on power sector reforms out of a desire to improve sector performances and attract sufficient investment in power sector infrastructure. The standard model of reform involved unbundling, privatisation, and competition. Yet, as experience has shown, African countries have not fully implemented the standard reform model. This outcome mirrors experiences of power sectors in other developing regions. While power sector reforms have introduced IPPs into the Generation sector and some private energy traders have come into existence, incumbent SOEs have often retained their dominant market position within Generation.

What has emerged, in practice, is a hybrid power market which has profound implications for new investment in generation capacity. The theory and experience of power sector reform, therefore, frames the broader context for the South African analysis in this book, and for implications of attracting sufficient electricity generation investment in hybrid markets.

Part III: State Owned Enterprises

Secondly, the role of SOEs in hybrid power markets and in securing additional generation capacity remains seminal. Sometimes they may continue to invest directly in new generation. Alternatively, they are off-takers for IPPs. The performance of SOE utilities is thus critical. Nonetheless, as a result of the social and development role that electricity has played—and continues to play, power utility SOEs have become politicised and their complex relationships with governments have made it difficult to transform them. Institutional, regulatory and reporting frameworks are important in helping to elucidate how and why the functioning of SOEs is intricately linked to problems of insufficient investment in generation. Although power sector reforms have brought new institutional arrangements, as well as regulatory frameworks and changes in functional responsibilities which affect SOEs, improving their performance remains a formidable challenge.

Part IV: Independent Power Producers

Thirdly, private power producers, as the latest entrants in hybrid generation markets, have investment expectations. The degree to which host governments can meet these expectations determines the host country's ability to attract and sustain investment through IPPs. The challenges in attracting private generation investment in evolving power sectors as outlined in Chapter 10 of this book serve as an additional background for understanding and analysing the problems of insufficient investment in generation capacity.

Due to the limited scope and sharpness of focus required, this book does not consider investment theories or theory on Foreign Direct Investment. Rather, the discussion jumps straight to the issues that are immediately related to generation investments in reforming power sectors in Africa where investment conditions are less than favourable.

Part V: Electricity Planning

Lastly, the dynamics of hybrid power markets present new challenges that unless explicitly addressed will frustrate attempts to bring in new power generation investment. During power sector reforms, the importance of effective planning functions is often overlooked or neglected. Weak linkages between generation planning and procurement of power plants can result in delaying the commissioning of power stations and, thus, the provision of electricity to consumers. Under certain conditions, contracting arrangements hold the potential to discourage investment in generation infrastructure, instead of facilitating it. The responsibilities for detailed power sector planning, procurement, and contracting must be explicitly assigned in hybrid power markets—and sufficient human resources and skills competencies must be developed to undertake these functions effectively.

Part VI: Synthesis and Conclusion

The framework (as presented by Parts II, III, IV, and V above) is revisited to synthesise the reform experiences and understand the implications for future power sector reforms. Part VI summarises the information in the chapters describing the experiences in South Africa. It provides insights on understanding the domestic problem of insufficient electricity generation.

The South African experience enables an extension of the framework for analysing the problem of insufficient electricity generation and providing a deeper understanding of hybrid markets. Furnished, are insights for guiding future power sector reforms to increase investment in generation in hybrid electricity markets in developing countries. Additionally presented, are implications for Generation planning in power sectors that are in the throes of reform.

PART II

POWER SECTOR REFORM

CHAPTER 3

THE EVOLUTION OF POWER SECTOR REFORMS

Industrial and developing countries implemented power sector reforms for distinct reasons. As a key objective however, reform across the globe has always been the achievement of greater efficiency in the provision of electricity. In terms of efficiency, the traditional belief was that electricity is a natural monopoly and should remain so to benefit from economies of scale in generation and to avoid duplication in distribution. This conventional notion was challenged when technological advances started to make economies of scale in plant construction and operation less important[18]. The optimal size for generation plants in certain instances became smaller, the time for constructing certain technology plants decreased, and an increase in standardisation of plant designs was achieved[19]. Competition thus posed an attractive option. Moreover, competition helped to address the problem of inefficient investment in—and functioning of—generation plant.

To offer a perspective on how power sectors evolved, this chapter gives a brief overview of the origins of electricity supply industry (ESI) transformation from state-owned vertically integrated monopolies to reformed power markets. The pioneers of restructuring, namely the United States of America (USA), Chile, England and Wales, and certain Nordic countries, were the first to spearhead reforms in their respective power sectors. Their experiences laid the basis for what would later be the blueprint of reform in other industrialised and developing countries. Although the drivers and paths to reform amongst the earlier forerunners differed, the reform outcomes were generally regarded as positive. The success of these reformers served as confirmation that electricity can be reliably supplied when the supply chain is broken up, while reducing costs through competition. Their successes became a driving force for subsequent reformers to initiate restructuring processes in their own markets to achieve similar benefits.

The Early Reformers – How it all started

The section below provides brief descriptions of early reformers. The text is not intended to be exhaustive, but rather to briefly inform on the origins of power sector reform. It provides sufficient information to reveal the historic context of global power sector reforms and how these initial reformers prompted reforms in developing countries.

United States of America

In 1978, the United States Congress passed the Public Utility Regulatory Policies Act (PURPA) as part of the National Energy Act to promote greater use of renewable energy[20]. Creating a market for non-utility electric power, this law obliged electric utilities to buy power from independent generators at the avoided cost of generation. An outcome of PURPA was the increased prevalence of unregulated independent co-generation plants[21]. Thereafter, a number of states permitted distribution utilities to enter into contracts with IPPs to secure the required capacity for these utilities to serve their customers. Certain regulated utilities also set up unregulated subsidiaries to develop IPPs in and outside of their service territories. By 1992, IPPs accounted for 60 percent of new capacity in the USA[22].

Another event that changed the operation of the sector was the institution of a rule by the Federal Energy Regulatory Commission (FERC) in 1996, requiring that each utility or utility pool allow non-discriminatory transmission access, thereby paving the way for wholesale competition. The result, roughly twenty years after the PURPA legislation was enacted, was unbundled generation and competition in the sector amongst power producers—with investor-owned generation accounting for about three quarters of US retail electricity sales[23]. At the Distribution level, municipal, federal, and customer-owned distribution companies still exist. Despite little switching of customers amongst retailers overall, by 2007 retail competition was available in almost half the states[24].

Chile

In 1982, in a more deliberate effort to restructure the electricity supply industry towards competition, Chile enacted a new institutional framework for a decentralised electricity supply industry with greater private participation. Generally recognised as the pioneer of electricity market reforms, the Chilean electricity supply industry managed transmission on an open access basis giving generators non-discriminatory entry to the national grid as power generation was subjected to competitive forces[25]. By 1996 there were eleven privately owned generation companies. By 2000, twenty-six private generators supplied all the country's power. Wholesale competition was implemented at generation (and distribution) levels as new investor financed projects were left to market forces and facilitated through legal and institutional changes[26]. While the initial market structure and regulatory arrangements have not been without problems, the Chilean experience was largely hailed as a developing country success story[27]. It was therefore used to persuasively argue for private ownership and operation in the power sector[28].

England and Wales

The British experience with power sector reform has been among the most widely referenced reform cases to date for industrialised and developing countries alike. Since nationalisation in 1947, the electricity supply industry was under the control of the Central Electricity Generation Board, which was responsible for Generation and Transmission functions[29]. Although reform was driven primarily by an ideological pledge to reduce the role of the state and increase private participation in the sector, another key reason for change was the high electricity prices. These had come about largely due to obligations by the Central Electricity Generation Board to buy uneconomic British coal from suppliers, who enjoyed strong political influence from coalitions backed mainly by coal unions[30]. With the passage of the Electricity Act of 1989, the way was paved for privatisation in the electricity industry. Generation was vertically and horizontally separated and privatised. Only nuclear power generation, amounting to approximately 15 percent of capacity at the time, remained in public ownership. In 1996, the government eventually floated modern nuclear stations as British Energy. An electricity regulator exercised oversight of the transition toward a fully competitive industry to promote competition at the Generation level through market mechanisms, resulting in lower retail prices and private investment in Generation[31].

Nordic Countries

Starting in Norway in 1990, new legislation through the Energy Act 50 of 1990 provided a legal framework for the restructuring and regulation of the power sector—and the establishment of the joint Nordic Electricity Exchange, also known as Nord Pool[32]. The exchange officially began operating in 1993, gradually spreading to Sweden (1996), Finland (1997) and Denmark (2002). By 2003, when the utilities in these countries assumed approximately three-quarters of generation through bilateral contracts, about a quarter of electricity produced was traded on the spot market managed by Nord Pool. This coincided with a period (2002-2003) of reduced hydroelectric generation. Reservoir volumes from hydroelectric dams were roughly half that of the preceding twenty years, while spot prices reached two to three times the norm. Despite these supply side shocks the system operated reasonably well. Most analysts reached the conclusion that the market institution adequately managed the large supply variations in hydropower[33].

Although restructuring among the early reformers, as described above, namely, USA, Chile, United Kingdom, and certain Nordic countries, came about through different paths and despite their teething problems, they all generally resulted in *improved efficiencies in the industry* by reducing state involvement (except for regulation) and by introducing competition. Market mechanisms have held except for a few market shocks that resulted in changes to market rules and incentives.

The California power crisis in 2001 revealed early weaknesses in the initial market trading rules. Regulatory rules placed retail caps on distributors and precluded them from entering into forward contracts (i.e., moving bulk power trades into spot markets). In addition, flaws in the market design, encouraged market gaming (or the exercise of market power) by traders, utilities, generators, and even the state itself. This steered one utility into bankruptcy and another near bankruptcy[34].

In the case of Chile, a severe drought from late 1997 well into 1999 resulted in market price shocks. It hobbled the country's electricity sector where hydropower comprised half of installed generation capacity. These shocks were however not inevitable. While it was possible to manage the system without power outages, rigidity of the pricing system resulted in the system being unable to respond to the large supply-side shocks. Weaknesses were attributed to poor regulatory incentives and deficient regulatory governance.

In the England and Wales pool, shortly after the introduction of competition, generators soon learnt that they could manipulate prices and set bids for their power stations well above cost, forcing the electricity regulator to institute a mechanism to cap pool prices.

Over time, learnings and improvements took place in countries that pioneered power sector reforms to ensure that competitive electricity markets functioned effectively. As these markets matured, competitive power pools became the *end-state* of the standard reform model and the blueprint for reforming power sectors.

The Reform Process

Power sector reform seeks to address a number of issues. In most developing countries and in some industrialised countries, the motivation for power sector reform originated from dissatisfaction with the performance of public utilities, increasing fiscal pressure on the state, the need to remove subsidies, and the difficulty in attracting finance for new investment. Reforms in the sector aimed to address these problems sustainably. The goal was to optimise benefits to most stakeholders in the long-term. Reforms were expected to follow a process that would enable the sector to move from a vertically integrated monopoly. The intended outcome was that generators would be self-sufficient and operate at improved efficiencies, thereby achieving the promise of lower electricity prices.

A reform approach was loosely spelled out in the World Bank's 1993 policy paper for effective institutional regulatory and financial reform. It included these key changes[35]:

Regulatory change: to reduce government's involvement in the day-to-day operation of the sector, thereby increasing the autonomy and the accountability of staff responsible for managing the utility.

Organisational change: to facilitate the structural change from a vertically integrated monopoly into separate generation, transmission, distribution, and marketing functions. This also entailed the establishment of centres to monitor the effectiveness of the performance of these functions with respect to management effectiveness; operational, financial, and technical performance; as well as service quality.

Commercialisation and corporatisation: to orient the utility's business to operate more like a private company and less like the extension of a government department. This would entail enacting legislation allowing the utility to compete with other private companies on equal terms.

Increased private sector participation: to invite private investment in electricity in a number of ways, including sale of assets and non-utility generation; contracting and leasing; and stock exchange listings.

Numerous variations resembling the above elements took root to establish an accepted roadmap to reform. Some advocates for reforms have gone further: they include the number and sequence of the reform elements that would have a higher likelihood of leading to desired outcomes.

There are practical reasons for establishing optimum sequencing of reform elements. The rationale behind optimum sequencing of reform elements stems from the feasibility in enacting reforms, e.g., passing legislation before regulation. It is important to emphasise the value of not committing to changes too early by keeping options open and delaying 'irreversible' changes until their potential benefits outweigh their potential cost, e.g., having effective regulation in place before divestiture and competition. In such cases, although government ownership may be unattractive for various reasons, optimal sequencing of reforms still guards the option of a well-formulated future privatisation.

Over the years the steps for power sector reform came to be known as the 'standard prescription' for power sector reform. In following the 'standard prescription' of changing the industry structure from a monopoly to a fully-fledged competitive sector, intermediate industry models have been adopted to facilitate such an evolution.

Models of Industry Reform

Market structure changes have been at the heart of power sector reform. Since competition requires a market, the first step to transforming the market structure from a monopoly is the single buyer model, an intermediate step in moving towards wholesale competition, as illustrated in Figure 3.1.

Figure 3.1: Evolution of Monopoly to Single Buyer

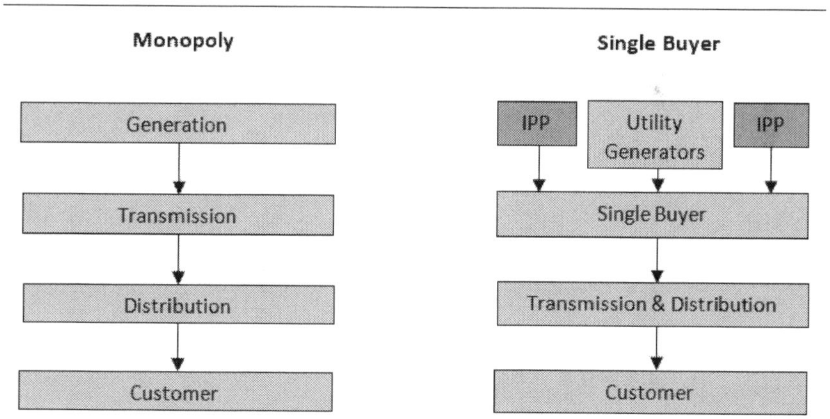

Arrows indicate the direction of energy flow. Payment flows would be reversed.

Under the single buyer arrangement only the existing integrated monopoly is allowed to purchase power from public and private generators, with purchases from private generators usually taking place through long-term contracts. Key advantages of the single buyer model have been its ability to attract capital through long term contracts; its ability to centralise purchases; and its ease of implementation. There are no fundamental changes to the market structure required to enable non-utility generators to participate in Generation. Once sufficient buyers and sellers emerge, the model is extended to full competition, as illustrated in Figure 3.2.

Figure 3.2: Generation Wholesale Competition

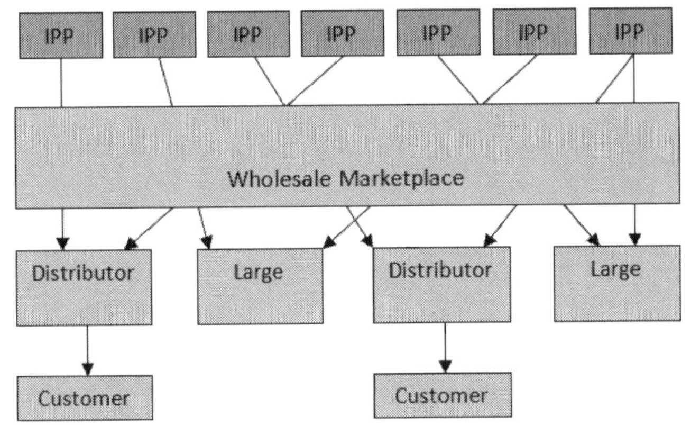

Arrows indicate the direction of energy flow. Payment flows would be reversed.

A further development of Figure 3.2 would be competition in the Distribution sector where commercial and residential customers would be enabled to choose their electricity supplier. The reform process as described above would be carefully synchronised with movement between the models from a monopoly to wholesale competition[36].

Shaping Reforms – Domestic Actors, the World Bank, and Policy Consultants

The standard prescription, as it came to be known, was adopted and advocated by numerous stakeholders. Although the model found domestic champions within developing countries and development finance institutions, a large network of consultants should also be credited with formalising and spreading the reform agenda.

With many developing countries dependent on finance from the World Bank and other development finance institutions, they were in many respects obliged to follow the policies as prescribed by these institutions. By the late 1980s, nearly three quarters of Sub-Saharan African countries would implement World Bank imposed structural adjustment programmes[37]. Continued commitment lending policies, aimed at improving power sector reform outcomes from multilateral and bilateral lending institutions, therefore played a significant role in influencing reforms in developing countries during the 1990s[38].

In addition, the World Bank supported funding for technical assistance missions and initiatives to address the shortage of expertise for restructuring and regulation. Many consultants who participated in the restructuring of the Chilean and British power sectors for instance, acted as advisors to development finance institutions as well as to governments of developing countries, often being directly drawn into the design of reforms[39].

Reforms in Developing Countries

Reform models and lessons learned from the early reformers were thus transferred to developing countries as they set out on various paths to transform their respective power sectors in search of improved performances. Chile, with a relatively small system, was an early case in point, serving as a model for electricity privatisation and competition in industrialised and developing countries with smaller grids. As positive outcomes of reform were realised in countries that adopted reform elements, momentum was gained. Thus, a wave of reforms was initiated. To date, the developing region that has reformed the most is Latin America with Eastern Europe following closely. South and East Asia, the Middle East, and Africa regions have seen significantly less reform.

A key reason for the large variation in the extent of reforms amongst developing regions is the diversity in the country and power sector contexts where reforms were instituted. The array of starting conditions for many developing countries and the range of endowments of developing countries made textbook approaches to reforming power sectors impossible for the most part. Reformers found it difficult to institute and sustain reforms in certain country contexts.

Two contradictory views were generally held with respect to power sector reform in developing countries. The one was that reform should be beneficial to these countries since the starting conditions were generally poor—and thus even a small change should have sizable positive effects on the sector due to the small base from which reforms are started. The other was that reforms were too complex an undertaking to successfully implement in smaller systems. In such cases the institutional capacity was already lacking, and the sector would be unlikely to support measures to institute reforms and sustain them[40].

Although the contradiction was mainly with respect to small developing countries with small power systems, larger developing countries have also had their share of difficulties in enacting and sustaining reforms. In 2004, authors Thomas Heller and David Victor conducted a survey of five developing nations that have the largest economies and power sectors in their respective regions (Brazil, China, India, Mexico and South Africa). The authors concluded that the difficulty of enacting reforms stems from the nature of state systems. They suggested that key political, legal, and institutional factors determined reform process outcomes[41].

According to Heller and Victor, efficiency improvements alone are not likely to be an adequate motivator for reform. They advocate that attributes such as financing, social functions performed by state utilities, and their systems of governance and control, ultimately guide the reform process as reforms become intertwined with reforms in other aspects of the economy. It is these reforms in other aspects of the economic, political, or social systems which tend to crowd out initial power sector reform drivers and result in insufficient momentum to sustain reforms. This may explain why many countries do not make it all the way through the entire reform process. The South African power sector reform experience detailed in this book is an example that illustrates this phenomenon.

Nowhere is this phenomenon of strong links to other pressing reforms in other areas of the economy more evident than in the least developed countries, most of which are found in Africa and South-East Asia. In these regions, restructuring has not progressed in ways foreseen by theorists. In most instances reforms have stagnated because the theory of power sector restructuring has not adequately mirrored the political and institutional realities associated with dismantling state-dominated systems and revolutionising them into market-oriented entities[42].

Reforms in Africa and the Emergence of Hybrid Markets

By any measure, power sector reform as per the 'standard model' has been difficult to implement in the African context. When contrasting reform progress of Africa with other developing regions, it is clear that the extent by which the region lags other developing regions is significant. There has been little unbundling of electricity supply industry functions to enable competition in African power sectors with the large majority of state-owned utilities remaining vertically integrated. There is no competition *in* the market. Amongst generators, there is no meaningful competitive bidding for dispatching generators to reduce electricity market prices in real time. In many cases there is also little competition *for* the market. Even where there have been invitations to introduce private participation, responses and outcomes have been mostly poor[43]. New investments in the generation sector have not always been brought in via competitive bidding practices to reduce electricity costs.

Several preconditions need to be achieved for a given country's power sector to be attractive to new investment. Few African countries have established independent regulatory agencies, which is key to attracting new investment and to attain financial viability within their power sectors. Even where there have been regulatory agencies established, their performances have been questionable, with the independence of regulators often undermined as governments exert pressure on regulators—and tariff setting becomes politicised[44]. Effective regulation is also impeded by limited human resources and inadequate funding.

A number of authors, policy analysts, and industry professionals have challenged the practicality and applicability of enacting power sector reforms up to and including wholesale competition in African and other developing countries where conditions are significantly different to those countries where successes have been achieved and power sectors have reformed in line with the 'standard model'. Despite three decades of reforms, nowhere in Africa has the reform end-state been achieved in accordance with the standard model for reform. This non-achievement is noteworthy, considering that a developing country like Argentina, for example, was able to reform its electricity sector to the point of wholesale competition in Generation in less than three years[45]. And this was done without the abundance of theory and experience in power sector reform currently available.

Problems Attracting Investment in Africa

Regardless of the theory and experience accumulated on power sector reform to date and the approaches proposed for various country contexts, the initial drivers for reform in Africa are still present. Operationally and financially, state-owned utilities are still underperforming—service delivery with respect to quality of supply and electricity access is poor and investment in new generation remains a key challenge.

In terms of attracting foreign investment into the power sector—a key reason for reforms in Africa—the continent attracts only small amount of global electricity investment into the sector, with even less going to Sub-Saharan Africa. This contrasts poorly to the Latin America and Caribbean region, and the East Asia and Pacific region, which attracts significantly more investment.

Not only has Africa attracted less investment in generation infrastructure than other developing regions, but investment is also on the decline. The downward trend in investment may be attributed to a number of reasons. In the late 1990s, private sector investors were negatively affected by the financial shocks of the Asian and Latin American currency crises that spilled over into most of the developing world. Many contracts were renegotiated in these regions, and some cancelled outright—leaving investors with less appetite for foreign power markets. The contracts that were not cancelled left many host governments, including those in Africa where currencies devalued significantly, with increased power charges due to the currency devaluations and inflexible purchasing contracts. Subsequently some governments, as in the case of Egypt, reverted to state funding of electricity infrastructure projects, bolstered by development finance institutions, which began to rethink their policies on conditional lending.

Poor investment performances and risk appraisals in developing countries also influenced private investors from industrialised countries to reduce their risk exposure in these emerging markets and return to their domicile markets.

Although recent development financing mechanisms, spurred on by carbon reduction objectives, have found ways to reimagine the financing of power sectors in Africa, investments in energy continue to remain chronically, and largely, inadequate.

Hybrid Markets – Solutions Giving Rise to New Challenges

Higher investment risks and economic shocks have not necessarily been the main factor for reduced investment in generation infrastructure. Countries that have not been adversely affected by economic shocks have not necessarily seen more reform than those that have experienced economic crises. Developing countries with IPPs that have not experienced significant currency shocks are still faced with the challenging task of integrating IPPs with rigid contractual arrangements into planned wholesale markets[46]. The transitional step to guide the industry structure towards competition—the single buyer—has proven tricky to move beyond. The issues of excess capacity, stranded costs and uneconomical tariffs prove to be difficult challenges for market designers and policy makers. Excess capacity often results in generators with higher costs finding it hard to economically compete in a competitive power market. Stranded costs represent reductions in asset values or lost revenues when fixed offtake agreements based on capital costs make way for new wholesale bidding practices. Additionally, uneconomical tariffs do not send the correct price signals to attract timely investment in generation infrastructure.

Due to these transitional hiccups, some reform proponents have suggested that it may even be better to skip the single buyer step and adopt a market model with multiple buyers immediately after unbundling due the complexity of moving away from a single buyer arrangement[47]. Despite the transitional challenges of the single buyer arrangements, in certain cases the single buyer is considered the only alternative to attract investment in power systems characterised by generation capacity shortages. Within this arrangement there are a few mechanisms that mitigate against its many drawbacks. These include increasing transparency; finding ways to accommodate the otherwise rigid contractual and institutional arrangements; and the reduction of contingent liabilities for host governments[48].

To their credit, in many developing countries, single buyer arrangements and IPPs have launched and sustained the reform process by demonstrating the benefits of private investment and management. Relatively easy to implement in power sectors that have not seen much reform, IPPs can enter wholesale power markets under any of the industry markets described earlier in this chapter. They have generally sold their power under long-term power purchase agreements to state owned utilities acting as the single buyer, affording private investors mitigation against market risk.

◈ ◈ ◈

With reforms having stagnated and levelled out at hybrid markets, it would appear that the single buyer arrangement will dominate the African power sector landscape in the foreseeable future. The end state of the standard prescription for power sector reform, i.e., wholesale competitive power markets, has remained out of reach for all power sectors in Africa. The need for private participation in generation infrastructure continues due to insufficient state funding and as political, economic, and social challenges in many cases continue to stifle further reforms. This is evidenced in the South African experiences examined in this book. The next three chapters will detail the South African experiences with power sector reforms, their links with other political, social, and economic policies, and the country's battle to keep the lights on.

CHAPTER 4

SOUTH AFRICAN ENERGY POLICY – A BRIEF HISTORICAL REVIEW

The development of the South African energy landscape is inextricably linked to its historic economic and industrial policies. The country's energy policy was strongly influenced by the gold rush that started in the late 1800s—fashioned largely by the need for cheap reliable power to extract minerals. This chapter describes specific historic features of South Africa's electricity and broader energy policies since the early 1900s, until political change occurred in 1994. It describes key factors that shaped energy policies, related environmental and mining policies, as well as social policies.

Also presented are the changes that occurred since the African National Congress (ANC) government assumed office in 1994, how more recent government policies have shaped the electricity landscape, and how policy reforms paradoxically contributed to the problem of insufficient generation capacity. Lastly, it sets out the challenges faced by the government in managing the most significant energy transition since the discovery of fossil fuels.

South African Energy and Industrial Policies (1910 – 1990)

It was clear from the outset that after the Union of South Africa was formed in 1910 and post-war resurgence occurred, the main goal of energy policy was to *provide a cheap source of reliable energy for national industrialisation.* Throughout the years of rapid economic growth and industrialisation, this objective was always central to economic development. Even after ESCOM/EVKOM transitioned into the new democratic dispensation in 1994, its bold vision was to provide *'the lowest cost electricity for growth and prosperity'*.

Industrial and Social Objectives

In South Africa, *affordability* and *reliability* were always the cornerstones of the national power sector policy. When the Apartheid regime was formally adopted in 1948, broader socio-political and industrial policies marginalised most of the population. Black South Africans were mainly used as inexpensive labour to keep mining costs—and therefore electricity production costs—low. To the detriment of most of its Black citizens, who did not necessarily benefit from affordable and reliable electricity, South Africa's minerals and energy policies formed the foundation for its national industrial progress. This contributed to the country becoming the largest and most industrialised economy on the continent.

South Africa's economic development centred around the development of mining and energy related institutions that spearheaded the country's initial industrialisation. The relationship between minerals and energy became known as the *minerals-energy complex*. While there was the introduction of other manufacturing and services sectors that over time significantly contributed to the growth and maturation of the South African economy, the minerals-energy complex largely dominated the drivers for growth in the domestic economy. Endowed with rich deposits of mineral resources, South Africa required large amounts of cheap electricity to extract and beneficiate these mineral resources.

Environmental Policies

Political and economic isolation during the Apartheid years meant that South Africa did not always have to play by the same rules as the rest of the world, especially when came to the environment, labour relations, and human rights. The country could therefore evade certain environmental obligations in order to meet its economic and industrialisation objectives[49]. The legacy of the Apartheid government's escape from environmental obligations in favour of economic and industrial objectives can still be seen today in the abandoned mine dumps that mark the Johannesburg skyline.

While South Africa did try to align with certain environmental protection objectives out of necessity, other priorities were often crowded out as the politics of segregation sought only to preserve and maintain the narrow interests of the whites-only government. The government, aware of its dependence on income from minerals, often exempted mining companies from appropriate environmental standards[50].

The electricity demand from the mining industry also meant that at times the provision of low-cost electrical power meant paying lip service to costly environmental imperatives. An example in the electricity generation sector was that of emissions from ESCOM's coal-fired power stations. The Duvha Power Station in Mpumalanga Province had high flue gas emissions for many years in the late 1970s, before the problems were eventually resolved (with retrofits) in the 1980s.

The political and economic isolation from the international community meant that environmental crimes could be suppressed along with human rights abuses by the Apartheid government, or ignored if the adverse effects thereof were not felt by their voting constituencies. Environmental activist groups were relatively few in South Africa during the Apartheid era. While during this period in South Africa's history, there were many positive environmental initiatives in certain sectors of the economy and society (such as the preservation of wildlife and the establishment of game parks), constructive environmental regulation initiatives were not always prevalent in the country's mining and industrial sectors.

Air quality was a case in point. In black suburbs, with or without access to electricity, air pollution was a common occurrence as inhabitants used wood and other fuels for heating and cooking. Moreover, many forms of active and passive advocacy against government policies were discouraged under the Apartheid regime. Environmental activism was therefore not prevalent due to the consequences of coming up against draconian Apartheid laws. Notably, some conservationists were implicated in the Apartheid system, whereas others were concerned about the consequences of openly objecting to specific environmental practices, which were often entangled in the trappings of related Apartheid laws and policies.

Environmental and climate concerns were not always priorities for the National Party. The ruling government disregarded adverse environmental impacts on Black citizens. Indeed, the global environmental movement had not yet ascended to a level of prominence where international pressures were exerted on sovereign countries to adapt their environmental policies to enable a more sustainable world-wide future—as is the case in today's modern globalised era. International support was mainly garnered for scrapping of the Apartheid laws, rather than for environmental protection imperatives.

After decades of political and economic isolation, however, environmental considerations rose in prominence after South Africa's reintegration into global politics and the global economy. For South Africa, making an entry onto the world stage meant adopting and adhering to more acceptable global standards, which would become more important. Its further inclusion into trade and other agreements (as well as participating in global oversight bodies) was dependent on its continued adoption of more widely accepted labour, human rights, and environmental policies. Progressive socio-economic policies and environmental considerations therefore only enjoyed higher prominence since the introduction of the country's constitutional democracy in the 1990s.

Energy and the Political Transition to Democratic Rule (1990 – 2010)

In February 1990, less than three months after the falling of the Berlin Wall, South African president, Frederik Willem de Klerk, announced the intention of the National Party government to release political prisoners detained under the Apartheid laws. De Klerk's landmark speech at the opening of the South African parliament signalled the start of a negotiating process towards a more inclusive political dispensation. The African National Congress, the country's largest liberation movement, positioned itself as a key player in the negotiations to end minority rule.

In the aftermath of the fall of the Soviet Union, and in the absence of a credible experiential outcome-based alternative of what life under a socialist system could be, the ANC and its alliance partner, the South African Communist Party, had no credible options for alignment to a former Soviet-styled political dispensation. The western world was waiting to welcome South Africa onto the global stage, and this set the expectation for adopting at least some western-styled economic and political principles. After the dissolution of the Union of Soviet Socialist Republics (USSR), many former Soviet states also sought to join western blocs. This signalled intent from former socialist states suggested fundamental changes to their political approaches, as it did for the ANC in South Africa.

As a liberation movement, before assuming political power the ANC adopted an ideology of centralism based on its adoption of the National Democratic Revolution. The three decades before the fall of the Berlin Wall, the Soviet Union had been the ANC's closest and most influential ally. The former USSR had taken a much more active role in supporting the struggle against Apartheid, than had many western states who opposed the racist ideology.

A strong supporter of the anti-Apartheid movement, the former Soviet Union supported the ANC with arms, as well as with logistical and financial aid. In addition to military training, the former Soviet Union provided professional non-military training for many ANC cadres and their families—and in many other ways protected ANC and SACP members from the specific struggles and dangers associated with life in exile. It was unsurprising therefore that among ANC and SACP cadres, there was a lot of admiration for the former Soviet Union, its ideology, its policies, and its achievements[51].

The demise of the former USSR was therefore a setback for the ANC, who started preparations for negotiations for a takeover of the government in the wake of the fall of the Berlin Wall. As negotiations started with the then-governing National Party, even amongst some ANC members and its allies in the South African Communist Party, they found themselves questioning the unswerving adoption of perceived outdated political and economic models that had incontrovertibly experienced the limits of their usefulness—its weaknesses demonstrated on a global scale.

With few political and economic policy alternatives, and despite the ambitions of many communist-aligned cadres to conform with USSR ideologies over the previous three decades, the integration of the country into the international community shaped the altered policies that the ruling party would adopt. In the absence of a significant socialist supporter nation (or a bloc such as the former USSR), South Africa was enjoined by western states to adopt more democratic political and economic models. The western world was ready to welcome South Africa back from its former isolation with promises of capital investment, market access to western economies, as well as opportunities take up a more leading role on the world stage and on the African continent. South Africa therefore made the required concessions to be ushered into western-styled global political and economic policy domains, rather than far-left socialist politics. This alignment had a marked influence on country sectoral policies spearheaded during the first administration of the ANC-led government from 1994 to 1999.

Since assuming government office in April 1994, the ANC-led government of national unity spent the next four years drafting new policies for various economic sectors. And despite a bold attempt to embark on power sector reforms as espoused in the 1998 Energy White Paper (and as followed in certain western states), there was little agreement amongst the ruling party and its alliance partners on its adoption. The 1998 White Paper on Energy Policy was issued at roughly the same time that Eskom repeatedly cautioned the government—that if the utility was not permitted to build more power plants, that the country would run out of electricity generation by 2007[52].

Policy uncertainty and indecision within the tripartite alliance itself, and in the government as a whole, largely contributed to the very late decision in 2004 to build additional generation capacity. The decision to develop additional generation capacity in the form of the Medupi and Kusile coal-fired power stations, as well the Ingula Pumped Storage Scheme, was therefore rushed.

The proposed change in energy policy introduced by the 1998 White Paper was subsequently not adopted by the government. Neither the state, nor the private sector, took the lead in developing new generation projects. Rather than creating the intended policy certainty, the 1998 White Paper did the opposite. The publishing of the intended policy document followed by the non-adoption thereof, was arguably the most significant policy contributor to the lack of generation investment (state sponsored or private) since the ANC government came to power. With insufficient supporters backing the proposed policy (inside and outside government), the indecision maintained the status quo, with state-sponsored generation projects eventually back in vogue.

Energy Policy Transition and the Environment (1990 – Present)

Regardless of the waves of environmental conservation, sustainability movements, and green politics, that swept the globe in the 1970s and 1980s, South Africa's political isolation meant that external environmental influences did not have the same profound effects on domestic environmental policies and practices.

Meanwhile, in 1992, while the South African political transition was being negotiated, a transition of a different kind was being tabled at the United Nations Conference on Environment and Development by the United Nations Intergovernmental Panel on Climate Change. The outcome was the United Nations Framework Convention on Climate Change (UNFCCC), effective March 1994. The stated purpose of the UNFCCC was to stabilise concentrations of atmospheric greenhouse gases to a level that would prevent dangerous anthropogenic interference with global and regional climate systems.

In 1997, the United Nations Intergovernmental Panel on Climate Change realised that in order to meet their desired goals, further cuts in greenhouse gas emissions were required. In August 1997, roughly three years into its new democratic transition, South Africa endorsed the UNFCCC. In 2002 therefore, South Africa acceded to the Kyoto Protocol, which would come into force in February 2005. Since the UNFCCC was non-mandatory on developing countries, South Africa did not have commitments under the first implementation of measures for the commitment period between 2008 and 2012.

In November 2011, at the 17th meeting of the Conference of the Parties (or COP 17) hosted by South Africa in the coastal city of Durban, it was clear that international greenhouse gas emission targets developed under the Kyoto Protocol were inadequate to achieve the desired projected reduction in global warming. As the Kyoto commitment period was coming to an end in 2012, according to the models of the UNFCCC a new deal was needed to stabilise the concentrations of future global greenhouse gases.

South Africa's showing at COP 17 was that it would commence its forays into changing its electricity mix by introducing renewable energy plants into its generation sector. As the host, South Africa was eager to show leadership. The Department of Energy hosted a number of side events at the South Africa Climate Change Response Expo, touting a range of measures. These included diversifying its energy mix towards a low carbon economy, promoting energy efficiency, and carbon capture and storage, amongst others. A few months earlier therefore, in August 2011, South Africa commenced with its Renewable Energy Independent Power Producers Procurement (REIPPP) programme.

Globally, however, an even stronger response to reducing greenhouse emissions and implementing the UNFCCC was required. This required response, in the main, was the impetus for the 2015 Paris Agreement (adopted at COP 21), whereby developing countries, like South Africa, would be required to set Nationally Determined Contributions to reduce greenhouse gas emissions, with financial and other aid provided by developed countries.

Unlike its predecessor (i.e., the Kyoto Protocol), the Paris Agreement was a legally binding treaty that committed countries to measures that would reduce carbon emissions. In April 2016, South Africa committed to change its standing policies and practices of large-scale coal-fired electricity generation in exchange for a range of power generation technologies that would promise reductions in greenhouse gas emissions.

By 2016, when the Paris Agreement was signed by the South African government, the country had already executed four bid rounds of renewable energy IPPs attracting roughly forty renewable energy IPPs for solar and wind electricity generation. At the time, South Africa was considered one of the leading developing countries with respect to integration of utility-scale wind and solar renewable generation—and the country's REIPPP programme was regarded a flagship programme. Advertised as a successful blueprint for future additional electricity generation, the REIPPP programme was generally hailed as a model to inform similar programmes in other developing countries, on the continent and elsewhere.

Headwinds for Renewable Energy Independent Power Producer Programme

The policy transition to renewable generation technologies did not retain traction with Eskom, when later in 2015 its Group Chief Executive Officer announced that the company will no longer sign on new renewable energy IPPs. Eskom cited that the PPAs were unaffordable for the utility and that the company could soon be left with excess generation capacity—once the Medupi and Kusile coal-fired plants (with a stated combined capacity of 9 600 MW) came into full operation. The long-term affordability of IPP charges on Eskom and its customers were questioned by executives and the continued impact of the REIPPP on Eskom's long-term financial sustainability was undetermined.

As part of the defence for the refusal to sign more IPPs, it was stated that Eskom would be responsible for the 'death of coal' and that the implications of this pivotal transition for the power sector as a whole—including the coal value chain industries and the economy at large—was not well understood. Caution was expressed over advancing moves to tamper with a symbiotic relationship between mining and power generation, a relationship which has spanned more than a century. Any sudden sectoral changes needed to be assessed technically, financially, and socio-economically, before embarking on a new generation paradigm.

It still remains unclear why and how the government as the holder of the policy to introduce REIPPs and sole shareholder of Eskom was so conflicted in its *environmental* policy formulation (which promoted signing of REIPPs) and its *energy* policy execution (which vetoed the signing of REIPPs). Some within the electricity supply industry have offered reasons for the unwillingness to sign REIPPs: they asserted that these same executives handsomely benefited from a coal future within Eskom, by receiving personal financial rewards from companies that would do business with Eskom. These suspicions were later validated after investigations by the country's National Prosecuting Authority found senior Eskom executives financially benefiting from shady dealings with dishonest suppliers and service providers, while they were in the employ of the utility.

Energy Transition - Preparation, Planning and Justice

Energy analysts have also speculated that the reason for the conflict could be that the environmental commitments made under the Ministry of Environment failed to adequately reach consensus with the Ministry of Minerals and Energy and the Ministry of Public Enterprises stakeholders. There was therefore no agreement on the adopted policy commitments from the national power utility—including policy implementation which would be required a few years later. At the time of signing the Paris Agreement, the implementation of commitments was more than five years away. Details of the agreements negotiated under the UNFCCC therefore did not yet consider it necessary to make other economic sectors (such as electricity) fully aware of the implications of what was negotiated on their behalf. The details of the agreement also did not spell out their respective future obligations in achieving commitments that were made on their behalf.

Still others have surmised that it was not necessary to provide comprehensive details on the full implications of the energy transition since South Africa did not have a choice under the UNFCCC. It simply had to change its carbon-emitting electricity landscape, and that those adversely impacted would be catered for under a *Just* Energy Transition.

It should be noted that South Africa's Just Energy Transition as a policy transition framework only formally came into being in 2020. The Eskom Just Energy Transition Office, as well as the Presidential Climate Commission, a commission tasked with advising on South Africa's climate change response, were both only established at the end of 2020. The first Just Transition Framework was only adopted at the Presidential Climate Commission's sixth meeting in May 2022. At the time when the commitments were made (in 2016), very little information was therefore available on the impact of the transition on communities, its timing, the coal value chain, as well as the operational and financial impact on the power utility.

It is contended that the effect of deciding on a policy transition in 2016 (after the Paris Agreement was formulated) and only ironing out the details five to seven years later, fuelled hesitation and apprehension that produced increasing resistance to its implementation. The resistance was expressed at the highest levels of the ruling ANC and within the executive levels of Eskom. The time chasm between policy adoption and understanding its full implications contributed to hesitation, opposition to the transition, and even resentment, amongst key stakeholders who were affected by the transition and whose assistance was needed to give effect to the policy transition.

Without a detailed plan for the implementation of the energy transition, the dawn of the death of coal, ushered in an uncertain era in the country's energy future. While it offered opportunities to those IPPs who already started to capitalise on alternate forms of generation, for many it spelled the end of an era because their livelihoods were integral to the minerals-energy complex.

While many communities would certainly benefit from cleaner air in the medium-to-long–term, the future health benefits were considered less pressing than immediate needs of protecting livelihoods. For poor communities, the trade-off between livelihoods and health was in the balance as they were contemplating an uncertain future of an industry that had supported their incomes for more than a century.

For many decades, at the heart of South Africa's industrial and economic expansion was the provision of low-cost electricity partly due to the abundance of cheap coal. Many commercial, industrial, and agricultural electricity consumers were also concerned about the effect of the transition on the long-term electricity tariff trajectory. Questions remained unanswered regarding what the energy transition meant for future investment in energy intensive industries and for the many South African residents for whom electricity was already unaffordable. Therefore, while many businesses, communities, and citizens, did not in principle resist or oppose the energy transition, the lack of adequate transparency and resultant increased ambiguity, resulted in fewer voices coming out strong in favour of the energy transition.

Much of the resistance to the energy transition came from the Minister of Minerals and Energy, Gwede Mantashe, a former coal miner, a former member of the South African Communist Party, and a former labour union representative. As the country's energy policy custodian, he found himself presiding over a coal sector in decline, as daily electricity shortages were clearly hurting the country's economy. The country lacked a cross-sectoral, all-encompassing and comprehensive blueprint for how to make the energy transition a just one. Environmental professionals and activists mainly interpreted the policy from an environmental and climate change perspective, Eskom only spoke to the policy from an electricity generation perspective, and the Ministry of Labour provided scant details on the unemployment impacts. Rarely were the detailed integration aspects of the proposed energy transition sensibly formulated and sufficiently communicated to show that short, medium, and long-term social risks for communities were addressed—and that the benefits to the environment, continued employment, and sustainable economic growth, were not mutually exclusive.

◈ ◈ ◈

South Africa's historic energy policy was anchored to using cheap coal to provide affordable electricity to power the country's industrialisation. To this end, environmental objectives were not always the main consideration. As the country transitioned politically in the 1990s, the reintegration of South Africa into the international community coupled with the advancing global decarbonisation movement, challenged the country's continuance of its historic energy policy—a policy that, in no small part, contributed to its past economic successes.

CHAPTER 5

COORDINATION OF ENERGY AND RELATED SECTORAL POLICIES

South Africa faced an uncertain energy future due to insufficient policy transition mechanisms, inimical related policy choices, and poor cross-sectoral policy coordination and implementation. These factors ultimately contributed to unsatisfactory power sector outcomes.

Incoherent cross-sectoral policies without any coordinated priority order, optimisation, or integration, make government policies difficult to implement effectively. This is even more so without deliberate policy harmonisation processes—to determine, moderate, or enhance the impact that policies in one sector have on policy objectives in other sectors of government or the economy. This is not to say that policy implementation in one sector would, or should, never slow down the achievement of policy objectives in other sectors. Often social objectives and economic objectives contradict. This could be the case when social policy objectives such as keeping tariffs low to support the poor threatens the financial sustainability of the state-owned utility.

Given the limited resources in any economy, it is expected that cross-sectoral policies could contradict. However, it is important for policies in one sector to be pre-assessed or stress-tested in other sectors, where they are anticipated to influence, in important ways, the outcomes of other policy or related objectives.

This chapter presents a discussion on the need for improved policy integration and harmonisation across various economic sectors—both outside and inside the power sector, as well as improved coordination and management of the sub-sectors within the South African power sector.

Policy Harmonisation and Coordination Across Economic Sectors

Where there are potential cross-sectoral policy contradictions, special provisions can reduce the impact of policy failure in a sector or in other spheres of government. Phased or temporal implementation of policy instruments (implemented by one Ministry, for example) could be one of the solutions offered to ensure that one sectoral policy instrument does not undermine another policy objective elsewhere in government, society, or the economy.

Policy harmonisation seeks to better integrate governmental policies and regulations of various jurisdictions to maximise overall cooperation and benefit from positive catalyst effects. The optimisation of policies seeks to leverage policy mechanisms, timing of implementation, and policy outcomes, to ideally have a synergising effect towards the achievement of positive outcomes in all sectors. Conversely, where there is the potential for one policy instrument in one sector to delay the achievement of policy objectives in other sectors, policy harmonisation seeks to minimise the retardation effects. Policy harmonisation is one of the responses governments can exercise to deal with problems arising from potential policy conflicts among government departments. It is a form of inter-governmental or inter-sectoral cooperation whereby various government sectors have a clear understanding how their sector-specific policy objectives would still be achieved despite the impeding effects of other sectoral policies.

Unfortunately, the degree of policy harmonisation in South Africa has been insufficient, especially in the energy sector. As an example, due to affordability concerns, electricity tariffs are maintained at a level whereby customers are protected from severe increases. The National Energy Regulator has been careful to keep tariffs low to protect the poor and to prevent the economy from stagnating. However, a carbon tax is levied on these same consumers of electricity to reduce reliance on fossil fuels.

By themselves, most residential, commercial and industrial consumers in South Africa have no real leverage to influence the speed at which Eskom changes its generation primary energy mix towards lower carbon sources. It can be argued that the timing of the carbon tax policy mechanism is therefore mismatched between energy affordability (poverty alleviation) and environmental (carbon reduction) policy outcomes. The use of ineffective (or blunt) policy instruments have been seen in many other sectors in South Africa.

Timely Updating of Policies and Plans

By 2016, South Africa was a signatory to the United Nations Framework Convention on Climate Change and the Paris Agreement on Climate

Change. Yet the country's updated electricity Integrated Resource Plan (IRP edition 2019) still indicated that fossil fuelled power for coal-fired power stations would be developed. Even five years later in September 2021, when South Africa pledged to reduce its Nationally Determined Carbon Contributions, its Energy ministry still did not timeously revoke the country's IRP. By November 2023, there was still no approved updated Integrated Resource Plan, despite South Africa's National Climate Change Response Policy being published as a White Paper as far back as October 2011.

Significant delays in updating related energy policies and plans have contributed to policy indecision and delays in setting the power sector on a correction course. Outdated policies, poor integration, and static plans, failed to provide the desired policy certainty and direct clear trajectories for key economic sectors—especially sectors that were fast changing, like the country's electricity supply sector.

Cross-Sectoral Influences

Broader industrial and economic policies linked to the energy sector were also fragmented in their approach towards achieving their stated objectives. The high tariffs levied on imported electric vehicles were inconsistent with the policy objective of reduced carbon emission—where renewable energy could be used to power such electric vehicles. Matching future transport policy with environmental and energy objectives therefore still lacked compatibility.

Also in the motor vehicle manufacturing sector, where protectionist policies stifled the pursuit towards a domestic lower carbon trajectory, the domestic economic conditions for creating foreign direct investment were in discordance with their key objectives (i.e., gross domestic income and employment growth). Motor vehicle manufacturing is a major exporting sector in the country. Delays in the expansion of existing manufacturing plants for the manufacturing and assembly of electric vehicles due to policy uncertainty was a lost opportunity for South Africa.

Poor cross-sectoral coordination was also prevalent in upstream power generation manufacturing sectors. Even though South Africa signalled its intention to reduce its carbon footprint as far back as 2011 when the REIPPP programme was introduced, the full upstream benefits of locally manufactured renewable generation plant components were not achieved. In 2016, after Eskom had suspended the signing of PPAs, local companies that invested in factories, machinery, and processes, to manufacture renewable generation components for wind and solar were left uncertain about their future investment outcomes. A few solar PV panel product suppliers who set up production facilities in South Africa closed their factories[53], as did a wind turbine component manufacturer[54]. As the prospects of locally produced wind generation equipment reduced due to Eskom's moratorium on the signing of new REIPP contracts, so did the expectation of increased domestic renewable generation component sales—and the expected return on investment for equipment manufacturing companies. Only in 2019, when Eskom resumed the signing of PPA, was there sufficient certainty for some suppliers of local content to return and reinvest in a growing market sector.

In July 2022, when the local content equipment requirements were reduced to permit more rapid deployment of renewable generation (amid severe national loadshedding), a solar PV parts manufacturer in South Africa was left with uncertainty about its immediate future.

Local content requirements for renewable generation projects were reduced to enable more rapid deployment of generation capacity and reduce power shortages. The impact that these relaxations in local content requirements left local manufacturers unsure about their future prospects in the short, medium, and long-term. Planning, especially planning linked to upstream manufacturing sectors, therefore failed to adequately consider critical linkages to changes in local content requirements. Investors in local manufacturing facilities were no longer sure about the investment potential of domestic manufacturing—thereby stalling further local investment in manufacturing capacity. This was due to policy uncertainty, as well as incoherent and contradictory signals received by domestic and foreign investors in renewable manufacturing facilities.

South Africa therefore not only lost out on much-needed investment in generation infrastructure. The country also lost out on investment in manufacturing facilities for renewal energy generation equipment.

Towards Harmonisation Within the South African Power Sector

Poor coordination *within* the power sector—between Generation, Transmission, and Distribution—also contributed to undesirable outcomes, including intensifying the rolling blackouts.

One of the key steps to reforming the power sector in accordance with the standard model of reform, is establishing an independent network operator which permits indiscriminate access for all generators (public and private) to supply their electricity to the transmission grid. This requires splitting up vertically integrated power utilities and inviting private sector participation into the electricity generation sector.

The creation of an independent transmission company, dissociated from Eskom's generation fleet, could help avoid the conflict of interest that occurred in 2015, when Eskom stalled the signing on of IPPs to favour operating its own plants. However, in the year 2023, eight years after the stalling of the contracts, while Eskom has embarked on vertical separation, the company had still not created a functional independent transmission company to resolve the potential conflicts of interest.

Taking Steps to Reform

Government stated that, when legally separated, the intention is that the independent transmission company would be wholly owned by Eskom Holdings. However, this leaves many questions unanswered. Even with legal separation, how would conflicts of interest be avoided if the National Transmission Company still reports into Eskom Holdings? And if the independent National Transmission Company reports into the same government ministry, as does Eskom's Generation Division, could this ensure sufficient independence, or would it amount to the same potential for undue political interference? Even if the two companies report to separate ministries, given the amount of state involvement in South African state-owned enterprises, would the intended legal separation as espoused under the standard model of reform yield the anticipated benefits under a 'commanding heights' paradigm?

The move to separate Transmission from Generation and Distribution is indeed a step towards liberalisation of the power sector if wholesale competition at the Generation level is to take place in the market. The separation of Transmission from Generation and Distribution within Eskom Holdings is therefore considered a step toward liberalisation, as long as the separation contributes to Eskom not displaying a bias to its own generation.

Currently (in 2023) no private generators actively compete with Eskom plants. IPPs are permitted to enter into Power Purchase Agreements with the utility. Thereafter IPPs are guaranteed of their financial returns, devoid of the risk of not being dispatched. Competition *within* a Generation electricity wholesale market may still be a long way off for state-owned generators and private generators.

Introducing Private Participation and Competition in the Generation Sector

In the standard model of reform, competition has been touted as a means for private and state-owned generators to compete side-by-side with the objective of state-owned generators eventually achieving the levels of efficiency of their private counterparts. In South Africa, however, private investors have mainly invested in renewable generation, and are unlikely to *directly* compete with Eskom's coal-fired plants. The concept of competition between state-owned generators and IPPs therefore still remains unclear, and uncertainty remains on how the price reduction objective of competition between SOE and IPP generators could be realised under this arrangement.

In the future there could, however, be competition in the coal generation sector. The country's National Treasury has indicated its preference for increased private sector participation to induce an improvement in the performance of some of Eskom's coal-fired generation plants. However, it remains to be seen whether the concessionary terms and conditions would be attractive enough to persuade private investors to take stakes in coal-fired generation.

Private investors could be reluctant to operate existing Eskom plants, unless significant concessions are made by the government. Financial institutions have increasingly come under pressure for promoting the continued operation, or funding, of coal-fired plants. It is unlikely that financial institutions would provide the private sector with the capital to invest in carbon emitting coal-fired plants, without significant government backing. Even with government backing, many domestic and international financial institutions have been wary about the reputational risks associated with investments in fossil-fuel sectors.

Given that the remaining design life of some of the oldest Eskom plants is only a few years, it is also questionable whether private investors would want to be saddled with widely publicised expectations of improved coal-fired plant performances—or the decommissioning of these plants. Internationally, the public have often visibly turned against private investors if performance requirements were not achieved, or when resultant higher tariffs were perceived to be due to private interests.

In addition, obtaining insurance coverage at an optimal premium is another problem that investors could encounter. Not only would insurers want to have assurances about the condition of older plants, which according to Eskom was poor. Many coal-fired operators globally have had their insurers question the continuing rationale for insuring coal-fired plants, which insurers argue contribute to climate risks—risks which the same insurers have to insure and re-insure against. Furthermore, under Eskom management, the plants have been plagued by abuse, corruption, sabotage, and there appears to be a reluctance from law enforcement agencies to speedily bring offenders to book.

It is unlikely that private investors would assume these same risks if the law enforcement capacity and political will for dealing with crime and corruption remains lacklustre. Eskom board members and executives have often stated that the company did not receive the requisite support from their political principals to ensure that Eskom plants operate optimally. This could therefore leave little appetite for legitimate private investors to step in.

Irrespective of the extent to which the private sector will be part of the solution to keep Eskom's ageing power stations operational for a few years longer, it could be a tough decision for the government, and for the National Energy Regulator of South Africa, should they decide to keep Eskom's coal-fired fleet operational for longer than their design lifespans. It could be difficult to determine when the reserve generation capacity will be recovered to a point where these plants are no longer required—and hence there could be uncertainty of the life extensions required for these plants.

Replacing a few old components with new components in ageing plants that have run their course complicates the investment decision, since a power plant is only as reliable as it most unreliable components used in power generation process. The investment decisions therefore require a number of questions to be answered with a reasonable degree of certainty. Which components should be replaced, and which components could be retained? How long could plants realistically be expected to operate after refurbishments? If investment decisions do not deliver the expected plant availability outcomes, this could have further adverse financial implications for Eskom. Worse (from a government public relations perspective) would be if government bailouts were still required after the private sector stepped in. It is for this reason that many stakeholders inside and outside Eskom have advocated for rather investing in new plants.

Because energy security must remain the primary objective, the overall impact of coal-fired plant life extension decisions must be determined. Questions abound: How would the life extensions impact on the Nationally Determined Carbon commitments made under the Paris agreement? What if the plants did not realise the expected increases in energy availability factors? How would fraud and corruption be avoided in capital investments to improve the performance of dated plants? What would be the optimal point of reinvestment for each power station? How long would the process take to approve contracts linked to life extensions, given that there are so many stakeholders (and much resistance to coal generation life extensions) in the power sector's political economy. What impact could the reinvestment have on the utility's finances, on the government's finances, and on future borrowing costs? Would reinvestment costs cover equipment required to reduce the company's emissions, or would future emission exemptions still be required?

Eskom does not have the funds to decommission all its ageing plants. The prospect of plant life extensions, therefore, could solve more than one problem. Out of necessity, such a move could perhaps help to kick the proverbial decommissioning can down the road, in order to prioritise the immediate problems of insufficient generation. Regardless of whether Eskom or the private sector will be responsible for decommissioning of coal-fired power stations, tariffs may have to increase to cover costs. Private investors may be reluctant to assume this responsibility if decommissioning commitments from government are not forthcoming.

Lastly, the approval of associated electricity tariffs could also become problematic if tariffs increased sharply to adequately cover the real cost of power generation for private investors who would take over the ageing coal fleet. The review and pre-authorisation for allowing private sector costs could be required from NERSA and a revised methodology for approving tariffs may have to be developed and be subjected to public participation. The political temptation of meddling in tariff and other regulatory determinations could also be challenged. Equally difficult would be to obtain concurrence for private sector takeover from ANC alliance partners, a grouping that has been opposed to increased private sector participation in a sector that has seen state dominance for over a century.

Vertical Separation

Breaking up the vertically integrated power utility into separate businesses has not been unanimously supported by ANC alliance partners, especially by labour unions who accused the government of privatisation by stealth. Irrespective of the form of private sector participation, the splitting of Eskom into three separate legal entities, will however allow increased and controlled focus of the separate Generation, Transmission, and Distribution sub-sectors within the electricity supply industry.

While the preparation for the organisational separation is fairly simple, there are factors that encumber the proposed legal separation. The large amount of debt has made it hard to apportion debt between Generation, Transmission and Distribution. Who would be best placed to assume what portion of the debt? Bondholders and holders of utility debt, including many pension funds, would have to agree to the transfer of their bonds to the new companies.

If the risk profiles for debtholders (and each individual Generation, Transmission and Distribution holding company) increase substantially, bondholders may be hesitant to approve the move unless more debt could be underwritten by the state. Too much debt on Generation and the future availability of Eskom's generators could be in jeopardy since there is already a shortage of funds to adequately maintain the existing generation fleet. Too much debt in Transmission and the transmission company may be unable to raise the required funding to transform the transmission grid to allow large renewable energy IPPs to connect and transmit energy to off-takers. Although the government agreed to take over a sizable portion of Eskom's debt, on its own Eskom's Transmission Division does not have the ability to finance the required transmission expansion to accommodate all future renewable IPPs. The electricity minister has indicated that private investment would be required to support transmission infrastructure expansion[55]. Too much debt in Distribution, and the continued non-payment from municipalities and Eskom customers could make it hard to sustain investment in vital upgrades and expansion of distribution infrastructure.

Although power sector debt is undoubtedly an important consideration for debtholders, there have been signs that private investors may be less concerned with the levels of debt in Eskom. In June 2022, Eskom announced that eighteen renewable energy contracts would be signed without PPAs. Although these contracts were for projects on Eskom leased land, it was an encouraging sign that independent power producers were willing to invest without state guarantees or long-term offtake agreements[56].

While it was not announced what the price per MWh would be, this apparent willingness may have been an indication that there are IPPs that may well be ready for some competition in real time amongst generators, and that investment risk devoid of guarantees or PPAs was considered sufficiently low for future investment. Although the projects would be using Eskom land, it was noteworthy that these projects were agreed on without any unbundling of Eskom. While this potentially puts into question the notion that unbundling is essential to facilitate market entry of new independent power producers, it does demonstrate that there may be sufficient appetite for power generation investments without long-term PPAs, provided that other assurances can be provided by the government and by Eskom.

Diversifying Electricity Generation Technologies

The reforms required to introduce more generation capacity into the South African power sector has been significantly hampered. This is the common thread throughout this book. At a Generation level, the power sector needed to undergo major changes as renewable energy generators would be added at a pace and scale that could be accommodated by a national transmission grid—a transmission grid that was originally designed for accommodating mostly large baseload plants. The predicted change in the mix of generation technologies has significant implications for investment in co-generation technologies.

Therefore, in order to advance the energy transition, it is not only the reduction of coal-fired carbon emitting technologies and the promotion of renewable energy generation technologies that need to be carefully managed.

Gas Generation

The intermittent electricity generation associated with increasing renewables such as solar and wind require dispatchable generation to make up for periods when the wind does not blow, and the sun no longer shines. Globally, gas-to-power is often offered as an interim or a transition electricity generation source. Despite its lower carbon footprint (compared to coal-fired generation), there are a few problems associated with the use of gas for electricity generation within the South African context. The insufficient domestic gas and gas transport infrastructure for additional power generation means that it could take many years to attract investment to develop gas infrastructure on a large scale. Gaining sufficient customers to make such projects bankable would require a long-term commitment from key off-takers.

During the energy transition however, it is not yet clear what time horizon is required to make gas projects bankable—or considered feasible to meet the net-zero objective. Getting to net-zero carbon emissions by a set target date means that over the longer-term certain gas power generation projects could potentially become obsolete even before such projects have sufficient time to reach their payback periods. If it is later decided that gas should be phased out as a transition fuel, it could put the initial gas infrastructure investment sunk cost at risk. Natural gas pipelines are typically designed for a fifty-year lifespan. With an assumed 25 years until net zero, this could significantly decrease the investment period, requiring investments to achieve higher rates of return over a shorter time period. It is therefore hoped that the transportation sector, as well as other industrial sectors, could stand as potential off-takers to provide sufficient impetus to the establishment of a sustainable domestic gas supply industry.

In addition, the high costs associated with using gas as a means for electricity generation means that gas is normally the last power generation technology to be dispatched when electricity demand increases (at least in some settings). To offset the high cost associated with gas generation, IPPs that combine renewables and storage could therefore be encouraged to enter the market to keep costs in check. This action could have the effect of placing downward pressure on the overall electricity production costs and result in gas volumes remaining low. These implications may keep away long-term investors and lenders in gas infrastructure development (due to the uncertainty on the future off-take of gas volumes). Imported gas can be exposed to fluctuations in international commodity fuel prices and volatile exchange rates. Nevertheless, staking energy security on uncertain gas infrastructure investment could be risky, given the success rates of large-scale infrastructure investments in South Africa and elsewhere.

Even if the gas infrastructure design, financing, and procurement plans are approved, the likely delays in an enterprise of this scale will result in further energy supply shortages when gas delivery is late. Although gas power needs to be part of the energy mix, the optimism on the development of gas supply infrastructure to enable gas generation plants within the timelines (as required for the planned energy transition) may be misplaced. In addition, how sustainable would the long-term payment arrangements be, if in future South

Africa's exposure to gas imports is in hard currency? Without domestic gas, given the steady devaluation of the South African rand, this could in future weigh heavily on South Africa's balance of payments.

More recently, prospecting for offshore oil and gas finds along the Atlantic coast of Namibia and South Africa has delivered promising discoveries. South Africa also has significant amounts of inland gas resources that remain untapped. However, it could take a number of years for these projects to come to fruition. Even with domestic discoveries in South Africa, it still remains unclear whether the optimal policy and regulatory environments could be achieved in time to effectively manage the energy transition in the interim.

With greenfield coal-fired generation investments no longer being viable options, gas or diesel plants appear to be the only dispatchable generation (that can be developed over the short to medium term) that can be available for periods when renewables are not generating electricity. Given the lower capital costs for gas power generation infrastructure, it will be a worthy insurance even though gas prices may be volatile—*the option of expensive power is often better than no power at all.*

South Africa could develop diesel generation plants that can easily be converted to gas-burning plants when, and indeed if, affordable regional or domestic gas supplies become available. Disinvestment in coal and decisions to decommission coal generation should therefore only be made once there are sufficient lower-carbon generation sources that have been proved to take the place of coal generation effectively and timeously.

Irrespective of whether South Africa performs brownfield life extensions on existing coal generation plants or whether it transitions to gas, the investment costs associated with any future power generation choices are considerable, and South Africa's capacity to take on more debt is limited.

In 2022, the country's sovereign debt stood at R 4.3 trillion, which roughly equated to 70 percent of Gross Domestic Product[57]. Its annual debt service costs exceeded R 300 billion. Infrastructure investment, especially in energy services contributed a large part to this debt. Domestic energy policy therefore must also consider credible finance options to fund generation infrastructure and upstream fuel investment.

A report by the Blended Finance Taskforce of the Centre for Sustainability Transitions at University of Stellenbosch estimated that South Africa will require more than US$ 250 billion over the next three decades to achieve the Paris Climate Agreement targets[58]. If this can be achieved with affordable finance options from developed countries, South Africa will do well to take advantage of such concessional finance offers.

Energy Storage

In addition to gas, to accommodate increased renewable generation, batteries are often hailed as an alternative to smooth intermittency and supply stored energy when renewable generation technologies cannot be dispatched. Although battery prices have steadily reduced over the last decade, battery storage technologies remain costly. While it is expected that batteries would continue to become more affordable over time, it is important to consider the practical extent to which this technology could be deployed as a viable option for periods when renewables are not generating electricity. Due to the short period to develop battery storage facilities, it remains a feasible option. Given the rollout of renewable energy in South Africa, battery storage would remain an attractive option to shift loads on the grid. The demonstration of large-scale distributed battery storage could therefore provide some interim relief until gas infrastructure projects can supply gas to thermal generation peaking plants.

Another energy storage technology that has been successfully deployed in South Africa (albeit on a limited scale) is molten salt energy storage for thermal plants. This technology is however not expected to be extensively deployed on a large scale in the short to medium term (i.e., roughly a 5-year horizon). It can however be easily integrated with Concentrated Solar Power generation, as implemented in the Northern Cape province.

Distributed generation, especially the combination of solar and batteries, have increasingly been used among residential and commercial customers and have enabled some households and businesses to generate their own electricity and mitigate the consequences of intermittent power outages. Solar photovoltaics and batteries have contributed towards the democratization of power generation. Whereas costs are still relatively high, combined renewable generation and battery storage is an exciting feature that could enable more distributed generation not only being inserted into the national transmission grid, but also into downstream distribution grids.

The role of distributors is therefore changing considerably as distributors endeavour to evolve into smaller versions of transmission utilities that not only buy from wholesale transmission companies but purchase electrical energy from multiple small-scale generators. Distributed generation allows more electrical power to be made available, especially to residential, commercial, and some smaller industrial users, provided that the renewable energy from solar, wind, or other primary energy inputs remain available.

Reforming the Transmission Sector

Renewable energy generation outputs from wind and solar are largely dependent on the location of wind and solar resources. If electricity demand centres are geographically far from the supply, larger and longer transmission connections are required to transport electricity to the centres where it is consumed. This requires significant investment in transmission infrastructure.

Servitudes for transmission lines can take a long time to acquire due to the processes for purchasing land parcels, and the implementation of transmission expansion projects can be challenging over the South African terrain. In 2022, Eskom estimated in its Transmission Development Plan, that approximately R 130 billion would be required to add approximately 8 500 kilometres of transmission lines and build roughly 100 additional substations by 2030. The slow pace of transmission expansion was seen as a stumbling block to bringing onboard additional renewable energy generation, especially in the Northern Cape, Eastern Cape, and Western Cape, where wind and solar resources could be found in abundance.

To enable the development of renewable energy generation projects, a new national transmission company must be well resourced to fund these investments (since the entity would own the transmission assets, even though private generators will be using the infrastructure to transmit their power). The new transmission company could also carry the risk of non-payment from defaulting distributers and municipalities, potentially perpetuating the current dependence on state funding in the form of direct access to finance or through government guarantees.

As a starting point, the new National Transmission Company must have a (relatively) clean balance sheet to start raising the capital required to finance new transmission infrastructure in accordance with the needs of the energy transition to a low-carbon power sector.

While the objective of creating an independent transmission company without bias and devoid of any conflict of interest with regards to electricity generator or distributor companies is clear, the policy, regulatory and governance frameworks for the functioning of a purported *independent* transmission company and system operator has not yet been finalised. It therefore remains to be seen the extent to which the transmission company will be able to move the power sector towards the end-state of a competitive power exchange market—one that would allow indiscriminate access to the national grid, drive down wholesale electricity prices, and realise timely investment in generation capacity.

Also not clear, is whether the transmission company will be sufficiently financially resourced to sign PPAs without government guarantees, nor whether the generation planning function will be taken over by the new entity. Still to be unpacked is the extent to which the government will allow the new transmission company and system operator to truly operate independently and devoid of unnecessary government interference. Or whether undue political interference will be encountered with respect to choosing generation technologies that must be added to the national grid, selecting suppliers of equipment to the national transmission company, choosing service providers, and signing on of IPPs based on factors that align to parochial interests.

While significant changes are required in the national transmission sector to realise the objectives of sustainable energy transition and achieving technical, environmental, and financial sustainability, most of the new generators (by number) was being added in Eskom and municipal distribution sectors.

Reforming the Distribution Sector

The importance of the financial and operational health of the Distribution and Customers Service sectors, as well their contribution to the problem of insufficient capacity, is often underestimated. The distribution sector can assist with the alleviation of rolling blackouts by having more targeted Demand Side Management programmes. These programmes incentivise respective industrial, commercial, and residential consumers to change consumption patterns—to improve coordination and balancing between power demand and supply. The distribution sector can also permit more Small-Scale Electricity Generators (with battery storage options) in the sector—to better manage consumer load profiles and alleviate grid congestion.

It is also in this sector where significant potential exists for matching electricity demand and supply through customised technology. Technology advancements have significant upside prospects for electricity wheeling, reducing producer-consumer interfaces, demand-side management, greater energy efficiency, revenue recovery, and the introduction of smart-grid technologies.

The operational health of the power sector to ensure that energy demand is being met, is largely dependent on the financial health of the Distribution sub-sector. And the financial health of the power sector starts with an efficient payment and revenue collection system. Nevertheless, many customers do not pay their bills when they are financially incapable and when service delivery is poor.

Low Revenue Collection Rates and Poor Service Delivery

In South Africa, distribution of electricity is mainly performed by municipalities. For those customers that are not directly served by municipalities, the service is provided by Eskom. However, more than half of municipalities in South Africa are unable to fully deliver on their overall service delivery mandates. In May 2023, a report issued by the country's Auditor General, revealed that only 38 out of 257 municipalities received a clean bill of health[59].

Most municipalities are dysfunctional and are not financially sustainable. Significant backlogs exist in infrastructure investment and development, as well as backlogs in maintenance. Municipalities suffer from acute shortages in technical and public sector managerial skills. This combination makes it unlikely that many of these institutions will be returned to even a modest level of functionality in the short-term, especially with respect to the distribution of electricity.

Due to poor service delivery and poor electricity quality of supply from local municipalities, some customers have requested Eskom Distribution to take over the electricity distribution functions in their areas. Eskom has already taken over the distribution of electricity in the Maluti-a-Phofung Municipality in the Free State, although concerns remain on the finances that will remain for other nonelectricity municipal functions[60]. Similarly, in the Eastern Cape, the Nelson Mandela Bay local business chamber has asked the National Energy Regulator of South Africa to intervene by having Eskom take over the electricity distribution function[61].

A concern for struggling municipalities, including those that are not yet technically insolvent, is that many of them depend on selling electricity for their financial viability. If revenue from electricity was ring-fenced and separately accounted for, insufficient funds would remain available for other municipal services. Many municipalities use revenues received from electricity sales to subsidise other municipal services like potable drinking water, sewage treatment, and refuse removal.

Many customers have complained of the poor quality of power supply, low responsiveness to customer needs, and tariff increases in excess of what is recommended by the National Energy Regulator of South Africa. Passivity to customer responses invariably resulted in two problems. Those consumers who could not afford to pay but continued to consume electricity put a strain on the financial resources of the municipalities. Those that could afford to pay for services, usually opted to generate their own electricity and reduce their dependence on the distribution supply, resulting in less revenue for the distribution utility or municipality.

Should more paying customers move away from municipal service providers by supplying their own power (such as from solar PV) local municipalities could lose a substantial share of their revenues that are used to fund other municipal functions. This trend not only has a negative impact on the electricity distribution function, but it also adversely affects other municipal functions.

Impact of Inadequate Municipal Distributor Capability on Eskom

Since most municipalities have not been able to collect sufficient revenues, they remain a risk to Eskom since the utility is ultimately saddled with bad debts which these municipalities are unable to fully settle. For this reason, it has been proposed that the revenue from electricity sales be ring-fenced, and separate accounts be allocated for servicing electricity distribution revenue and expenditure. Likewise, because Eskom is unable to pay all its debt (on its own) and dependent on government bailouts, the company also cannot continue to provide electricity without expecting debtors to settle their accounts.

The city district of Soweto, located south of Johannesburg and covering roughly 200 square kilometres, on a few occasions (since 1994) had its electricity debt written off. The city district has the largest accumulation of black townships in the country and has grown to historically symbolise the struggle against apartheid. It is home to roughly two million residents, with many unable to pay their electricity bills. In 2022, it was reported that less than half of Soweto consumers pay their municipal bills[62]. Like Soweto, many other municipalities find themselves in a similar situation where low revenue collections, coupled with weak municipal capacity has resulted in unpaid debts. In 2023, the national municipal debt to Eskom was more than R 63 billion[63].

Customer Defection and Potential Revenue Losses

For fear of losing out on revenues, municipalities have also contributed to the problem of insufficient electricity by frustrating private producers from legally connecting and selling their supplies to local grids. Tardiness to provide approvals for Small Scale Embedded

Generation and the inclusion of *net consumer* clauses in contracts with Small Scale Embedded Generators have contributed to the levels and durations of loadshedding.

In the City of Cape Town for example, a metropolitan area that is governed by the country's official national opposition party (the Democratic Alliance), residents bemoaned the City's net-consumer requirements for residential customers who have Small Scale Embedded Generators. Net consumer clauses help ensure that some degree of electricity dependence on the City of Cape Town is maintained, even during times when the metropolitan municipality itself cannot provide consumers with sufficient electricity. Revenue collection rates, however, are in an improved state in the City of Cape Town and the city was one of the few metropolitan municipalities that received a clean audit from the country's Auditor General.

Even if the ill-fated policies that have contributed to the poor state of South African municipalities were jettisoned and progressive policies are adopted, it could take many years before the fortunes of those municipalities significantly improve. A key question is: what can be done to improve the conditions in which South African municipalities function in order to stem the rate of defection, as well as improve revenue collection and the overall financial status of municipalities?

Looking Ahead – What the Future may Hold?

The largest number of distributed generators, albeit small-scale, are (and will continue to be) in the distribution sector, mainly in the form of solar photovoltaics. This trend is expected to continue as the energy crisis continues and as the cost of PV generation equipment reduces. The introduction of time-of-use smart metering to permit electricity charges that more accurately reflect the time-related price of power will be required in the distribution and customer services sector—to help alter consumer consumption patterns and permit more efficient energy management.

The distribution sub-sector has expanded steadily for over thirty years, and the country's electrification programme has been relatively successful. Despite the country's impressive rate of electrification over the last three decades, the growth in power consumption (and in the number of residential customers) must continue if South Africa is to realise its goal of irradicating energy poverty and providing equitable electricity access to its people[64].

While the electrification rate resulted in more poor households having access to electricity (when power is available) the failure to create conditions for sustained economic growth, investment, and meaningful employment, has meant that many poor households were still not able to afford electricity. A proposal to provide sufficient residential incentives for solar PV panels, could also yield positive spin offs such as reducing dependence on municipal grids during the daytime. Related benefits are providing revenue generation opportunities by selling excess power into the grid, and making users more aware of their consumption patterns in a manner that optimises electricity production costs.

Distribution Infrastructure and Further Consequences of Rolling Blackouts

In many parts of South Africa, loadshedding contributed to *other* problems that affected the power sector. Cable theft increased in areas where rolling blackouts were occurring. The absence of electrical power in key areas, led to inadequate surveillance and protection of power infrastructure. During loadshedding, when power lines are electrically dead, crime syndicates targeted copper and other materials from public and private infrastructure—to strip their value and sell it off as scrap metal. The interruption of power permits a window of opportunity whereby copper cables, transformers, and other components on the low voltage networks can easily be stolen by criminals. These acts in turn lead to greater opportunities (longer than the typical two or four hours of loadshedding) to plunder more infrastructure. Due to an increase in crimes and violence in certain areas due to load-shedding, there are fewer law enforcement resources to tackle the crimes linked to cable theft. The downward spiral continues. In 2022, the South African Chamber of Commerce and Industry estimated that copper cable theft costed the South African economy in excess of R 7 billion. The distribution sector's asset base must be protected.

It is hard to recover from these criminal acts. In some cases, any rebuilding of infrastructure to its state prior to loadshedding will take years—and in certain extreme cases, decades. In many instances, the refurbishment cannot start until the problem of loadshedding has been eradicated and resolved. In some high-crime neighbourhoods, it was decided to exempt districts from loadshedding due to the inherent risks that loadshedding poses to the safety of communities. In effect, unequal loadshedding between geographic areas (causing animosity between electricity consumers who have their power interrupted and those who do not) became an easier problem to deal with than loadshedding-induced crimes.

Even where distribution assets were not at risk of thievery, most municipalities lacked the required maintenance and investment expenditures, and distribution networks have not kept up with the required upgrades to accommodate growth in consumer demand. Many consumers have illegal connections, and it has become difficult to police the increasing electricity theft. Between 2016 and 2021, Eskom distribution energy losses have steadily increased from 6.9 percent to 10.1 percent. Eskom further reported that in 2022, that it lost over R 22 billion in revenue from theft due to illegal connections[65]. These unlawful activities put more strain on the low voltage electricity reticulation systems of Eskom and municipalities.

Impact of Distribution on the Power Sector as a Whole

The flow of money from consumers to the Transmission company, and in turn to Generation companies, starts in the Distribution sector. The distribution sector (including municipalities) account for the majority of consumers, and a significant portion of electricity sales revenues. Insufficient investment in distribution, continued overloading of existing infrastructure, illegal connections and damage to infrastructure, are all signals that the health of the infrastructure is declining. To arrest this decline, financial resources are needed.

A financially struggling distribution sector means that there will be insufficient means to invest in transmission infrastructure, and in turn, to accommodate more generators (state-sponsored or private). There may not be sufficient revenues to pay Eskom to cover its maintenance, staff, and fuel costs. It also means that there could continue to be insufficient revenues to pay IPPs and honour the PPAs. Citizens and taxpayers will continue to shoulder the financial risk as government provides bailouts to Eskom and financial guarantees to IPPs. If issues like electricity theft, cable theft, bad debts and growing unpaid bills persist and are not urgently addressed, recovery from the problems of insufficient capacity will be slow at best—and the problems associated with a shortage of generation capacity will deepen.

With increasingly more customers generating their own electricity, it means that fewer paying customers remain to subsidise poor customers for their power needs. As well-off consumers produce their own power and Distributor electricity sales decrease, this trend contributes to the unsustainable financial decline of Eskom since less revenue is available to provide for the cross-subsidisation. This phenomenon is known as the *utility death spiral*. The utility death spiral occurs when the economic growth in electricity sales is too low to compensate for the effects of higher tariffs. Eskom has already experienced a decline in its customer sales, and this decline is set to continue as long as the poor quality of electricity supply brought about by load-shedding continues.

Proposals for getting municipalities to pay their bills have been tabled but have proved difficult to implement. These includes increasing the payments terms (i.e., providing more time to pay) and decreasing the interest rates for overdue accounts. However, these actions have yet to result in an overall improvement in payments.

Regulating Distribution Tariffs

NERSA regulates electricity tariff increases for Eskom, as well as for municipalities. Since Eskom supplies almost all electricity to municipalities, this has resulted in all municipalities obtaining roughly the same tariff increases over time. However, given the disparate state of distribution infrastructure amongst municipalities, similar disparate financial resource provisions would be required for future distribution infrastructure investment, upgrades and maintenance. For municipal distributors to fulfil their mandates to their consumers and ensure the provision of reliable electricity, many municipalities will also require larger tariff increases to be off-takers of power from municipal-contracted IPPs and offset costs from power purchase agreements. The tariff-setting role and activities of the electricity regulator is therefore expected to become more complex over time as the nature of the distribution sub-sector is evolving.

If power rationing continues or intensifies, and municipalities wish to protect their customers from increasing levels of loadshedding, they would have to financially dig deeper to make up for the insufficient electricity provision from Eskom. To cover for the increased cost of generation (from municipal-contracted IPPs), tariffs will have to be increased to reflect the increased municipal cost of power provision. In such instances, in order to ensure a fiscally sustainable distribution sector, new regulatory mechanisms for municipal tariff increases would be required.

◈ ◈ ◈

South Africa suffers from the effects of a government with ministries and departments, alliance partners, as well as institutional and regulatory stakeholders, that were unable or unwilling to converge on policy priorities. This incoherence in policy formulation, poor policy implementation, and a lack of policy harmonisation, contributed to the dilemma of insufficient generation capacity.

In the power generation sector, poor coordination amongst stakeholders were a common feature and stakeholders were numerous. These included governance and oversight bodies such as the

Departments of Mineral Resources and Energy, Public Enterprises, Cooperative Governance and Traditional Affairs, Forestry, Fisheries and the Environment, National Treasury within the Ministry of Finance, Labour, the National Energy Regulator of South Africa, the South African Local Government Association (representing over 250 local governments), the National Planning Commission, the Presidential Climate Commission, the President's National Electricity Crisis Committee. Added in 2023 was a new Electricity Minister appointed specifically to resolve the electricity crisis (with vague legislative powers, executive mandates, and key performance indicators). The potential for role ambiguity, poor coordination, and incoherence may continue.

CHAPTER 6

THE ENERGY TRANSITION

Above all, the key objective of domestic energy policy in the modern era has been to ensure energy security, and if possible, to ensure energy independence. The importance of these two policy objectives was arguably the most important lessons learnt during the first post-war global energy crisis. During October 1973 and March 1974, the Organisation of Petroleum Exporting Countries proclaimed an oil embargo that targeted nations supporting Israel during the Yom Kippur War. This event resulted in soaring international oil prices and shaped the energy policies of many nations, irrespective of whether they were primary targets of the embargo or not. Many countries without abundant domestic primary energy resources such as the those in western Europe, Japan, as well as some states in the USA, increased their share of nuclear power plants in order to keep up with electricity demand and avoid their economies being hamstrung by the drastic reduction in global primary energy supplies. In the modern era, the triadic principles of *energy security*, *energy independence*, and *energy affordability* still inform the design of domestic energy policy for most industrialised countries.

Energy Security, Independence, Affordability, and Reducing the Carbon Footprint

Renewable energy generation technologies offer exciting alternatives to secure domestic electricity and present opportunities to limit the amount of mining and drilling required for producing fossil fuels. Renewables also permit traditional primary energy supplies, or fuel supply chain, to be eliminated or reduced. However, one of the potential problems associated with intermittent renewable energy generators such as wind and solar is that on their own (i.e., with no dispatchable cogeneration) their daily and seasonal generation supply profiles do not match sporadic quotidian electricity demand profiles required to enable a stable grid where demand matches supply.

In the absence of cogeneration or sufficient back-up generation, electricity supply shortages will be experienced during times when primary input energy resources (i.e., wind and solar) are no longer present and electricity generation supply is unavailable to match consumer demand. From a strictly engineering standpoint, the transition from fossil fuels to low-carbon electricity generation technologies is not difficult to achieve. However, the energy transition amounts to more than just the narrowly defined technical challenges.

A Just Energy Transition

Socio-economic, environmental, and labour concerns are at the heart of a Just Energy Transition. The concept of a Just Energy Transition has its origins in the United States of America (USA) in the 1980s, where tensions between labour and environmental movements required resolution in an effort to balance what appeared to be mutually exclusive interests[66]. In many states, labour unions called for a framework that would inform discussions for how social and economic issues linked to transitioning to environmentally friendly economies could be managed[67].

Just transitions in the energy sector sought to limit inequalities and reduce adverse impacts on the livelihoods of workers brought about by sectoral changes. In the USA, transition programmes managed mainly between labour and environmental movements were in many instances able to balance outcomes and align seemingly polar interests of labour unions with increased protection of the environment. The issues surrounding an energy transition and what constitutes fairness, were reasonably well defined between labour and the environment, serving as a basis for the achievement of its objectives.

According to most Just Transition frameworks globally, a just and inclusive energy transition should generally have four essential components of justice[68]. *Procedural* justice involves fairness in the process of obtaining agreement on the various aspects of the energy transition. *Restorative* justice refers to redressing the inequalities and the harms inflicted from previous policies. It engages communities in the process of resolving issues and seeks to hold offenders responsible for their actions. *Distributive* justice involves the perceived fairness by which costs (and benefits) are distributed to those communities impacted, considering income, wealth, and social status. *Participatory* justice involves the direct inclusion of those communities that are most affected by the decisions and decision-making processes in the energy transition.

While the elements of justice can be applied on a global stage to all sovereign states that have commensurate stakes in the energy transition, the four components of justice are also applied to the various country, regional, and community stakeholders that are involved in—and impacted by—the energy transition.

It is often stated that a Just Energy Transition is steeped in the principle of *leaving no one behind*. But what does this mean? Who are these individuals that should not be left behind? What does 'not being left behind' mean? Is leaving 'no one' behind an absolute imperative? Or is it simply a broadly stated objective? These were the questions that greeted the Energy Transition when its processes were launched in South Africa.

Domestic Characterisation of an Energy Transition

In South Africa, for certain interest groups the high-level concept of a Just Energy Transition may have been broadly understood when these stakeholders believed that their interests would be catered for, whereas for others it remained somewhat nebulous—especially if their interests were not specifically catered for. In the South African context, the risks and benefits for an energy transition was referred to in the country's electricity production framework as well as in the electricity Integrated Resource Plan. However, the upstream mining related concerns from certain labour and capital sub-sectors went largely unheeded.

The Department of Environmental Affairs led the transition charge with the signing of the Paris Agreement and committed the country to a transition. With Eskom following this cue and developing its own plans for transitioning to a low-carbon economy in 2020, it turned out that certain interests of relevant marginal groups had not been adequately considered.

Generally, labour unions in Eskom were amenable to an energy transition due to reasonable employment security assurances provided by Eskom management. Company employees could be absorbed into other areas of the business or into ventures that would support the utility's energy transition. However, similar assurance could not be provided for the company's sub-contractors, suppliers, and service providers involved in the generation of electricity. Even less assurances could be provided for miners in the Mpumalanga province. The province supplies more than 80 percent of the coal production in South Africa and is home to twelve of Eskom's fifteen large coal-fired power plants.

Mining in the province accounts for roughly a quarter of the province's economic output, and the formal mining sector employs over 90 000 workers. With the expanded value chain that includes transport and support industries it was estimated that more than 150 000 workers would be impacted by the energy transition[69]. The coal sector was therefore a relatively large economic sector within the province and the livelihoods of communities was at the heart of making any energy transition work.

Between 2008 and 2015, as many as 42 000 mining jobs had already been shed in the province, largely due to gradual reductions in coal exports[70]. This decline in employment occurred as developed countries reduced coal imports and started their own journeys to meet their commitments under the Kyoto Protocol. From 2015, with the adoption of the Paris Agreement, the effects of decreasing international exports started to intensify, as developing countries also reduced coal imports. As these local communities were still feeling the effects of a sector in decline (due to lower international demand for coal), the prospects of further job losses from a domestic decline in coal demand were distressing.

In September 2023, the research organisation Krutham, reported that up to 120 000 jobs could be affected in various coal value chain companies, and that energy transition studies conducted at the time had paid little attention to the coal-dependent *informal economy*. Commenting on donor funded initiatives, the research group announced that the government had no specific budgeted line item that showed how resources would be allocated to support communities affected by the energy transition. The informally employed, as well as unemployed citizens, were largely dependent on the formal mining sector[71]. Information regarding the impact of the energy transition on the informal sector was not readily available. Given the dearth of tangible and detailed information (supported by local data) to explain to communities the impact of the energy transition, it was often difficult to garner support for the energy transition, irrespective of its label – *Just*.

As the world's fifth largest coal producer, the impact on the South African economy was significant. The regional impact of a declining coal sector on local communities within the timeframe of the net-zero targets until 2050 is expected to be significant in the Mpumalanga province. Already the impact has been felt due to reducing coal exports to Europe, Africa, and Asia, as industrialised and developing economies were embarking on their own energy transitions. Domestically, the energy transition was not experienced as one that was equitable for local communities because the adverse impacts were disproportionately felt at home due to reduced coal exports followed by increasing unemployment. The effects were not experienced as abroad, where the declared benefits of fossil fuel reductions were presumably being realised. Therefore, with the promise of domestic benefits, even when there were clear benefits of the energy transition for local communities, sufficient backing for the transition was still lacking. In spite of reduced health risks associated with decreased coal-fired electricity generation, nationally self-determined reductions in coal mining were not universally welcomed by locals. It soon became clear that the term 'justice' meant different things to various communities and individuals with varying interests.

Inequality and Restorative Justice

In 2022, the World Bank ranked South Africa as the most unequal country in the world. The vast pre-existing inequalities in South Africa presented many socio-economic and political obstacles, even before the energy transition was formulated[72]. Between 1948 and 1994, Apartheid policies under the National Party significantly contributed to increasing social and economic injustices. Based on a review of Gini coefficient trends over the last three decades, it is clear that the level of inequality has continued to grow significantly since the ANC assumed government office in 1994.

Given pre-existing inequalities and the label of a *Just* Energy Transition, the expectation of some kind of restorative justice and redress was expected, especially amongst poorer communities. It is therefore hardly surprising that there was profound disappointment with the early energy transition outcomes within some communities and interest groups. Although the shutdown of coal-fired power stations was expected, there was much fanfare about the new employment opportunities that would be created as renewable energy generation projects were developed. These opportunities did not materialise for many people in communities that lived close to the Komati Power Station in Mpumalanga when the plant shut down for final decommissioning in October 2022.

Justice for Employed and the Unemployed

In 2022, the official unemployment rate reported by Statistics South Africa for the Mpumalanga province was 38.6 percent; the second highest unemployment rate of the country's nine provinces. The expanded unemployment rate—which accounts for those who are unemployed, but who are no longer actively seeking employment—was as high as 51.6 percent[73]. This meant that Mpumalanga had more citizens that were unemployed, than the province had citizens that were employed. There were therefore strong sentiments that the poor, most vulnerable, and the unemployed, were largely excluded in the building blocks of a reputed just energy transition.

There was initially little transparency regarding planning phases of the transition and how it would affect communities. While it was not clear to what extent the lack of communication contributed to resistance to the energy transition, it did result in an indifference at sufficient levels of society and industry—and this ambivalence contributed to the lack of needed support for the energy transition.

Communities in the coal region claimed that they were not consulted on the permanent closure of the Komati coal-fired power station—Eskom's flagship decommissioning project to usher in the energy transition to a lower carbon future. Six months after the Komati Power Station was shutdown to enable the energy transition, communities were reportedly disillusioned about how the transition will ensure ongoing employment—and what they ought to do while the funds that South Africa has been promised by western countries are waited upon. Even environmental groups initially in favour of the permanent plant shut down reported that there was confusion and concern for the communities—as locals were finding it harder to survive after the plant was shut down and the justice to ensure an equitable changeover was not forthcoming[74].

Many of the meetings to discuss the Komati closure, the Just Energy Transition tenets, and the future closure of other Eskom plants, were held centrally in the town of Middelburg to reduce the average travelling distance from most of the older coal plants that would be decommissioned. In the case of Komati Power Station that is located approximately 50 kilometres away from Middelburg, many community members did not have the means to travel and attend these meetings. It was alleged by campaigners that only one meeting was held in Komati, and that this meeting was held only after the power station had already shut down for decommissioning.

In 2023, when the communities in the town of Balfour near Eskom's Grootvlei coal-fired power station learnt about the experiences at Komati, they too threatened to stop the energy transition. Grootvlei Power Station was set to reach the end of its operational life in 2027 and residents of the area were concerned about their future livelihoods.

They believed that if they did not speak up, they would end up like the communities around Komati Power Station, who they felt were indeed *left behind*.

A few citizens did secure jobs in renewable electricity production, but many—especially those in mining—did not. Some were gainfully employed, but others were not. Some had skills that they could transfer to other industries, but some did not. Some were young enough to move on and start learning skills in new industries, but some were not. Some were legally employed and could probably be part of the energy transition, while some were working illegally and would be overlooked for inclusion in the South African Just Energy Transition benefits. Some mine workers were foreign migrant workers from countries outside the borders of South Africa and were not likely to find formal employment in South Africa.

The energy transition therefore failed to acknowledge the unequal starting point within the South African energy sector context, especially in the coal province of Mpumalanga. Despite the announcement of a Just Energy Transition, distrust between labour and capital, between government and citizens, and between environmentalists and mining companies, added to the complexities of understanding a Just Energy Transition: what it could look like, who it would benefit, and what would be the actual outcomes (on paper and in reality) for stakeholders and their constituencies.

Therefore, while a western-based Just Energy Transition asks what the transition means for mainly workers, the South African starting context was starkly different. It needed to be adequately acknowledged that it was not only unionised workers that were impacted. Given the context in South Africa, it is argued that a Just Energy Transition should have asked much broader questions not only about justice between workers and the environment (as in the United States of America)—but also about justice for non-workers (unemployed who in Mpumalanga province outnumber the formally employed); justice for women (who have historically been economically disadvantaged); justice for coal communities that were more adversely affected by the energy transition than communities that were economically active in other sectors, such as agriculture and manufacturing; justice for black entrepreneurs (such as miners and transport bosses) who had only recently (i.e., within the last two decades when the coal contracts with traditional investors expired) been formally integrated into the industry and were still waiting to achieve a return on investment on their capital; justice for those citizens that have never experienced what it is like to live with and use electricity; justice for unemployed and unemployable youth, who were numerous in a province that has high youth unemployment and who risk remaining economically marginalised; and justice for many more for whom it was clear that the energy transition would fall short on the elements of *restorative* justice.

It is acknowledged that the purported Just Energy Transition initiative was not intended to solve everyone's problems and rectify inequalities of all kinds. After all, its origins were specifically aimed at mainly resolving an apparent conflict between the labour and environmental objectives. However, without the requisite clarity regarding which parties would benefit to a greater or lesser extent (and who could be worse off), the announcement of a *Just* Energy Transition risked creating unreasonable expectations which, if expectations remain unfulfilled or insufficiently clarified, could cause further opposition.

Incentives for the Energy Transition

So why was the starting point of the Energy Transition in South Africa so poorly characterised by policymakers? And why did South Africa move so fast and make commitments for an energy transition without a comprehensive understanding of the local complexities that could undermine the commitments made by the government? Surely buy-in from local communities should have been obtained before the government committed South Africa to the Paris Agreement?

Being a first mover amongst developing nations and demonstrating that South Africa was indeed committed to the Paris Agreement did have some advantages that the country would have wanted to benefit from. The lure of fiscal support from western nations may have contributed to a hasty acceptance of financial assistance offers before the South African context for a Just Energy Transition was comprehensively understood.

Limited financial support was available to developing countries. Collectively, developed nations were unable to fund energy transitions in developing nations to the extent initially envisaged or promised. Both Eskom and the South African government had weak balance sheets to raise capital for additional electricity expansion—and the concessionary finance by developed countries was one of the few ways which could ensure that the required investment to replace ageing coal-fired power generation with low-carbon sources could continue. The threat of carbon border taxes from the European Union, South Africa's largest overseas trading partner, contributed to South Africa moving quickly to appease principal investors in —and consumers from—their target export markets.

In addition to insufficient characterisation and understanding of local conditions preceding an energy transition, in South Africa more general questions around the global energy transition began to resurface. How equitable was it to expect developing countries to make significant sacrifices toward the energy transition, when poorer countries have less significant historic contributions to carbon emissions? And given that most industrialised countries had failed to take concerted action under the UNFCCC and Kyoto, was it fair to disproportionally place the decarbonisation burden on developing countries? How could the transition be fair for communities that were dependent on coal value chains in areas where geographically concentrated renewable energy sources were not as abundant?

The energy transition reopened old wounds of imperialism amongst those who felt that neo-colonial outsiders were once again the ultimate decision makers on their domestic social fates, their economic fortunes, and their political futures. This resentment intensified as European economies increased their coal imports from South Africa, when faced with energy security fears brought on by the conflict between Russian and Ukraine. Those adversely impacted by the energy transition, including governments of other developing economies accused western states of hypocrisy for using climate arguments for refusing finance for oil, gas, and coal projects in developing economies, while continuing to burn fossil fuels at home and expanding fossil fuel industries due to concerns over energy security.

It must be highlighted that the Energy Transition was a domestic choice made by the South African government, not by the western states that promised to partly fund the transition. However, communities internalised the transition as one that was imposed on them from outside. In the eyes of many, these external forces were also seen to be partly responsible for loadshedding, as they saw the last unit of Komati Power Station being closed in order to attract low interest and concessionary finance.

In June 2023, after mounting pressure from various societal sectors, Eskom finally issued a tender notice to address the socio-economic impact of the Komati plant closure. The following month, the Presidential Climate Commission visited Komati Power Station to better understand the process of decommissioning and repurposing, as well as make recommendations on the lessons learnt from the process.

Conditional and Temporal Finance for the Energy Transition

The promised funding from wealthy nations was—in theory implicitly, and in practice explicitly—conditional on South Africa retiring its coal-fired fleet. Komati Power Station, one of Eskom's oldest operational coal-fired generation plants was the first to be decommissioned under concessional arrangements. It didn't help that the last operational Komati generation unit was ironically still functioning at a performance level that made it one of Eskom's top performing units. The situation led to the questioning of the logic of shutting down operating units for decommissioning while the country was experiencing record levels of rolling blackouts. Why should long-term decarbonisation considerations be prioritised above short-term energy security when energy security has more pressing immediate impacts on lives and livelihoods?

While Eskom committed to close down older plants based on their age, it later became clear that the performances of the coal-fired units were not necessarily correlated with age, but with operational factors such as coal quality, the degree to which maintenance had been performed, and the extent to which sabotage and corruption had infiltrated into their operations. It was also questioned why in the context of carbon emission reductions, more efficient coal-burning plants like Komati with dedicated mines, were shut down in lieu of more polluting stations.

Conditional finance does raise an important chronological issue with regards to the problem of insufficient electricity generation. If coal plants must first be shut down *before* funds become available for renewable electricity generation plants, which constituency is served first? How fair is this conditional requirement to communities when the retirement of these plants contribute to communities experiencing rolling blackouts and being left with insufficient generation capacity? Not to mention lapses in employment opportunities.

Even if the coal plants are only gradually shut down *after* there is sufficient renewables available, there could still be a time lag between one technology sector maturing and becoming available versus another being retired. How then will the detailed temporal linkages of this transition be managed? Why should activities be sequenced in a manner as prescribed by financiers? How can interests be more equitably balanced between funders of the energy transition and those who are likely to be adversely affected? These are important questions that must be addressed in order for the energy transition to gain endorsement amongst those whose support is required to make it sustainable.

If workers in the coal value chain must first give up their employment before carbon emission reductions are realised, then where is the justice for workers? Will the increase in employment in the renewal energy sector exactly match the reduction in employment in the coal value chain to ensure that employment rates at least remain constant? If not, at what level of job shedding and job uptake is the energy transition considered to be just? Which communities will transition immediately into new jobs, and which communities will experience a transition to unemployment before being re-employed as part of the transition to renewables? Wage compensation under the two generation technologies may not be comparable, increasing the potential for disappointment amongst re-employed workers who could be financially worse off after the transition.

Even if there is a net increase in employment, those that are not immediately re-employed in the green economy will not necessarily perceive the transition to be fair. The faster the transition and the closing of coal-fired plants, the more there could be dissatisfaction amongst labour stakeholders, who perceive themselves as having more to lose on two counts. Firstly, they lose their jobs in the coal value chain; and secondly, they have to endure higher levels of loadshedding due to the shutting down of existing coal-fired plants before replacement generation has been commissioned. Community members questioned the perceived higher priority placed on the environment, than on their own livelihoods. This sentiment underscores the complexities of simplifying the energy transition on paper, while inadequate attention is paid to the real implementation challenges amongst impoverished communities.

It could have been a more acquiescent compromise to release funds for the energy transition and delay the decommissioning of coal-fired stations until the replacement renewable generation came online, or until the country's power crisis was resolved. This would have ensured that energy security was not undermined. With the understanding that energy security has the highest priority, renewable energy funding could rather have been used as a *carrot* to fast-track the displacement of fossil-fuelled electricity production—rather than be used as a *stick* and compromise socio-economic and development objectives.

How Previous South African Experience Informed Responses to the Energy Transition

Under the Apartheid government, black communities were seldom consulted on issues that affected them. Since 1994, even under the post democratic ANC rule, there had been times where communities were upset because they were not consulted on issues that affected them.

Many communities already had high levels of unemployment and the expectation amongst community members was that the transition will bring more jobs and reduce the unemployment in their region. The promise of employment remained fresh within the memory of some communities within the coal mining province of Mpumalanga.

In the mid-2000s, when Eskom decided to recommission the previously mothballed plants (Komati, Camden, and Grootvlei coal-fired power stations), much of the skills and expertise were not readily available in the geographic region. Eskom had to bring in skills from other areas inside the country. Despite the increased employment due to the return-to-service of these units that had been mothballed since the 1980s, many communities were still disappointed because the projects did not result in mass employment for locals as they had envisioned.

Even in the area where the new coal fired Kusile plant was constructed, there was dissatisfaction about the number of sustainable local jobs created by the Kusile construction project. In 2022, communities were still demanding that their members be employed at these sites. Despite seeing the largest infrastructure investment project in the province for several decades, communities were still troubled that not enough of their inhabitants were employed. Community members blocked the entrances to the coal-fired power plant and police had to be called in to manage the stand-off[75].

Communities were therefore wary of transition promises when their previous lived experiences did not match the promises made by government.

Justice between Economic Sectors Responsible for Carbon Emissions

The energy transition to lower carbon emissions had a disproportionate increased focus on the coal mining and electricity generation sectors—without a comparable focus on other carbon emitting sectors such as transportation, the built environment, and other mining and industrial processes. Similarly, the *justice* aspects were more focused on the operational period of electricity generation than on upstream value chains during the production of generation technology hardware. Likewise, less focus was placed on future downstream decommissioning of various electricity generation technologies (including renewable generation technologies), together with waste disposal and site rehabilitation.

Amongst some consumers in the South African coal mining sector, the feeling was that the sector was an easy target for the government and that those working in the sector had to pay the price, while other emitters in other sectors were left alone or got away scot-free. To make matter worse, the sacrifices by those who felt that they were being unfairly targeted, was to make space for other carbon emitters such as diesel or gas-fired plants—plants needed as part of the energy transition to keep the lights on.

Generation Technology Cost Comparisons

The prices for renewable power generation have gradually decreased in recent years, largely driven by steadily increasing technology efficiencies, the lower cost of capital due to concessionary finance, and maturing markets for green investments. Yet, the remaining investment in storage or dispatchable generation to ensure grid stability, was not always priced into overall generation cost comparisons. This is partly due to the manner in which generation plant bid specifications are drafted and announced.

This incorrect direct comparison often confounds the debate between intermittent renewables and dispatchable generation technologies. Comparisons of levelized system costs for renewable energy generation technologies often exclude back-up generation or storage, increased transmission costs, as well as exemptions from certain taxes and levies. The time horizons for Levelized Cost of Electricity calculations can distort evaluations used in generation technology comparisons.

The hidden costs of green power, which often exceeds the publicly cited costs, are therefore passed on to consumers (or taxpayers) and are still for the account of the off-taker utility, and do not accrue to the private producers who have developed most of the renewable generation capacity in South Africa. Long-term guaranteed PPAs lock in private profits for decades, whereas the full wholesale metered costs to consumers or taxpayers are seldom in the public domain when PPAs are signed. This is because the cost for making the power network

work with increased penetration of renewable generation (i.e., the cost for the transmission utility) is much more than the cited charges for renewable generation plants (i.e., the PPA charges).

State-owned and private generation utilities provide cost estimates which exclude the costs for transmission connections. And where they are publicized, they often fail to accurately reflect the real cost to the off-taker from project development through construction up to the point of commercial operations, the externalised costs for the duration of the PPA, and the end-of-life decommissioning phases of projects. This often results in opposing parties (renewable versus fossil fuel generators, or state-owned versus private generators) claiming to be disadvantaged by the manner in which generation requirements are specified and services are priced.

For South African consumers feeling the effects of increased tariffs, the financial costs associated with an energy transition to renewable generation remained unclear. This made consumers uncomfortable with the future impact of increased renewables. Despite lower energy charges from renewable energy IPPs, the potential impact of the energy transition on the long-term tariff trajectory was not communicated to stakeholders. This presents a risk for some consumer stakeholders: only later would they discover the real tariff implications once the policy decision is locked-in and when unintended tariff consequences can no longer be easily reversed.

Government subsidies, tax incentives, import tariffs, and economic programmes that support socio-economic and environmental objectives, all have the potential to skew information used in comparative analyses informing practices and policies for dealing with the energy transition. In the absence of the kind of transparency that will enable the public to be better informed on energy policy and generation technology decisions, it makes it hard for the energy transition to gain traction with consumers and the public in general. In a country like South Africa, where confidence in the government has fallen sharply in recent years, the trust deficit has contributed to an increasing number of guarded citizens that could not find the resolve to support government policy in any direction, whether with renewables or with carbon emitting technologies. This contributed to the stalling and cancelling of many generation projects, as discussed in Chapter 13.

Justice for Prosumers

One way to obtain greater buy-in to the energy transition and ensure that a transition remains equitable for many consumers of power, is to allow users of power who are willing and able to employ embedded renewable generation to produce their own power. Unlike fossil fuels, where relatively large capital investment is required to produce affordable power, the sun's energy, photovoltaic (PV) collector panels, an inverter, and limited auxiliary equipment allows almost anyone to produce much of their own electricity. Small scale rooftop PV does not require lengthy environmental approvals and complex regulatory permit approval processes.

However, despite the lack of sufficient electricity generation, innovative ways to sufficiently incentivise greater adoption of solar PV amongst consumers has not gained sufficient traction in South Africa. Greater government relaxations on equipment purchases, subsidies, tax exemptions, and feed-in tariffs to all prosumers of power could have averted a large portion of the daytime loadshedding. For users that do not use all their daytime power, selling excess power to the distribution grid could have empowered ordinary citizens to generate revenue in this manner.

Justice for Emerging Black Investors

The Energy Transition may also have gotten off to a rocky start due to its timing. Just as black entrepreneurs have entered coal mining and coal transport sectors, the energy transition presents a real risk of their assets becoming stranded. Historically mining was reserved for white-owned businesses, and the energy transition introduced a new element of racial polarization amongst new black investors that have recently entered the coal mining and coal transport sectors. Moreover, the coal industry is seen as a success story for Black Economic Empowerment. Some traditional white-owned companies and investors in the sector have retreated from the sector—ostensibly to allow for more black investor participation, but most probably in anticipation of a protracted decline of a previously booming coal industry.

Because the energy transition starting point was insufficiently characterised, whatever the Just Energy Transition meant—or was understood to mean for various stakeholders—was lacking the required clarity to move forward with its large-scale adoption. Policy makers, eager to adopt a western model of a Just Energy Transition, failed to adequately read the situation on the ground and consult accordingly. They were therefore faced with sufficient detractors to derail, slow down, and outright reject, the planned energy transition.

To be just and leave no-one behind, the energy transition must place energy security and energy independence at the apex of national energy policy. Given the local conditions, a just energy transition must be mindful of the base (or starting point) of inequality within the country, and any transition plans must be adapted to meet the basic needs of vulnerable citizens and communities. In South Africa, there remain questions about the ability for an energy transition to truly be *just*.

A just transition can possibly be implemented and centred around fewer complex interplays between labour unions and the environment in relatively more resourced and stable western developed countries. However, for more complex and lower resourced developing country contexts with heterogenous populations and high initial inequalities, it may mean that the current existing models and frameworks for achieving justice in energy transitions are inadequate.

With the journey to a low carbon energy future, the South African case has shown that obtaining clarity on the starting point and the envisaged final destination is as important as the journey itself—if the energy transition is to be just. And without good knowledge of the terrain (i.e., the evolving context) and a detailed energy transition roadmap, the road ahead will continue be filled with obstacles.

Under different circumstances, the energy transition could have provided South Africa a faster route to connect more generation capacity onto the national grid. However, the South African experience was characterised by poor environmental and energy policy integration, poor communication and context characterisation, as well as inadequate stakeholder engagement. Hence, efforts towards reducing the carbon footprint and integrating more low-carbon technologies exacerbated the problems of insufficient generation capacity—rather than mitigate or prevent it.

Although the triadic principles of energy security, energy independence, and energy affordability still informs the design of domestic energy policy for most countries, many nations will do well to improve broader socio-economic, environmental, and industrial policy harmonisation, now that the fourth principle (i.e., the net-zero objective) has been added to the equation.

PART III

STATE OWNED ENTERPRISES

CHAPTER 7

THE FOUNDATIONS OF STATE-OWNED ENTERPRISES

State-owned enterprises (SOEs) have remained dominant in nearly all African countries and continue to be the providers of most of the electricity generated in Africa. The rationale for SOE existence, how they came into being, and how they function is connected to the problem of insufficient generation capacity. In many ways, SOEs have frustrated investment, both due to their own limited financial position and by discouraging entry of private generators.

This chapter briefly describes the rationale for SOEs and the reasons behind their poor performances. It gives an account of the two rounds of reforms which were intended to address the problems of poor SOE performance: the first between the 1960s and the 1980s, and the second from the 1980s onwards. Also included is a discussion of why efforts to address the poor performance of SOEs have been largely unsuccessful and the implications for continued investment in the sector. While SOE reforms have had a long history dating as far back to the immediate post-independence era of many African states, it sets the context for today's public utilities.

In the South African experience, which follows in the next chapter, it is demonstrated how the manner in which the utility SOE was managed and supported by government, had strong links to how investment in generation (private or public) was sustained or stifled.

The Rise of State-Owned Enterprises – The Rationale for Public Champions

In the late 1950s and early 1960s, when many former colonies and independent territories gained their independence, a belief existed that government involvement in the economy would be crucial for development. This notion was, in part, due to the experience with previous colonial regimes (in which central economic planning often was the standard) and also to the successes achieved through centralised economic planning in many western states[76]. Western economies in Europe and North America had adopted centralised state planning and control in many strategic sectors of their economies, especially after the Wall Street Crash in 1929 and the Great Depression of the 1930s.

In the period between the two world wars, the national enterprise model dominated. The ideology continued to gain popularity even after World War II through the works of John Maynard Keynes, as government involvement became an integral part of reviving economies after the war. Many development finance institutions also channelled their aid and loans to governments through state-owned enterprises that formed part of the socio-economic development organs of poorer nations, thereby providing funds for the expansion and, at times, creation of SOEs[77].

It should also be noted that especially in Africa, significant state involvement had its legitimacy in development economics in an era which encouraged strong government engagement. In the absence of local capitalists and private domestic investment institutions, political control was needed where large inflows of foreign investment or significant foreign interests were prevalent. A position amongst many African countries was that the gains in self-confidence and national pride would outweigh economic growth and 'supposed' technological advantages gained from association with industrialised nations through foreign ownership[78]. The practice of public ownership and management of utilities, established as a result of governments' development strategies, was near universal in African countries. Apart from international views backing public control of infrastructure industries, the small size of economies and the lack of private capital markets made the state-owned enterprise a logical policy choice for most African states[79].

Even if domestic private capital existed, the notion among developing countries was that they could not rely on a laissez-faire approach toward industrialisation, especially in strategic sectors of the economy. Instead, late developers needed the state to have strong levers of control over the economy (including via import substitution strategies) to overcome the technological gap separating them from early developers. This development strategy was key to nationalisations that occurred after independence in African states.

While profit maximisation was generally regarded as the primary objective of private corporations (particularly from a shareholder perspective), profitability was only one of many goals of SOEs—and evidence would suggest that it was not the most important one. In developing countries, SOEs were expected to create employment, keep prices down artificially, help develop laggard regions, and be at the vanguard of social progress, even if these goals hurt their financial and operational performance.

Welfare economics played an important role in social and economic development and these functions reflected the ideological preferences of state leaders to guard against social inequality and promote social stability. To ensure allocative and distributive efficiencies, the state was therefore considered to be better placed than markets. State corporations could also attract loans at a lower rate than their private counterparts, thereby reducing the cost of capital, and theoretically providing goods and services at lower prices.

During the 1950s and 1960s, as the demand for electric power increased dramatically, coordination procedures for system operations were consolidated and a national self-sufficiency theory prevailed, implying that electricity should be controlled as a strategic resource. Financing the electric power system became dominated by the state or state-controlled banks. As economies of scale in the power sector increased during this period, it reinforced the conventional political and developmental driving forces for state ownership and control. In addition, it suggested that electricity supply was indeed an integrated natural monopoly.

Inefficiency, Poor Performance and Financial Distress

In the mid to late 1960s, many African public enterprises started to register poor financial performances, which led to increasing government debt. Through state subventions to support loss-making entities, SOEs were drawing down the state's fiscal resources, instead of contributing to them as originally intended. The fiscal strain of SOEs on the national finances, in turn, translated into minimal investment in infrastructure expansion and general maintenance—negatively impacting on the quality of services provided to customers, and subsequently, discouraging private investment in other industry sectors.

The causes of poor performance were multifarious. However, the fundamental conclusion was that public enterprises were managed according to too many divergent objectives. The combination of commercial and social objectives invariably led to political meddling in company operational decisions to the extent that commercial performance and organisational efficiency were severely compromised[80].

The vagueness in objectives may be considered a managerial problem since managers became unclear on what was really expected from them. The vagueness in objectives may also be considered an opportunity for managers since the multiple objectives provided a built-in excuse for not fulfilling a specific objective. In such a system, where an enterprise is managed directly by a state department and its officials are likely to be political rather than industrial experts, officials are hamstrung. They thus cannot be held responsible for the success or failure of the enterprise.

Political interference stemmed from arrangements whereby ministers often served as chairmen or held seats on SOE boards[81]. This led to a push towards the political and social objectives of the respective ministry (an organ of the state) at the expense of the commercial and performance goals of SOEs. In addition, board members often lacked training in the specifics of the industry since their appointments were based more on their political associations rather than industrial competence[82].

Weak and sometimes absent performance evaluation monitoring meant that there were few indicators that would alert external controllers and SOE stakeholders of business areas displaying unsatisfactory performance[83]. The lack of credible evaluation criteria often stemmed not only from the knowledge that profits were not the overriding objectives of SOEs, but also from the inability to translate clear social objectives into measurable performance criteria. Few governments were capable of providing SOEs with clear-cut performance goals and credible trade-offs amongst conflicting objectives. Conventional accounting and reporting systems, which were developed and used in the private sector, were incompatible with SOE objectives. Where employed, they often gave external controllers performance measures that were inappropriate and inconsistent with the overall goals of SOEs[84].

SOE managers lacked the autonomy to change inefficient relations with business associates such as suppliers and service providers. These business relations were often with other public enterprises in search of partnerships that would increase the performance of their own undertakings. Executives also had difficulty in shedding labour where public corporations were clearly overstaffed and were sometimes obliged to add more workers than needed or wanted to their payrolls[85]. The limited control that executives had over labour and other costs contributed to the resulting lack of profitability of their utilities.

To make matters worse, governments frequently failed to increase tariffs to the point where they were below levels of cost recovery. This, in turn, limited growth in terms of network expansions and related service improvements. In 1990, based on a survey for over sixty developing countries, the World Bank showed that electricity tariffs fell by roughly 35 percent between 1983 and 1987 in constant US$ terms and that developing countries generally faced tariff levels that were too low to encourage efficient use of electricity, and utilities were unable to raise sufficient revenues to finance their expansion needs[86].

The World Bank's *Review of Electricity Tariffs in Developing Countries in the 1980s* showed that in 80 percent of developing countries, tariffs were found to be below the Long Run Marginal Cost (LRMC) of production and two thirds of African countries surveyed did not plan to base their tariffs on the economic cost of power. Low revenue collection rates further strained the financial situation of SOEs, with government departments and other SOEs sometimes being the worst defaulters. Even with the help of tax-exempt status and despite most of their investment income coming from government budgets, many SOEs could not maintain positive cash flows.

In the most perverse cases, it could be argued that SOEs became an apparatus for misappropriation of funds, corruption, and nepotism, to further the interests of the ruling elites. This, in turn, led to SOEs becoming even more inefficient, as their control reflected less the interests of the corporation and more the parochial interests of a select few. In extreme cases, SOEs were created deliberately as a cover for political party fundraising. This was the case with the National Development Company in Ghana (which was investigated by the Azu Crabbe Commission), and the National Investment and Properties Company in Nigeria (which was investigated by the Coker Commission).

Reform – A Prescription for Poor Performance

Given the performances of SOEs, in addition to consumers and citizens that felt the brunt of poor SOE outcomes, lenders and financiers were equally perturbed about the status quo at many public utilities.

Reaction by Development Finance Institutions

Development finance institutions that lent money to SOEs, most notably the World Bank, became concerned and gave much attention to the predicament by—examining the underlying causes of the problem in more detail; assisting governments to improve performance through instituting monitoring methods; making further borrowing conditional on improved policy formulation and implementation; and making institutional changes to improve governance functions for SOEs[87].

The focus on the problems relating to SOEs corresponded to the period of the World Bank's structural adjustment lending programme in the late 1970s, where infrastructure sector performance featured prominently in the bank's objectives. African states were prominent amongst developing countries that accepted the terms of the loans from the Bretton Woods institutions. Due to their ailing SOEs, African states hence attracted noteworthy technical assistance operations and training assignments, which would carry on well into the 1980s to improve SOE performance[88].

Structural adjustment policy changes and conditions were instituted by the World Bank and the International Monetary Fund (IMF) to ensure that lending would be done in a manner that would meet the initial objectives of the loans. To correct for borrowing countries' fiscal imbalances, Structural Adjustment Programmes (SAPs) were instituted to reduce protectionist behaviour through the reduction of trade barriers and the promotion of free market principles[89]. Critics of the World Bank's SAPs contend that the acceptance of SAPs was merely as a result of pressure exerted by the World Bank and IMF since developing countries had limited alternate access to funds and complied due to a lack of options.

The First Round of Reforms – SOE Performance Improvements

Reforms proposed to address the poor performance of SOEs took the form of adopting a 'modern enterprise system' by transforming SOEs into shareholding corporations, all within an overall framework of public ownership. Corporatisation, in part, was intended to clarify the rights of SOEs and free them from ministerial and administrative interference by establishing them as separate legal entities run by professional managers[90]. Furthermore, reforms focussed on operational analysis to determine the array of factors leading to SOE losses, including a wide range of restructuring and performance improvement measures which excluded ownership changes in infrastructure sectors such as electricity. Specific reforms requested included:

- Classification studies to clarify the role of the state and categorise SOE portfolios into companies that should be retained, restructured, sold, or closed.
- Legal and administrative reforms aimed at making public enterprises more commercial in nature by rationalising control procedures, increasing the autonomy of SOE managers, and altering the form, duties, and roles of boards of directors.
- Changes in determining pricing formulae for infrastructure service tariffs, including review periods and criteria for ad-hoc reviews.
- Labour studies and policies for determining the correct levels of staffing, the funding of retrenchment mechanisms, as well as training and redeployment schemes.
- Rationalising of financial systems to reduce automatic or concessionary access to credit.
- Creating or bolstering SOE monitoring bodies and strengthening the scrutiny of SOE expenditures and borrowing.
- Reviewing the competence and qualifications of managers in infrastructure SOEs and studying and improving management procedures.
- Performance contracts were used to provide a means to clarify performance objectives and to monitor and judge performance against prior agreed criteria.
- Privatisation or preparation for privatisation of non-strategic SOEs, which were of a commercial nature.

Implementation and Reform Outcomes

Although many initiatives were called for to address the operational and fiscal troubles of state corporations, implementation proved challenging. In many cases, tariff hikes agreed on by governments were later rejected; pledges from government agencies to pay their bills were not kept; commitments to make investment capital available to infrastructure SOEs were not honoured; and, contrary to agreements, managers were not allowed to fire workers, change suppliers, or cut off service to non-paying customers. Where price increases were realised to recover the cost of commodities or services, the culture of non-payment persisted. Where charges were paid to recover the cost of commodities or services, it often translated into inflationary pressures within the fiscal system—an unintended consequence of the increases. Resistance and disillusionment also came from customers who found themselves paying more for no notable increase in service quality.

Often, the ill-coordinated cessation of subventions to loss-making SOEs strained working capital, leading governments to arrange extensions of loans with state-owned banks to ailing SOEs[91]. In these cases, the problems of poor fiscal discipline were *shifted* rather than *resolved*. Retrenchment of excess workers also proved to be easier said than done, with reductions in salaried costs being modest. In many cases, public enterprises have been subject to gross overstaffing in the past, and in general governments wanted to avoid the already high levels of unemployment that were prevalent in most African states. Collective bargaining arrangements concluded between unions and SOEs granted employees generous retrenchment pay-outs. Given that the liabilities of some SOEs exceeded their assets, the inability to pay termination provisions brought reform to a halt[92]. Side-stepping by governments and frequent recanting on initial commitments to support SOE rehabilitation were common obstacles to restructuring efforts since they were politically risky and socially upsetting.

In some cases, written performance contracts provided a means to clarify performance objectives and to monitor and judge performance against prior agreed criteria. In other cases, agency problems between governments and SOEs persisted in contributing to the poor performance of SOEs as information asymmetry caused problems of moral hazard and adverse selection. Moral hazard is the notion that an entity largely insulated from risk will behave differently when exposed to the whole or a significantly larger stake of the risk. SOEs managers are normally exposed to less risk due to soft budgets and insufficient retrenchment disincentives. Information asymmetry occurs when one party to an agreement has more or better information than the other party. This impairs the balance of power in the agreement and could result in the agreement going awry. SOE managers often know more about the operational aspects of the business than government officials who they engage with during performance contracting. They could be tempted to demand huge bonuses for relatively soft performance targets. Adverse selection is the tendency for a higher risk group to seek coverage more than less risky groups. In the case of SOEs, adverse selection occurs when the state decides on the future of loss-making corporations in the absence of complete information.

Thus, it was difficult for the state to set and enforce equitable contracts that required a reasonable amount of effort on the part of managers for a commensurate reward. In its report on *Information, Incentives, and Commitment: An Empirical Analysis of Contracts between Government and State Enterprises,* the World Bank analysed the impact of twelve written performance contracts between SOE managers and their governments in six developing countries and found no evidence to support the argument that improved performance could be credited to contracts[93].

In half of the cases, pre-contract productivity performance trends continued—and in a quarter of the cases performance deteriorated after the contracts were in force. Problems encountered were that contract targets changed too frequently; there were too many objectives from too many principals; and governments pledged actions that they were not motivated, or politically able, to implement. A reason for the pledges that government could not—or would not—fulfil was the lack of credible alternative options as the helpline from the World Bank was often the only one extended. In Ghana and Senegal, for example, promises were made to obtain foreign aid, which may not have been forthcoming without such concrete pledges.

When managers put a high probability on government reneging on its commitments such as providing support, increasing tariffs, or paying incentives, they invariably would not exert the effort to effect performance improvements. Such weak incentives therefore led to shirking by managers. The World Bank ascribed the problems in contracting between government and managers to contracting maturity (or immaturity) since government agencies were in the early phases of a learning process on how to contract successfully. The bank also noted that commitment to honour the contracts when circumstances changed was a problem—it was difficult, if not impossible, to force the state to comply.

Despite some successes from the wave of reforms to address SOE performance, outcomes were largely ineffective in bringing sustained change. By 1990, development finance institutions concluded that a new approach to SOE performance improvement was required. Despite the reluctance of African governments to move towards privatisation in commercial and manufacturing sectors in the 1980s, development finance institutions pushed for private sector involvement to become the driving force of SOE reform in the 1990s.

Privatisation (involving a change in ownership) was prioritised for SOEs that exhibited an improvement in performance under the first round of reforms for the following reason. In times of crisis, governments committed to hard budgets, granted managers autonomy, and gave priority to commercial objectives. However, as the crisis disappeared, gradually government commitment also faded. Therefore, even in cases where previous reforms not involving ownership changes yielded positive results, privatisation was still thought to be beneficial since it would lock in the gains from earlier reform efforts[94].

The Second Round of Reforms – Privatisation

Just as the rationale for SOEs (in the preceding half century) had come from western states, the motivation for privatisation also came from industrialised countries. In the United Kingdom and the United States of America during the 1980s, in a departure from Keynesian economics, the Thatcher and Reagan administrations instituted liberal economic policies informed by the works of Hayek and Friedman[95]. These largely successful privatisations resulting in improved sector performances in industrialised nations, as well as the transition economies of Latin America, helped make a case for privatisation in less endowed countries—including those in Africa.

The change in Western economic policies and a growing sense that previous performance improvement policies had failed, made some officials in developing country governments question earlier commitments to state-led development and sparked debate on the possibility for more far-reaching market reforms, including divestiture. In Ghana, for example, it was observed that the low political cost of government interference was a main reason for failed reforms, and that divestiture (partial or full disposal of public enterprises through a sale, closure, or bankruptcy) was thought to be a more efficient way of dealing with poor SOE performance.

Towards the mid-1990s, a number of developing country governments thus focussed on divestiture, especially within infrastructure industries—sectors that had been spared in an earlier wave of reforms due to the fact that they were considered natural state-owned monopolies (unlike other commercially oriented enterprises in manufacturing)[96]. It is important to reiterate that the World Bank and other development finance institutions lent strong support to privatisation as a change of ownership in order to improve the performances of SOEs and meet the objectives of reforms[97].

It was expected that divestiture would address the question of ownership, which was believed to be at the root of the problem of poor SOE performance, and also bring in foreign exchange receipts that would alleviate pressure on the balance of payments. Furthermore, privatisation in the form of divestiture held the potential to stimulate the economy and yield additional tax revenues by the entry of a rejuvenated private sector. Lastly, it could promote open markets and reduce the inordinate power of trade unions.

By the mid-1990s, the concept of improving SOE performance under government ownership was therefore exchanged for privatisation and private participation in infrastructure amongst development finance institutions in transitional and developing economies. In Africa,

Cote d'Ivoire was the first country to invite private participation in its Electricity Supply Industry, first via a management contract to a private consortium to manage its state-owned utility in 1990, and then with an IPP four years later[98].

Reform Loses Flavour and SOEs Survive

Although divestitures in electricity generation infrastructure were few in Africa, by the second half of the 1990s, IPPs, where contracts were entered into with utilities and host governments to add capacity and supply power, were on the increase. Many African countries formulated reform plans to privatise and introduce competition at a Generation and a Distribution level, but efforts were in almost all cases stopped short thereof. Publicly owned utilities have thus remained dominant in almost all African power sectors. Although in some cases SOE performances improved, the utilities of most countries were still not able to finance capacity additions to support the increased demand for electricity. Although the private sector had a role to play in additional investment, the poor financial state of public utilities hindered investment.

Whereas privatisation of SOEs became common in commercial and manufacturing sectors, infrastructure sectors— particularly the electricity supply industry—have been among the most difficult to reform. Changes in ownership were difficult to implement for a number of reasons, as detailed below, and were reminiscent of earlier attempts starting in the 1960s.

Comparing Ownership Performance

While privatisation was largely associated with increased performance objectives, there was evidence to suggest that in certain contexts there was little difference between the performance of private and state-owned companies—putting the factor of ownership as the single determinant into question. Instances where divestitures hardly showed an improvement by private capital (compared to state ownership) merely increased the mounting resistance to privatisation.

For example, in 2003, US-based AES bought a 50 percent stake in Kelvin power station, a coal-fired plant supplying roughly a quarter of Johannesburg's electricity in South Africa. During the Enron scandal, AES reassessed its international operations and decided to pull out of its South African operations. The shareholding was then sold to a consortium led by CDC Globeleq, but by 2006 CDC Globeleq abandoned its stake in Kelvin power station, citing technical problems after it recorded financial losses on the plant. After significant investment spending on refurbishing the plant, the plant could only generate 25 percent of its rated 600 MW capacity[99]. Such ambivalence to outcomes between public and private ownership, in turn, slowed the momentum of privatisation as intellectuals, government officials, non-governmental organisations, academics, and other interest groups, started to challenge the appropriateness of divestiture as a means to performance improvement.

A caveat is that any comparison between state and private corporations needs to be made with caution. Public companies are often required to fulfil some societal objectives which their private counterparts are not necessarily obliged to fulfil. Governments may have acquired loss-making companies for non-economic or strategic reasons, thereby nullifying comparison on a profit basis. Therefore, even when the financial performance of private firms has been found to be superior, it does not necessarily mean that they were more productive. Comparison also becomes problematic when the review or comparison period is too static. This could be the case when a new and inexperienced public enterprise is compared with a well-established private company. Finally, while large profits may indicate efficiency, they may reflect market distortions and monopolistic pricing.

Even in instances where private participation did not involve a change in ownership (e.g., through management contracts), performance was questioned by stakeholders, whose expectations were not realised by the contract outcomes—as was the experience in Tanzania. In the management contract involving the Tanzania Electricity Supply Company Limited (TANESCO) and NetGroup Solutions, an agreement was reached that aimed to prepare the national utility for privatisation. It was found that the management contract outcome was highly dependent on how governance and performance incentives were structured[100].

Revenue incentives made up more than 99 percent of contract fees that were awarded. The contract failed to place sufficient emphasis on customer service, as it was assumed that it would automatically follow from other objectives. With customer service standards and incentives largely omitted from the contract scope, it was hardly surprising that end-users were disappointed by the customer service outcomes of the management contract despite the contractor improving collection rates and nearly doubling utility revenues in two years.

Negative Perceptions about Privatisation

Speculation about the lack of transparency, including allegations of corruption in the management of divestiture, also negatively impacted the overall impression of privatisation. Many of the transactions were never publicised, contributing to this impression[101]. Furthermore, in many cases, absent or weak regulatory frameworks after divestiture allowed privatised business to continue protecting their monopolistic positions rather than increase their competitiveness. Many African states lacked the resources and skills to negotiate with multinational or domestic private firms in such a way to ensure that the public interest was protected during the sale, or to institute and sustain credible regulatory institutions after the sale. Persistent claims that assets were sold at artificially low prices also added to negative perceptions as uncertainties clouded valuation methodologies, as did buyers who delayed payments.

Even where there was no transfer of ownership, rumours and accusations of embezzlement by foreigners fuelled negative perceptions relating to the practice of private participation as happened in the case of Cameroon and reported by the United Nations Economic Commission for Africa. In 2000, a bid was launched to sell off 51 percent of the Cameroon electricity utility, Société Nationale d'Electricité (SONEL) de Cameroun, for which the government of Cameroon was expecting a purchase price of US$ 80-90m[102]. AES was the only company among five pre-qualifying consortia that submitted a bid and subsequently bought the majority stake in SONEL for US$ 70m. In March 2002, AES' parent company was reported to be in financial difficulty, and AES was accused of diverting funds from SONEL to its parent company. Despite an improvement in the relationship and a turnaround in the performance of the utility, the period shortly after AES took over the management of SONEL negatively impacted on perceptions of privatisation due to the accusations. This made it difficult for government and investors to rally mass support for further private sector participation. Although such instances were uncommon, their occurrences did slow momentum to privatisation as they were widely cited by opponents to privatisation.

Weak Regulatory and Tariff Reform

Non-cost-reflective tariff structures have been key obstacles in attracting private sector investment. This was observed in Zimbabwe, where in 1991, as part of wider SOE reforms, the Government of Zimbabwe embarked on reforms to improve the performance of the national utility, the Zimbabwe Electricity Supply Authority (ZESA). While there were subsequent improvements in the technical operations and customer service areas, little reform progress occurred on the legal and regulatory fronts. Failure to raise tariffs affected the utility's financial performance and frustrated the government's efforts to attract private sector investment. Furthermore, the failure to increase tariffs to the Long Run Marginal Cost (LRMC) was directly linked to the failed negotiations of the Hwange Privatisation and Expansion Project and the Gokwe North Project[103].

In September 1996, the Government of Zimbabwe issued a letter of intent for the sale and expansion of Hwange power station. The joint venture between YTL Corporation of Malaysia (51 percent) and ZESA (49 percent) was expected to finance the expansion of two 300MW units to the value of US$ 550m on a non-recourse basis. The value of the existing plant, as stated by the government was US$627m. In order for the investment to attract a 20 percent return as asked from the investor, tariffs needed to be increased from 2.97US c/kWh in 1996 to 6.2 US c/kWh by 2000. When the proposed tariff increase was considered to be too high by the government, YTL proposed to pay US$ 184m for the existing plant. Having already publicly put US$ 627m as the fair value of the plant, the government could not accept the large discount on the plant and called off the negotiations, without reaching an agreement.

Not long thereafter, in April 1997, the Government of Zimbabwe signed a letter of intent with National Power and Rio Tinto of the United Kingdom to develop a 1 400 MW plant at Gokwe North. Inclusive of finance charges, the coal-fired development would cost US$ 1 600m. Project viability was conditional on achieving tariffs reflective of the LRMC by the year of commissioning of the first unit. With the government unable to fulfil the commitment, the project failed to attract the financial support and negotiations were abandoned in early 2000.

Zimbabwe is only one example of many that illustrates how tariffs that are insufficient to cover the economic cost of production hamper efforts at transforming SOEs and increasing investment. Later, in the case of South Africa it is further shown how policy uncertainty, weak regulatory reform, and uneconomic tariffs, continued to cast a shadow on financing prospects for continued generation investment.

High Perceived Risk and Lack of Private Sector Interest

Many emerging and developing countries have not been able to attract quality private investors due to the perception of high country and sector risks. In 2001, the World Bank financed the bidding process for

51 percent of the shares of Mauritania's national utility, SOMELEC, after making privatisation a condition for debt reduction. After two pre-qualifiers for the bid withdrew, only Morocco's Office Nationale d'Electricité (ONE) was left in the running. ONE subsequently put in a low bid in the hope that the Government of Mauritania would feel compelled to acquiesce. Realising that the country would be incurring a significant loss in accepting the offer from ONE, the government renegotiated its debt reduction conditions with the World Bank, which, in turn, agreed that Mauritania could not be held liable for the failed privatisation[104].

Mauritania was not the only country in the West African region to have difficulty in attracting credible private investors. In 1996, with the support of the World Bank and other donors, the Senegalese government embarked on reforms, which were aimed at eventually privatising the national electricity utility[105]. Eager to transform its ailing electricity industry, it initiated institutional, legal and regulatory changes. By March 1999, it had sold off 34 percent of the Senegal Electric Company (SENELEC). The partial privatisation of the utility lasted only eighteen months mainly due to conflicts over investment and pricing issues.

A new government bought back the shares from Hydro-Quebec International and Elyo, the consortium which initially secured the bid. In 2001, the new government tried to re-privatise the utility under a new framework to address the shortcomings that strained the first relationship. Only two consortia responded. Despite active discussions, successful negotiations did not lead to any deal closures. Ultimately, the privatisation effort was abandoned, with private partners losing financially and the Senegalese government saddled with utility subsidisation[106].

Economic Nationalism and High Political Costs

The lack of private sector interest also has roots in economic nationalism. Many host countries must share the responsibility for the lack of investment appeal to the private sector due to its hostility towards Private Participation in Infrastructure initiatives. This antagonism may partly be explained by the idea that privatisation was 'forced' onto countries with hardly any credible alternative options since Africa, in general, was a policy taker, not a policy maker. *"In very few cases was the decision to privatise totally home-grown or strongly endorsed or supported by domestic decision—and opinion—makers. While African proponents of privatisation could be found, the main impetus for divestiture came from the donor community in general, and the [development] finance institutions in particular"* (as reported by the Centre for Global Development)[107].

A key problem in infrastructure is the perception of loss of sovereignty. When infrastructure in strategic sectors is placed into the hands of foreigners, it conjures up fears of neo-colonialism. There is a strong link between the antagonism to the privatisations of the 1980s and the nationalisations that preceded reforms in the 1960s. There was a pattern across the continent—Africans wanted control of their own house[108].

Thus, the sale of publicly owned infrastructure assets was often politically sensitive. The desire to appease economic nationalist opposition influenced the appetite for privatisation. Even where local capital was possible, privatisation was often viewed as being against the political interest of leaders in government since divestiture could undermine the government's ability to use public corporations as instruments of employment creation and patronage.

Governments were reluctant to shake up the management of SOEs unless they were sure that new managers could take over smoothly and swiftly. The fact that skills in utilities were in short supply (especially knowledge of the local industry) gave managers some bargaining power with governments. In Ghana, for example, to allay the fears of opposition parties, the government maintained minority shareholdings in divested SOEs and undertook fewer divestitures during election years. Even in newer companies, despite the Ghanaian state having limited resources to partner in the country's first IPP on a 50:50 equity basis between the government and the private sector as initially intended, it still pushed for a shareholding. Ghana only managed to raise cash which could give it claim to a 10 percent of the project's equity[109].

Despite a sense of economic nationalism in Africa, where the popularity of officials (and ultimately their political survival) was more dependent on enacting reforms to reverse the downward trend of SOE performance than on political patronage, there was generally greater reform momentum than in countries where the political survival of governments depended on defending SOEs. Nevertheless, in many cases, political considerations shaped the outcomes of the privatisation process, as the political costs of privatisation swayed governments into action, or inaction. In Egypt for example, despite net foreign aid diminishing from 5 percent of Gross Domestic Product (GDP) in 1980 to zero in 1988, and trending into negative in 1989, the SOE workforce was important enough in the leadership's support base to condone poor SOE performance (in the short term) and the aid crisis was not considered a strong enough imperative to lead to successful reforms[110].

There were thus many investor, sector, and country related factors that aggregated. These factors complicated divesting of monopoly SOE electricity utilities; challenged the implementation of management contracts; and restricted broader private sector participation. In addition to the overview presented here, many of the challenges were also prevalent in South Africa. These challenges will be expanded on later in this book.

Views Regarding Future Reforms

Despite the previous rounds of reforms, the power sectors of many developing countries still lack the investment climate that would create sustainable electricity generation investment. So, what is to be done next? What should be the focus of the next round of reforms to bring about sustained improvements in African power sectors? Should countries revert to the non-divestiture reforms instituted from the 1960s to the 1980s given the problems encountered with privatisation, or should the last three decades of reform failures with state ownership be reason enough to do away with state ownership altogether and take away *the government of business* from the *business of government*'?

In spite of the number of African countries that embarked on reforms, the fact that nowhere in Africa have governments been able to fully dismantle the public apparatus in the power sector, suggests that there is still a need for SOEs in electricity. The question at the heart of the issue remains: *How can the financial and operating flexibility needed for the successful conduct of SOEs be compatible with the need for measures to assure consistency in public policy and public accountability?*[111]

While at this stage the road to future SOE reform efforts remains opaque in terms of how SOEs will be dealt with, various authors, policy analysts, and industry professionals, have presented broad views on what the next round of improvements should entail.

In a 1999 policy research report entitled *'Bureaucrats in Business'*, the World Bank analysed the political economy of state enterprise reform. They concluded that because privatisation has similar political costs as corporatisation (instituted in the first round of reforms from the 1960s to the 1980s), the two (privatisation and corporatisation) tend to succeed or fail together. Where reform was politically feasible, desirable, and credible, countries corporatized and privatised successfully. Whereas where countries were not politically ready to reform, substitute ownership strategies were not successful in improving performance.

A corollary could be that any kind of reform should only be embarked on in countries that are ready politically, socially, and perhaps economically for such transformation, and where government commitment to reforms is compelling. This implication, however, does not address the situation in many African states where reforms are sorely needed, but where governments are politically numbed into inaction.

Another perspective offered by policy analysts are that the SOE model should not be jettisoned, given the difficulties in making Private Participation in Infrastructure (PPI) work effectively in Africa. However, the limitations of the PPI approach should be recognised, and stakeholders should work harder at creating the conditions to make it function effectively. This view is widely held among domestic nationalists, given that earlier reform efforts did in some instances produce moderate successes[112]. Some of these reform efforts, when carefully applied, may help in improving the performance of infrastructure SOEs.

With the difficulties encountered with privatisation it may be a reasonable prospect to give reform under government ownership another chance in selective cases. The support for giving SOEs a second chance stems from the idea that experience over the last three decades has taught governments, donors, and other institutions valuable lessons, allowing them to proceed with caution. Due to the advances made in the theory of performance and management contracts, corporate governance, regulatory arrangements for SOEs in less endowed country contexts, centralised and decentralised ownership functions, the impact and functioning of institutions, the management of managerial incentives—five decades later we are armed with new and more current knowledge on how to tackle the old problems of poor SOE performance[113].

Policy analysts and observers favouring nationalism but who remain sceptical about the prospects of performance improvement in electricity SOEs without privatisation, maintain that improvements in corporate governance may still be worth pursuing to create an arm's length relationship between the government and the utility. What is needed are changes to the rules and the structures that govern the relationship between governments and SOEs. These changes should, in turn, impact on the long-term performance of the SOEs and the sector. Again, given the advances made in the theory and practice of corporate and SOE governance, there may be a way forward.

A distinction and qualification must be made here; classic corporate governance has two important built-in assumptions. Firstly, the right of free exit of shareholders and the threat of a hostile take-over is relied on by an efficient equity market. Secondly, the maximisation of shareholders' wealth (as opposed to social benefits) is the principal criterion for efficiency. These assumptions may contradict the realities for SOEs in most African states where private equity in SOEs is absent, and where social objectives feature heavily due to the gap in development.

One way advocated that SOE performances could be improved through better formulated governance arrangements is tailoring governance guidelines to the specific infrastructure sectors and to reflect market structures and regulatory arrangements in which SOEs operate. Both internal and external governance factors need to be holistically addressed since partial remedies—such as focussing only on one governance dimension—is not likely to yield improved SOE performances in a sustainable way[114].

The difficulty in reforming SOEs stems from the nature of state-centred systems. This includes their systems of governance and control, their financing, and the many ancillary societal functions that are performed by SOEs. Unlocking SOE performance improvements lies in better understanding how institutions discourage sector progress, and in strengthening the institutions (formal or informal) that govern their existence and operations to achieve sustained progress[115]. Institutions do matter, especially the institutional links between government and utilities. They ultimately have a pervasive influence on the long-run character of the power sectors within economies[116]. Good economic management, therefore, depends on the effective design and quality of public sector institutions that are responsible for executing reform policies and providing public service. Good economic management depends on the effective design and quality of public sector institutions that are responsible for executing reform policies and providing public service[117].

◈ ◈ ◈

SOEs have survived despite attempts at divesture. However, despite their continued existence, governments have struggled to put SOE utilities on sustainable operational and financial performance trajectories. This outcome has negatively impacted their ability to attract infrastructure investment into the power sector.

It is clear that governments alone will not be able to finance the expansion of electricity infrastructure to meet the objectives of development—at least not in the foreseeable future. The private sector will have to play a key role in adding capacity to African power grids. In order for private investment to be attracted to the power sector, however, public sector capacity must be enhanced. How this will be achieved in the next cycle of reforms is still unclear. What is clear is the following—unless frameworks are effectively geared to achieve the required synergy to promote mutual partnerships between the state and the market, the next round of reforms will be doomed to fail.

CHAPTER 8

ESKOM – STATE OWNED CORPORATION

In May 1910, as soon as the Union of South Africa was incorporated, the Power Act came into force. The Act provided for the future expropriation of private electricity undertakings. Under its authority, the state envisioned electricity provision as a public service provision that should in time be placed under its control. From 1948, under the country's Apartheid policies, the National Party government established many state-owned companies to moderate the impact of sanctions against South Africa. After 1994, the African National Congress (ANC) government inherited these State-Owned Enterprises (SOEs).

Just like broader country policies were shaped by the National Party from 1948 until 1994, after the country's transition to democracy South African domestic policies were strongly influenced by the ideologies and political leanings inside the ANC and its alliance partners. This chapter provides insights into the policies that directed how SOEs like Eskom were managed and it provides an appreciation of the real outcomes of such policies.

The Changing of the Guard

While the ANC government initially sold stakes in some non-strategic SOEs and intended to reduce the role of government in many sectors, by 2008 the ANC reversed this policy and wanted SOEs to play a more expanding role in the country's economy. This reversal originated from the ANC's 52nd National Conference in 2007, where President Jacob Zuma was elected as the new leader of the party[118]. Unlike his predecessors, Presidents Nelson Mandela and Thabo Mbeki—who ushered in macro-economic policies to reduce the country's debt and expand private sector investment, President Jacob Zuma and his supporters backed the state-dominant model to increase the role of the state in the domestic economy[119]. This policy choice continued under the subsequent administration of President Cyril Ramaphosa and was supported by resolutions at the ANC's National Conferences in 2017 and 2022.

Within the ANC, the role of state-owned enterprises as a vehicle for economic development was enshrined in the governing party's adoption of the National Democratic Revolution (NDR), an ANC/SACP ideological strategy document. The NDR positions state-owned enterprises to take on a developmental role in the pursuit of national development and industrialisation[120]. Despite the weaknesses of the state-dominant model within the African context and displays of its misfiring on the continent and elsewhere, there were sufficient actors within the ruling party and its alliance partners to push for the developmental state as a model for economic development.

Amongst these were socialist actors who genuinely believed in the promise of the ideology as a model for economic progress. There were, however, players supportive of this model due to the parochial benefits that they could derive from its implementation, especially when implemented alongside the ANC's preferential procurement policies for SOEs.

While the NDR remained the primary script for economic policy and transformation, there have been diminutive economic improvements that have occurred during the period of its adoption. In the main, the NDR has not delivered on its intended outcomes with respect to broader policy goals such as economic growth, employment creation, income inequality, and poverty alleviation[121]. On the contrary, these indicators have deteriorated during the period of its implementation in South Africa since the global financial crisis of 2008.

With the ANC at the helm of government business, the party has trailed down a similar path as many other post-colonial freedom-fighting movements that have emerged victorious after the advent of democracy but have failed to sustainably improve the conditions for its citizenry[122]. The ANC was initially successful in promoting and improving the conditions for its population. And in the early years of ANC rule under the policies of Nelson Mandela and Thabo Mbeki, it appeared as if South Africa would buck the trend—but since the Jacob Zuma and Cyril Ramaphosa presidencies, the country has been unsuccessful at maintaining the initial successes. To wit, the scores of almost all meaningful progress indicators have been in decline. SOEs have become a drain on the South African fiscus. Rather than contribute to the nation's economic growth as intended, many SOEs have become the reasons for the country's economic stagnation[123].

Government Hegemony and Undue Interference

Like many large South African SOEs, Eskom operates within a complex framework of government policies spanning many jurisdictions. Its spending is directed by government in the form of preferential procurement frameworks and the Public Finance Management Act. Its labour guidelines and how these are implemented are directed by its shareholder. The company's four greatest cost inputs are: 1) investments in infrastructure and the interest on the loans to enable these investments; 2) primary energy; 3) operating and maintenance expenditures; and 4) human resources costs. For these significant expenditures, there is considerable government input or involvement in directing how these should be managed.

With the provision of electricity being centred in socio-political and socio-economic spheres, Eskom operates in highly constrained business operations and regulatory environments. The extension of government bureaucracy into Eskom's business operations has weighed heavily on the effectiveness and the efficiency of the utility. The number of areas where government involvement is prevalent has often been underestimated and the extent of the state's involvement in South African SOEs has not always been sufficiently appreciated—especially by those who operate mainly in the private sector.

Given that all facets of power sector operations are, in some or other way, governed by the state, it was fairly easy for the state or the ruling party to extend its reach further into Eskom's operations with decisions on the awarding of tenders and setting unrealistic and onerous targets for SOEs to be the champions of social progress. Ironically, there were times when the government's assistance was required, but government action was conspicuously absent. A key example of such instances was when various state organs (including government departments and other SOEs) were not paying their utility bills owed to state-owned companies, including their electricity bills to Eskom[124].

State involvement in day-to-day operations was substantial. With organised labour allied to the ruling party through the tripartite alliance, it added another level of complexity to SOEs achieving autonomous governance with clear performance objectives. Traditionally, labour acts in the role of being gainfully employed to perform certain functions within an agreed set of equitable principles. With organised labour, through its alliance partnership with the *de jure* shareholder, organised labour was therefore also indirectly a *de facto* principal to the Eskom board and the executive, rather than an equal partner.

The blurred lines between principal and agent in the form of the shareholder and the executive respectively, as well the blurred lines between the utility executives and labour bosses (quasi 'shareholders' through the alliance) resulted in power imbalances that were often not in the interest of the utility's other stakeholders, including its customers.

Since the introduction of Eskom Conversion Act 13 of 2001, electricity customers were no longer the *de facto* shareholders. As previously stated in Chapter 2, the Eskom Conversion Act 13 of 2001, provided the legal framework for government to have significantly more involvement in the power utility. Prior to this, ESCOM was created essentially for the *consumers* of electricity, with minimal executive government involvement—apart from board, parliamentary, and regulatory oversight. Hence, in various ways the interests of consumers in particular—and the ability of broader stakeholders to protect their interests in general—were diluted with the Eskom Conversion Act. With the Conversion Act, electricity consumers effectively handed over their proxy to the government of South Africa—to exercise the requisite authority over the power sector (and over Eskom) on their behalf. The utility therefore lost its distinctive organisational autonomy that provided the leeway for it to deviate from government and private corporation objectives[125].

Losing this independence and persevering against an increasingly dominant state was initially not easy for some SOE executives who were previously used to arms-length approaches taken by traditional financiers and shareholders. Over time, however, increasing relations with government became part of the job. As the reach of the state into Eskom operations increased, opposition to overreaching political interference was not expected from appointed company executives since the ruling party had a strong hand in placing board members and senior company executives in their respective positions. Even where company executives wanted to resist unwarranted government or organised labour demands in order to achieve more balanced outcomes for consumers and other stakeholders, their efforts were not supported, often countered by alliance partners.

Brian Dames who served as Group Chief Executive Officer between July 2010 and March 2014, stated that his exit from Eskom was, in part, due to political interference, including pressure from former Public Enterprises Minister, Malusi Gigaba, to do more deals with the architects, main actors, and beneficiaries of state capture[126]. Even after

Dames' departure from Eskom, when contractor strikes interrupted construction during the early civil works at Medupi Power Station construction site, former Minister Malusi Gigaba would intervene and settle disputes by giving into their demands[127]. This set the stage for further labour strikes, with the inferred understanding that further increases in benefits could come from unlawful industrial action, and impunity for those who were striking illegally and intimidated workers who refused to go on strike[128]. The capitulation to contractors' demands played right into the hands of certain contractors and beneficiaries of Eskom contracts that had questionable related technical experience, lacked sufficient managerial expertise to execute projects effectively, and gained their contracts through dubious commercial processes[129]. Perversely, their contracts were extended, and cost escalations ran into billions of rands.

While there may be justifiable reasons why government ministers should step in to avert some form of calamity, the question of under what conditions this interference should be required or condoned, and why it had ostensibly become necessary for certain kinds of intervention, was often not clear. Equally unclear was how the fiscal discipline objectives of the company could still be achieved.

Former Minister of Public Enterprises, Barbara Hogan, testified at the Zondo Commission on State Capture (a commission that endured from August 2018 until June 2022), how key members of the ANC and others lobbied for the appointments of heads of state-owned enterprises, despite the boards of these companies having already applied the appropriate selection criteria and shortlisted their preferred candidates[130]. In a number of cases, the candidates that were lobbied for ended up facing corruption charges after being implicated in the capture of these entities. In the light of the expectation to provide political favours for appointments, many capable candidates retreated from applying for public office positions, especially in state-owned companies.

In South Africa, the appointment to office within a state-owned company was likened to a poisoned chalice that left a curse on the future careers of those who drank from it. Sources within the government itself, indicated that most black executives did not want to have anything to do with state-owned companies—and that due to political interference and unrealistic expectations SOEs have ruined many careers of otherwise highly capable individuals.

So dire was the situation at Eskom that in 2019 after the departure Phakamani Hadebe as Group Chief Executive Officer, when the Ministry of Public Enterprises was specifically looking for a black CEO, it struggled to obtain applications from suitable black candidates. While there were some candidates who could have stepped into the role and steer the organisation, many of them declined the invitation to apply for the position, citing their disfavour to political interference.

Media outlets reported that 27 potential candidates were asked to apply for the position—they all declined[131]. These included at least two non-executive directors who were at the time serving on the Eskom board of directors. Following the dearth of interest from the proposed black candidates, the company decided to employ a white Group Chief Executive Officer—a move the ruling party would later come to regret. A bit more about this in the next Chapter.

Appointments to Leadership Positions

At the Zondo Commission on State Capture, country president Cyril Ramaphosa was also called to testify and provide details on the ANC policy of appointing its officials to leadership positions within government, including state-controlled institutions. Since 1997, within the ANC, its *cadre deployment policy* had the objective of having political party loyalists occupying influential positions in the public sector. The Zondo Commission found that the contentious policy is a key enabler of state capture since it blurs the line between state and party[132]. Serving party members exploited the policy as a promotion instrument for corruption in government institutions, SOEs, as well as in independent institutions set up specifically to guard and defend the country's democracy in accordance with South Africa's constitution.

At the Zondo Commission it was heard how the ANC cadre deployment committee selected individuals who would be appointed to various organs of state, including many SOEs, to influence decision making, and thereby protect and promote the narrow interests of a few influential players. Board and executive appointments to SOEs were therefore a crucial part of the machinery that would accelerate the decline of the once globally well-respected state-owned utility[133].

Once the board and executive levels were filled with deployed individuals, often under the guise of socio-political transformation, lower-level senior management appointments were made to ensure that the necessary support for nefarious activities was obtained at levels low enough in the organisation—in order to oil the state capture machinery and execute its extraction mandate[134].

Capable executives, as well as senior and middle managers were often replaced with those who could –and would– act as agents who ensured that parallel and intertwined political and shady parochial objectives were foregrounded while performance and sustainability objectives moved to the background. This happened in very subtle ways.

Frequently, company restructurings with changed appointments of candidates were instituted with the stated objective of improving organisational responses to company challenges. This could be to bring in individuals purported to be more suited to the tasks at hand, or to enable professed sideways movements to grow and broaden the skills base within the company. Within a framework of pursuing credible and reasonable employment equity objectives, such moves were rarely questioned—broader socio-political objectives of addressing and rectifying past inequalities were universally accepted and enshrined in legal statutes and company policies.

To further the ends of state capture, there were also instances where ethical senior and middle managers would be suspended from work for claimed contraventions of company rules, or for no plausible reason at all, to allow morally flexible candidates to temporarily occupy these positions to obtain contracts or approve irregular payments. The precautionary suspensions would later be lifted with no evidence presented of investigations having been conducted. These seniors who instituted the precautionary suspensions would also benefit from false accolades of being 'tough on performance' since they were prepared to suspend lower-level managers for projects which were 'problematic'.

These actions therefore earned crooked senior managers and executives further ill-gotten praises with their own principals and the public. In some cases, employees were suspended on full pay for many weeks, months, and even years, without proof of completed investigations into their cases[135]. In many of these instances, there were no justifications for the fruitless and wasteful expenditure for ongoing salary payments while the suspended employees were 'waiting' at home to be reinstated[136]. These fruitless and wasteful expenditures were not reported in accordance with the country's Public Finance Management Act.

It is acknowledged that legitimate paid suspensions were at times required to swiftly investigate allegations and decide on a just outcome; however, the use of precautionary suspensions was abused within the public sector[137]. While there were often discussions to limit the suspension periods and provide adequate justification for their use, the practice of extended paid suspensions was common in state institutions in South Africa. The result was that billions of rands was lost to the state due to this easy-to-use and unchecked practice, which did not mandate any serious accountability from those who instituted such suspensions[138].

Relationship with Organised Labour

Party aligned and emboldened organised labour unions were accustomed to getting their salary increases honoured, often through unprotected worker strikes. This further invigorated labour unions and reinforced the belief that they were unstoppable—and they were.

In an environment of constrained finances, where Eskom was dependent on National Treasury for bailouts, the Eskom executive and the board determined that it was not feasible to pay salary increases. Between June and August 2018, employees staged demonstrations over a wage dispute. The utility entered into a three-year wage agreement, but due to financial losses, could no longer honour this agreement without government or taxpayer support[139].

Incoming Chief Executive Officer, Phakamani Radebe, communicated to labour unions that the company was no longer able to pay the stated increases and therefore no increases could be on offer. This set off the worst power sector industrial action and widespread protests in the post democratic era and resulted in national rotational blackouts. Intimidation by union members allegedly caused staff to stay away from work. At some plants where staff did report for work, they could not enter their sites due to physical blockades preventing them from doing so. When power station middle –and first line– managers stepped in to assist with keeping generation units operational, coal trucks were stopped from delivering coal. As coal stockpiles were decreasing and conveyor belts were reportedly damaged at some power stations, generating units were eventually taken out of commission. At Duhva Power Station, the media reported that a coal truck was hijacked, and the coal was dumped at the entrance to the site, impeding access to the plant[140]. The wage deadlock was ultimately eased with a renegotiated wage agreement for another three years. The three-year wage agreement ended in 2021.

In 2022, when the company was in deeper financial distress than three years prior, a new round of wage agreements was under discussion for the period July 2022 to July 2023. Having learnt their lesson from three years earlier, under a collective bargaining agreement Eskom executives offered unionised employees salary increases of between 4.5 percent for higher earning employees and 5.3 percent for lower earning employees[141].

Once more, certain labour unions were not prepared to take the offer and the dispute resulted in unprotected industrial action. Since Eskom is an essential service, the utility was able to obtain a court interdict against the labour strikes. However, it was not until at least 4 000 MW was lost to the national grid, in large part due to the labour unrest. Widespread media reports circulated of groups between 50 and 100 people protesting at nine Eskom coal-fired power stations[142].

Again, protestors barred their colleagues from reporting to work. In certain instances where employees reported for work, they were forcibly removed from their offices. In some cases, managers stepped in to assume the roles of employees who were either on strike, or employees who could not be at work due to being blocked or due to intimidation. Selected staff members who returned to work reportedly received text messages and threatening calls cautioning them not to return to work. Certain managers who did return to work, reportedly had their cars stoned. Others had their homes and cars targeted with petrol bombs—and still others had their vehicles set alight and their tyres were slashed. The Minister of Public Enterprises, Pravin Gordhan, reported that at some power stations, more than ninety percent of workers did not report for duty, some taking part in the unlawful industrial action, and others out of fear of intimidation[143].

These acts of industrial action led to the worst bouts of rolling blackouts that the country had experienced at the time. Plants that were scheduled for maintenance during this time could not be shut down for the scheduled maintenance to continue. Plants that were already shut down for maintenance could no longer continue with their planned maintenance schedules. This contributed to future bouts of rolling blackouts due to inadequate maintenance on Eskom's ageing coal fleet.

In many ways the frustrations on the part of organised labour can be understood as they were not directly responsible for the poor financial state of the utility brought about by the government's handling of SOEs. However, despite the expressed empathy for the some of the lowest paid workers in the company, during the periods of labour unrest their actions significantly contributed to the problems of insufficient electricity generation in South Africa. The protests eventually subsided after Eskom endured one of its worst bouts of loadshedding. As much as 6 000 MW of electricity demand could not be served, resulting in electricity consumers not having electricity for as long as 12 hours daily.

Constrained Finances

Constrained finances have not only been an obstacle to workers obtaining pay increases. The tightening of the purse affected the available generation capacity due to insufficient funds being available for maintenance for the coal-fired fleet[144]. Constrained finances also prevented important strategic activities from being performed—such as long-term planning and training. While the neglect was not immediately felt in the short term, it was felt over the longer term[145].

Tariff Increases, Increasing Debt Interest Payments, and Government Bailouts

Despite state bailouts, the poor operational and financial performance of state-owned enterprises, such as Eskom, led to significant increases in government debt. A significant portion of Eskom's debt was due to increased fruitless and wasteful expenditure, escalated costs in the development of its Medupi, Kusile and Ingula plants, as well as widespread corruption. Eskom was unable to convince the National Energy Regulator of South Africa (NERSA) to pass through all these costs.

While for many years Eskom attempted to pass through inefficient costs to consumers, NERSA was unwilling to pass through all the costs, citing that the costs were too high and that tariff increases would be too steep for consumers. While Eskom continuously claimed that it only expected prudent costs to be passed, NERSA was wary. NERSA was substantively correct in its argument for non-approval of tariffs requested by Eskom. After all, much of Eskom's cost increases arose due to corruption, malfeasance, and ineptitude. By prudent regulatory principles, these costs should not be passed through to consumers[146].

Over the decade from 2013 to 2023, on many occasions Eskom and NERSA have locked horns in South African courts over tariff increases. Eskom usually argued that procedurally, NERSA incorrectly applied its approved methodology for its tariff determinations. And in turn, NERSA argued that Eskom's costs were not prudently incurred and therefore should not be passed on to consumers. Both parties were correct. However, on procedural grounds the courts have ruled mostly in favour of Eskom. So, while NERSA had a substantive case in not passing through inefficient costs, on procedural grounds the energy regulator could not justify its tariff determinations. Consumers ended up paying for this procedural regulatory oversight.

When NERSA tariffs could no longer cover the total cost of electricity production, the government finally stepped in. In a series of bailouts, it allowed the utility to remain financially afloat with annual equity injections. The challenge for NERSA to protect the economy and consumers from unaffordable tariffs yet allow cost reflective tariffs for the power sector to recover and continue on a sustainable trajectory, remains formidable.

Despite having competitive electricity prices on the continent and among developing countries globally, what it cost Eskom to generate power may not be what was efficient or affordable for its consumers. Irrespective of the regulatory processes used to determine tariffs, under the government's state dominant model for economic development, it would take a long time before cost *reflectiveness* came closer to cost *effectiveness*.

An Uncertain Tariff Trajectory?

Eskom has been managed inefficiently. This is characterised by low revenue collection, corruption, as well as inefficient allocation and misuse of resources. The resultant high costs need to be covered either by revenues or by state bailouts. Irrespective of the acceptability of having consumers, or taxpayers, pay for the sins of poor SOE control, Eskom cannot navigate itself out of its technical and operational challenges, if it cannot manoeuvre out of its financial challenges (and be relieved from its huge debt burden). The utility is saddled with problems that need skills, new ideas, and finances to solve. No company can become operationally sustainable if it cannot reach long-term financial sustainability—and vice versa.

In spite of the need for cost reflective tariffs, the transition to cost reflective tariffs have met—and will continue to meet—with increasing resistance. In a country with high unemployment, high levels of inequality, and increasing electricity connections for the poor, any rapid plans to recover the full costs of electricity without regard for the poor will find it hard to garner broad-based support amongst voters.

While a longer transition period (i.e., enduring lower tariffs) does delay the financial recovery of Eskom, without understanding the impact on the poor it is understandable that significant short-term tariff increases can cause concern amongst various NGOs and community groups, as well as the government. Any move towards increasing tariffs therefore requires a plan that clearly shows the long-term tariff trajectory as well as the impact of long-term tariffs on the economy and society. The long-term consumer tariff trajectory becomes difficult to predict in an environment where so many other varied factors such as future investment, sector reform changes, decarbonisation target contributions, the financial health of distributors, and the speed of the utility death spiral, all have an impact on the outcomes of tariff reforms.

The Ministry of Finance has decided to take over most of Eskom's debt. While this does add to the burden of taxpayers, the assumption of Eskom's debt at least shields the poor from exorbitant tariff increases. However, some questions still remain: Will this be sufficient to put Eskom on a sustainable financial future path? And will this be sufficient to turn around Eskom's operational performance? How long before additional government bailouts could again be required? What stresses do financial bailouts put on government's other social obligations? And what does this mean for South Africa's future sovereign domestic and foreign debt?

In 2022, the National Business Initiative, in partnership with Just Share and the World Wide Fund–South Africa, conducted a study to determine the investment required to sustain the power sector over the next three decades. In part, the objective of the investigation was to determine the level of power sector investment required that would put the country on a sustainable path to encourage sufficient investment in other sectors of the economy, put the country on a sustainable long-term economic growth trajectory, and reduce unemployment. They estimated that South Africa could need as much as R 3 trillion over thirty years, to recover a power system that would signal sufficient available generation investment[147].

Taking over Eskom's debt (by the Ministry of Finance) therefore only provides temporary relief against steep tariff increases. It does not necessarily resolve Eskom's underlying problems. It is therefore conceivable that after the financial reset (i.e., state bailouts between 2023 and 2026), that Eskom could once again move towards an unsustainable financial situation over the next decade. Costly government procurement policies, poor revenue collections, and reduced sales spurred on by a utility death spiral, could land Eskom in a similar or more precarious position in the years to come. In addition, continued political overreach and corruption remain credible concerns.

The point made here is that while, in isolation, good decisions are seemingly made for Eskom over the short term, it still remained unclear what the long-term implications could be on the power sector as a whole and for the broader South Africa economy—especially when the underlying policy and structural obstacles remain. In this context, the future tariff trajectory will continue to be an unknown in South Africa.

Procurement by State-Owned Companies

Tough decisions to improve financial performance and reduce costs could also upset a different constituency benefitting from the status quo. In addition to pacifying the aligned organised labour constituency and the many poor consumers who are also voters, many companies legally and illegally benefit from SOE procurement supported by the country's preferential procurement policies[148].

In the absence of effective procurement governance systems to avoid corruption in the company, many Eskom staff and their family members were implicated in procurement activities that inflated costs to the company and resulted in further pillaging from the utility. Not only did illicit procurement significantly increase electricity costs, the introduction of middlemen also noticeably increased the time to procure much-needed products and services. In June 2023, Electricity Minister, Kgosientsho Ramokgopa, announced that the slow procurement of specific plant components through intermediaries reduced Eskom's output by 2 800 MW on average, thereby extending the levels of loadshedding[149].

The procurement expenditure for Eskom is significant and many high-cost components used in power generation are regularly procured as part of the utility's maintenance budgets. In the past, long-term agreements were entered into with Original Equipment Manufacturers in a bid to minimise costs. Once technologies are selected for plants, the operator is largely locked into specific technology options and cannot easily disengage in its relationship with suppliers, without costly plant modifications.

Original Equipment Manufacturers are often best placed to continue with servicing their own technology, especially when there is intellectual property related to the technology that would make it harder for competitors to compete. However, owing to preferential procurement policies instituted by the erstwhile Minster of Finance, Pravin Gordhan in 2017, the procurement process requirements created opportunities for middlemen to exercise rent seeking[150].

The company's internal procurement activities from the board level and various company committees down to functional department levels contained lapses in governance. Eskom became a company of enablement as unethical suppliers, illicit service providers, political elites, and the company's own employees, turned the company into a resource for all kinds of fleecing, corruption, patronage, and extraction. The absence of consistent criteria for when cost-adding economic empowerment objectives trump value-for-money, was lacking in many of the company's procurement practices. Equally absent was the recording of the additional costs (i.e., over and above fair market value) associated with the company's preferential procurement practices. The company, the public, and electricity consumers had insufficient grasp of how much government policies were costing financially (in terms of electricity costs) and in terms of its contribution to rolling blackouts.

It is important to emphasise that despite the abuse of preferential procurement processes leading to extensive corruption, the country's Black Economic Empowerment policies did yield its intended objectives amongst some of the company's suppliers and service providers. Many honest enterprises were developed and a number of companies that were contracted via the company's preferential procurement policies helped Eskom to stave off further bouts of loadshedding. These suppliers and service providers were more than just middle-men and had excellent capabilities and products which greatly assisted Eskom in areas where there was a shortage of products and skills. Still others helped with the fight against corruption. A few companies went as far as being whistle-blowers to acts of corruption. Some staff at these contracted companies reported fraud at the utility, at great risk to themselves and their families. In South Africa, whistle-blowers were generally not celebrated and were rarely supported by state institutions.

Declining Plant Performance

The company's operational performance eventually reflected its financial performance. The declining operational performance of the coal fleet was easy to hide initially because the time lag between cause and effect is long—although it is easy to predict. A well-maintained plant can operate for many years after preventive maintenance is stopped and plant improvements and repairs are indefinitely deferred. However, plant performance follows the quality of maintenance and operations, and performance eventually catches up.

Performance Indicators

As is the case for many production facilities, leading performance indicators are essential for managing performance towards desirable future outcomes, because they show the direction in which the business is heading. Unlike lagging indicators that focus on the past, leading indicators reduce the likelihood of future undesirable consequences. Leading indicators include human and organisation factors that will contribute to plant events. The purpose of focussing on leading indicators is to enable the identification and prediction of potential consequential events—in the direction of managing and reducing the likelihood of adverse outcomes.

Leading performance indicators help build resilience into organisational capabilities, and if used correctly, provide the correct information to decision makers to reduce the likelihood of significant undesirable events and reduce their consequences. Leading indicators are forward looking and project the likely future trajectory of company technical and financial performance.

As Eskom slowly ran out of generation capacity, the preservation of the long-term health of generation assets took a backseat. Rather than preserving the operational lives of its plants, Eskom was playing to keep the lights on. Leading (or long-term) performance indicators to ensure plant integrity were systematically reduced. Amongst others, these included indicators on personnel pipelining and training, plant condition monitoring, completion of in-depth failure investigations, and the development of comprehensive life-cycle asset management programmes. It was initially hoped that the tight balancing of priorities of keeping the lights on versus performing the requisite maintenance would be an interim arrangement. Slowly over time, however, the management of outcomes (i.e., lagging indicators) became the main focus areas (sometimes the only focus areas)—rather than the management of leading inputs that could predict future outcomes[151].

As the priority shifted from *sustainable plant performance* towards *keeping the lights on*, there were considerably less opportunities for preventive maintenance at coal units. In this kind of operational environment, accountability for plant performance became opaque. Plant technical managers were conflicted between their traditional technical objectives of ensuring long-term sustainable operations as the shift towards new objectives focussed on keeping the lights on.

This also spelled the end of traditional performance management within the company since it became difficult to hold managers responsible for long-term plant performance when they were explicitly told by superiors that there was no opportunity—and in many cases no funds—to perform preventive maintenance and ensure future reliable plant performance. While most managers believed that there had to be a middle road to balancing both objectives, this middle road often remained undefined. Even when there were strategies drafted to simultaneously meet these dual objectives, these interim strategies often proved difficult to follow in practice.

Interim strategies failed to consider evolving or deteriorating plant conditions, available skills required to execute work scopes, the amount of preparation required to ensure successful outcomes of contingency plans, the lead times to procure essential spare parts, and the amount of financial and human resources that were available versus what was required to successfully execute strategies for balancing opposing objectives. In other cases, objectives and processes changed so frequently that proposed strategies became obsolete even before they could be approved or implemented. Attempts to reintroduce a balanced scorecard and include both short-term and long-term performance focus areas proved extremely difficult.

By March 2022, the energy availability factor of the coal fleet decreased to a low of 55 percent as the utility grappled with planned and unplanned generation losses to catch up on maintenance backlogs.

Poor Coal Quality

Despite the low average Energy Availability Factor of the coal fleet, there was substantial variability in the energy availability performances amongst the individual coal-fired stations. Some power stations and units performed better, while others fared considerably worse. Coal stations with dedicated coal mines generally performed better than those power stations that received coal from multiple sources.

At generation plants without dedicated mines, Eskom started losing control of its coal quality supply when it started diversifying its coal procurement to include several small independent coal suppliers. While Eskom historically invested in coal mines to have greater control over coal quality and price, in 2015 the practice was significantly relaxed when former Eskom Group Chief Executive Officer, Brian Molefe, retreated from this practice, since [*he*] *did not want to buy the bakery,* [*he*] *only want*[*ed*] *the bread.* While the practice was intended to increase Eskom's coal supply options, reduce coal costs, and expand the number of black-owned coal companies, it came back to haunt the utility in later years when it lost control of its coal quality at certain plants[152]. It became increasingly hard to ascertain whether the poor coal quality was due to coal supply from emerging black-owned mining companies, or large mining companies that were opposed to the inclusion of smaller black-owned coal suppliers.

It later emerged that some unethical Eskom officials colluded with dishonest coal suppliers to pass and accept coal for Eskom consumption despite coal-quality concerns raised by Eskom technical experts. Often the coal did not meet the plant specifications, resulting in low unit electricity power outputs, increased use of oil to maintain boiler firing, accelerated deterioration of plant equipment sensitive to coal quality, higher environmental emissions, accelerated plant ageing, and significantly lowered plant lifespans.

There were suppliers delivering coal contaminated with metal and rubble, and these contaminants caused Eskom equipment to fail more frequently[153]. Eskom coal generation plants have few credible systems in place to monitor the quality of coal in real time or identify which suppliers failed to provide the coal at the correct quality—free of contaminants and foreign material. Due to increased equipment failures, generating units were frequently taken out of service for repairs, resulting in deeper levels of loadshedding. Despite planned maintenance to improve the reliability of plants, continued damage to units without dealing with the root causes after the maintenance was performed, hardly resulted in improved performances.

The foreign material resulted in damage to conveyor belts, mills, hoppers, and other materials handling systems. Non-coal contaminants also contributed to increased boiler tube leaks, the repairs thereof being costly and lengthy—since it required units to be taken out of service for extensive repairs. Metal objects not only damaged power station equipment, but it also increased the coal tonnage for which Eskom provided payment.

A burgeoning and thriving coal road transport industry had been established and there was increasing reluctance to use other, more cost-effective, means to transport coal to plants that were not served directly from adjacent mines. Sunk investment in coal trucks made it hard to convince new transport companies to accept Eskom's options to transition to alternate delivery methods. While rail options were more affordable for coal transportation to certain power stations, in 2022 rail infrastructure was vandalised amid resistance from coal mining and transport mafias. Organised crime networks destroyed rail infrastructure to ensure that future revenues from road transport contracts remain, despite the higher costs of road transport compared to rail transport[154].

Eskom lost many battles to regain control over its coal quality[155]. Where it was dependent on law enforcement agencies to assist, the sentiment was that there was insufficient will to act fast enough to stem the tide on what was believed to be the work of a coal mafia.

Even when there were no incidents of poor coal quality, there were still major problems experienced with the delivery of coal. In September 2023, eight weighbridge operators and one truck driver were arrested for coal theft and fraud at Kusile Power Station. It was reported in the media that weighbridge operators would authorise weighbridge verifications and process the transactions without the coal hauler ever entering the plant to offload the coal[156]. The power station would, however, be invoiced for the coal that was ordered but was never received. It is unclear how long such acts of fraud had been ongoing.

Acts of Sabotage

Reports of plant damage were not limited to power stations that sourced their coal from the many coal suppliers. Acts of sabotage to plant equipment also occurred at plants that had their own dedicated mines, where these acts caused countless interruptions to normal electricity supply from the generating units. A loss of generation at plants with dedicated mines meant that the difference in generation needed to be made up by plants that did not have dedicated mines. This manoeuvre turned out to be very profitable for mines not dedicated to specific power plants and for transport companies transporting coal to the various power stations.

Reports about crime syndicates were common, with cartels having invested in systems to divert Eskom coal for export, and in turn supplying Eskom with sub-standard coal. In August 2022, an encounter was reported in Middleburg, Mpumalanga, where in one day 65 trucks were robbed of their high-grade coal loads intended for Eskom power stations and the loads were diverted to Richards Bay harbour for an export price that reached roughly eight times the Eskom contracted price. Lower grade coal was subsequently sent to the Eskom sites[157].

In May 2022, Eskom reported that acts of sabotage had delayed the return to service of one of its coal generation units at Tutuka Power Station. At first, a cable was damaged and repaired whilst the country was experiencing Stage 2 loadshedding. Thereafter, once the unit resumed start-up operations, it was discovered that an air pipe was cut and an entire bend in the piping was removed from the system that supplied control air to the turbine. Eskom affirmed that these were deliberate acts of sabotage by someone who had access to the specific plant area—areas to which only normal employees would have access[158]. The utility proceeded to open a case with the South African Police Services. This had been the fifth case of sabotage at the plant reported to the police in ten months. A few weeks later, at the same plant, spares worth R 1.3 billion could not be accounted for and the company had to write off the assets. Tutuka Power Station regularly featured in the news media for sabotage, theft, and corruption incidents that adversely affected operations and presented a risk to electricity generation[159].

In November 2021, a pylon was cut at Lethabo Power Station (an Eskom coal-fired plant with a dedicated mine). Eskom reported that the evidence of sabotage was clear since nothing else was removed from the scene. The incident happened when there was already rolling blackouts occurring nationally. The event could have resulted in more frequent loadshedding if the 3 000 MW output from this plant was no longer available[160].

These acts prompted the utility to introduce measures aimed at improving security at these national key points. In addition to contributing to the problem of inadequate generation capacity to meet demand, the cost of additional security personnel and smart systems to enhance security, further strained the limited resources of the utility.

The increased security did not always deliver the desired outcomes of protecting Eskom's assets. The same security staff brought in to protect the assets of the utility, were often found to have been involved in the covert attacks. In June 2022, for instance, additional security guards that Eskom had hired to bolster its security and to protect and secure its cable assets at its Rosherville facility in Germiston, were caught and arrested for cable theft and related charges[161].

Response from Law Enforcement Agencies

The extent to which state institutions were compromised and under-resourced, resulted in inadequate support for the utility from law enforcement agencies to stem the tide against sabotage—including those from highly organised criminal syndicates (often aided by the utility's own staff). Despite numerous reports of sabotage, support from governmental crime fighting and intelligence agencies remained limited. Frustrations grew amongst many stakeholders for the lack of action, including Eskom's Group Chief Executive, who in mid-December 2022 resigned, citing the lack of political support in bringing criminals to book[162].

In December 2022, after the country experienced its worst bout of level 6 load shedding, the government finally gave approval for the support of the South African Police Services' Directorate for Priority Crime Investigation, which has the mandate for investigating organised crime, economic crime, and corruption—as well as the South African National Defence Force. Amid unprecedented levels of rolling blackouts, the country's National Defence Force was deployed at several Eskom coal-fired power stations in response to growing concerns that increased acts of sabotage could lead to higher levels of loadshedding, which at the time amounted to more than twelve hours of daily rotational blackouts throughout the country[163]. While some welcomed the deployment of the army at Eskom generation plants, others considered the government's efforts at preventing the escalation of the sabotage, vandalism, and criminality, as 'too little, too late'.

The country braced itself for its first Christmas day blackouts, but this was averted due to much lower national demand as industrial activity wound down for the end of year festive holidays. In the entire month of December 2022, Christmas day was the only day when there was no loadshedding. The country ended the 2022 calendar year with more than 200 cumulative days of rolling blackouts. This was the first year that the country experienced more days with, than without, rolling blackouts.

Of the fifteen coal plants in the Eskom fleet, many had reports of sabotage to some degree or another, including all twelve plants in the Mpumalanga province, resulting in system-wide risks to electricity production. Not only did these incidents result in more costly diesel being used for operating open-cycle gas turbines to meet some of the demand, but the financial strain of burning expensive diesel resulted in less funds being available for operations and maintenance at coal-fired units, further adversely affecting the future reliability of these generating assets.

Burning through Money and Diesel

Due to the extensive operation of open cycle gas plants, the financial strain became so dire that Eskom ran out of cash to procure sufficient diesel to operate these units. In December 2022, after the company had exhausted its financial allocation for diesel fuel, it approached the National Treasury department in the Ministry of Finance for financial support to mitigate Stage 6 rolling blackouts and avoid deeper stages of loadshedding.

The country's National Treasury responded that it did not have the funds and that the money should be sought elsewhere. Eskom was able to find diesel stocks with the country's Petroleum Agency. These stocks were held for extreme emergencies—and the situation qualified as an extreme emergency. During this time, when Eskom was drawing down the country's strategic fuel reserves, the media reported that South Africa had left itself exposed, as it no longer possessed minimum volumes of strategic emergency diesel reserves. Eskom was forced to wait until the new financial year until its budget allocation would permit spending on more diesel fuel. The Public Finance Management Act, to which Eskom is subject, prohibited spending when there was no budget allocation for such expenditure and without written approval from the National Treasury.

In January 2023, it was reported that Eskom applied for a wholesale import license for diesel fuel that would have helped the company save on its fuel costs, but the approval was purportedly denied by the Ministry of Minerals and Energy. Were Eskom to obtain the licence to import its own fuel, the company would allegedly have been able to import diesel directly from importers, or on its own. The savings for the ailing utility would mainly be in government taxes to the extent where 25 to 30 percent of the fuel price would reportedly be reduced[164].

While such a saving would have meant that rolling blackouts could be reduced during the last few months of the fiscal year, the application was not approved by the relevant ministries. At the time, the country experienced the most severe levels of rolling blackouts in its history—at least until the company's new financial year started in March 2023, and a new fuel budget brought some temporary relief.

Human Resources - Functions and Processes

During the period of the Jacob Zuma administration, increasingly board members and Eskom executives were alleged to have been appointed by outside influencers that were inserted into key positions for the promotion of narrow interests of those who benefited from state capture (as reported at the Zondo Commission into State capture). This period was evidenced by weakened technical and corporate governance, larger losses of technical and managerial skills, and general organisational decline and impropriety[165].

Technical managers frequently bemoaned the organisational recruitment practices as well as other *push factors* that caused many of the company's most skilled employees to leave the organisation.

Far removed from plant operations, while managing human resource policies from the company head-office in Sandton, Corporate HR professionals could not recognise their own role in the creation of a skills crisis. With few credible performance measures to link the impact of corporate HR practices and organisational performance outcomes, notwithstanding improvements in some areas, ineffective HR practices continued, unaffected by the impact that this had on the overall performance of the company.

Where Corporate HR did relinquished control of hiring practices and gave command back to individual power stations, the situation often did not improve either. It became clear that in many instances the reasons for staff leaving were due to poor leadership exhibited at individual Eskom plants.

Loss of Intelligent Customer Capability

The loss of technical skills in engineering, project management, and procurement, contributed to Eskom's challenges to keep the lights on. Certain company executives and senior managers believed that where skills were lost to the organisation, these skills could easily be replaced by contracting in the requisite skills and intellectual capacity from 'the market'. The problems arose when there remained insufficient skills inside the organisation to specify end-user services required from suppliers, actively manage contractors, and provide comprehensive oversight on external service providers.

While there were still departments which had excellent competencies within the organisation, areas where skills were depleted resulted in costly experiences for the utility. In many areas, Eskom lost much of its intelligent customer capacity, the in-house capability within the host organisation to take responsibility for ownership, management and implementation of projects or services. Since the organisation is usually the end-user of a specific product or service, it is the responsibility of the client organisation to manage the quality of service delivered to the organisation. When the skilled staff turnover rate at Eskom departments exceeded the rate to attract, train and maintain sufficient capability, the risks to company increased.

In many instances there remained few suitably qualified and experienced personnel inside the company to scope the range of services required, integrate the delivery of these services into related company processes, or adjudicate whether Eskom had received fair value for its payments. The inability to comprehensively understand the organisation's needs in relation to the products and services procured was of significant consequence to Eskom. When there were no longer enough suitably skilled people in the company, these risks normally materialised.

While this problem could be resolved with the aid of owner's engineers, this normally involved additional contracting of services, amounting to additional layers of contracted handovers, and increased reporting which significantly escalated costs. In a highly technical organisation such as Eskom, where its human capital is arguably the most important determinant of future performance and success, the company failed to take a measured approach to skilled staff attrition. Eskom risked the loss of sufficient technical and managerial acumen for long-term sustainability.

Recruitment of Talent

Key performance indicators for local human resources departments had insufficient focus on staff skills, related experiential capability, and their impacts on performance. Specific power plant equipment skills for boilers, mills, precipitators, pumps, compressors, fans, turbines, electrical switchgear, transformers, civil structures, control and instrumentation, and fire systems, were inadequately managed at many plants, in part due to the centralised control from the corporate head office.

Human Resource appointments required for improved plant performance was therefore often delayed by centralised Human Resource functional departments that accepted little to no direct accountability for plant technical performance. While the constraint from corporate Human Resources may have been necessary in certain instances to manage headcount and control manpower costs (which in some cases had spiralled out of control), in certain key areas these controls had numerous negative impacts on the achievement of the desired plant performance —and few positive impacts on the intended overall cost reductions.

In some areas the company also employed many younger staff with little experience in the hope that they could make a success of their roles. While this strategy allowed Eskom to reduce salaried costs and smooth employee age demographics by recruiting younger staff, departments provided insufficient support in assisting new recruits and their managers with ensuring that the requisite skills and experience levels were timeously obtained.

Such lapses ultimately came at a cost to company performance—it contributed to inexperienced leaders having to make significant technical, procurement, and financial decisions, when the stakes were high. While some appointees were notable and lived up to their potential, many failed to deliver at the desired levels of performance.

Many promising appointments were made, but often appointees were inadequately supported by the same leaders who appointed them. Many appointees were also poorly selected. The inefficient and inconsistent application in awarding employment opportunities and recruiting individuals into various company roles was widespread. Therefore, even when departments were adequately staffed with employee numbers, the management processes for ensuring the right skills, competencies, and attitudes for the job were not sufficiently aligned to achieve optimal performance outcomes.

Workforce Planning

While employee numbers at power stations remained relatively stable, the number of cumulative years of related experience in key functions dropped precipitously, as followed the levels of performance. Engineering training programmes were adversely impacted by budget constraints. Eventually formal engineer training programmes were either postponed, reduced in scope, or discontinued.

Eskom no longer trained engineers at the same level that it did in the past—and in practice, it no longer consistently implemented its 'commitment and undertaking' to ensure that its young graduate engineers-in-training were trained to the quality and performance standards of the Engineering Council of South Africa. HR skills pipelines for artisans, technicians and operators also ran into difficulties. At times there were insufficient or no candidates to train. When candidates did present themselves, there was often not enough instructors to train them, or training budgets did not allow training programmes to continue as planned.

A 2016 World Bank report on the *Financial Viability of Electricity Supply Sectors in Sub-Saharan Africa* stated that Eskom was 66 percent overstaffed[166]. While the World Bank was subsequently shown that it was incorrect with its metrics and methodology used to determine and compare optimal utility staffing levels[167], at the time there were hardly any clarifying responses from the utility—thereby perpetuating the public perception that the utility was grossly overstaffed. While certain areas within Eskom were overstaffed, some departments were indeed understaffed. Most business units lacked transparent, credible, and accessible organisational frameworks for how staff numbers were derived. This made it hard for managers to motivate for increases in employee numbers in an environment that saw a concerted effort to reduce headcount and employee costs.

Cost-cutting was performed in specific areas across the organisation, focussing specifically on human resources. In many cases staff number allocations were cut indiscriminately and important functions that were performed to ensure long-term sustainability were often the first casualties. The focus remained on short-term production issues and important longer-term functions such as plant reliability assessments, future plant life-cycle maintenance strategies, and long-term outage planning were 'postponed'—at times indefinitely.

Savings were made on capital and operating expenditures without knowing, assessing, or seeking to understand, how these *savings* would eventually impact the medium to long-term performances of plant components. An *'all-hands-on-deck'* call-to-action was often prompted. In many areas this normally meant that those staff members who were responsible for longer-term performance and planning were called in to assist with daily and weekly firefighting—often to the detriment of long-term sustainable outcomes.

Indiscriminate headcount reduction proved costly over the longer term, especially in environments where there was insufficient pipelining to ensure an adequate supply of new recruits. Where headcount was not determined by a specific decentralised function, but rather on a wider company or business unit level, it took considerable time to motivate for—and fill—vacancies linked to critical functions. The risks associated with inadequate detailed workforce plans and lengthy vacancy durations were not well understood or widely appreciated within the company.

It must be emphasised that since 1998, the uncertain policy and operational environments that Eskom was functioning in made it hard to predict what future skills the company would be requiring for each year of operation. For more than 25 years, it was intended for the Generation division to transition from a supplier of last resort to only one of many generation suppliers operating within a power market. It was therefore hard for the corporate HR department to have a firm timeline upon which to base their projections for workforce planning. This uncertainty will continue as details on the intended unbundling of the utility becomes clearer. Balancing the risks of excessive human resource costs; ensuring that there would be adequate human resources for operations and capital expansions; bringing in sufficient younger talent to mitigate long-term age-demographic human resource risks; meeting employment equity objectives; all while guaranteeing no forced company retrenchments; was a formidable ask of the company corporate HR planning department.

This aspect stresses the importance of careful human resource workforce planning during power sector energy transitions. The need to extend the operational lives of coal stations to limit energy shortages is likely to challenge the corporate HR department even further in the future. The planning horizon for power stations spans many decades—longer than the career lifespans of its employees. During transitions, therefore, the potential for getting HR planning wrong remains—and potentially increases during uncertain power sector reforms and unpredictable energy transitions.

Impact on Generation Plant Performance

Eskom could have benefited from improved organisational design and workforce planning functions—to ensure that important functions were catered for, and management control and oversight functions were being actively performed. Critical functions when not actively monitored and managed, especially during periods of transition or vacancies, created latent weaknesses in important asset management activities.

Eskom experienced several significant events that resulted or contributed to inoperable generation plants. In these instances, available generation capacity was no longer available to meet electricity demand due to insufficient experienced staff being available to prevent inappropriate operational decisions, provide adequate oversight, and correct ineffective asset management practices. Operating with insufficient staff to ensure plant safety had its consequences, especially when coupled with increasing pressure to keep units running to limit downtime during maintenance outages. The examples below provide reasons for why plants were unavailable for prolonged periods during the years of loadshedding.

Medupi

In August 2021, while an operator was bleeding off hydrogen from a generator cooling circuit at the Medupi Power Station, the hydrogen inadvertently mixed with air and caused an explosive detonating mixture[168]. This resulted in a catastrophic explosion on the unit 4 generator—a unit that had entered commercial operations only a few months earlier.

During the root cause investigation into the event, Eskom management cited procedural non-compliance and management failures. With this single failure about 720 MW was unavailable to the grid for an estimated three years, leaving the utility with an initial estimated repair bill of more than R 2.5 billion[169]. It is noteworthy to consider that the overall operational plant training and competence—as well as management safety processes, were so weak that an elementary operator error could destroy a costly asset during the execution of a routine plant outage activity. The effect of this generation capacity being unavailable to the national grid would be felt for many years.

Kendal

In September 2021, a fire at Kendal power station rendered two units inoperable, thereby making 1 360 MW unavailable to the national grid. A single generator transformer had caught fire and the fire had spread and damaged cables to the main cooling system, thereby taking two more units out of operation. While the two units where the fire did not originate from, were recommissioned later the following week, grid stability was maintained running costly diesel plants, while the extent of the fire damage to the other unit was assessed. The estimate was that the fire-damaged unit would be out of service for many months, with repairs pending[170].

Duvha

In March 2014, Duvha Power Station experienced a boiler pressurisation event that caused extensive damage to the boiler[171]. An explosion on Unit 3 was reportedly due to insufficient evaluation of a change in coal properties and insufficient maintenance. It took three years to appoint a supplier to effect repairs despite the initial plan for the plant to be back in service by 2020. Although a supplier was eventually appointed, in December 2020, a court set aside Eskom's decision to award the R4 billion tender for the repairs after General Electric accused Eskom of rigging the tender for building a new boiler to favour Chinese firm Dongfang[172]. Eskom subsequently announced that since the plant was scheduled to be decommissioned in 2034, it was no longer considered economically viable to effect repairs.

The event in 2014 was not the first catastrophic event at Duvha Power Station. In February 2011, three years into the national power crisis, the turbine on Unit 4 spun out of control[173]. The cause was reported to be 'human error and lack of personnel' and repairs took just under two years to complete.

Majuba

In November 2014, a silo collapsed at Majuba Power Station, thereby immediately rendering unavailable 3 000 MW of the plant's installed generation capacity. The cause was initially reported to be a design flaw, and the incident resulted in countrywide rotational loadshedding[174].

Fortunately, Eskom could find a way to bypass the collapsed silo and restore operations to minimise the generation production impact during the repair period. This workaround, however, required hundreds of trucks to offload coal at temporary conveyors close to the boilers every hour.

The repairs took more than two years to complete, and the six-unit plant could only return to its fully functional generation output in February 2017.

Koeberg

More alarming concerns were raised in October 2021 when the media reported that experienced staff at Koeberg Power Station were leaving the nuclear plant at a faster rate than the plant management could replace suitably skilled and experienced resources. While the company's Chief Operating Officer, Jan Oberholzer, expressed that he was *'absolutely horrified'* by the number of skilled personnel that the plant had lost[175], staff reported that he did not do anything to resolve the problem.

It was widely reported that suitably skilled technical staff were leaving the utility because of poor career prospects due to the manner in which the company implemented its employment equity rules, as well as a toxic work environment. What was particularly alarming was that employees were prepared to leave the utility while not having any employment alternatives lined up. Most employees who exited the organisation would leave for Europe and the Middle East where there was a demand for their nuclear skills.

Despite the dismay expressed by the company executive, the push factors inside the company that drove the exodus of skilled human resources remained largely unaddressed[176]. The loss of skills at Koeberg[177] subsequently contributed to longer maintenance outages[178].

Camden

The issue of inadequate staffing skills occurred again in September 2022, when an employee at Camden Power Station inadvertently shutdown all the generating units at the plant by opening a single valve. The action resulted in the chemical contamination of several plant systems[179]. Not only did these incidents highlight the issue of inadequate attention to issues of human performance at Camden, but it also highlighted the weak and antiquated plant design, as well as insufficient administrative processes, whereby one single operator error could disable the entire plant by incorrectly operating one single valve.

Kusile

In October 2022, a fire was reported at unit 5 of Kusile power station. The unit was still under construction and the incident was expected to delay the commercial operations date of the unit by a full year. A few years earlier a similar incident had occurred on Kusile's unit 2, also setting back the date for commercial operations by approximately one year. In two separate instances therefore, at least 800 MW of generation capacity at Kusile was delayed by at least another year, thereby exacerbating the rolling blackouts in the country during this time[180].

In the same month, a section of the flue gas duct on unit 1 failed while the unit was shut down for repairs to its flue gas de-sulphuration recirculating pumps. This single failure resulted in the unavailability of an additional 800 MW. As a precaution, a decision was made for unit 2 (which was also shut down and due to return to service) to remain shut down, thereby rendering a further 800 MW of generation capacity unavailable to the national grid[181].

These failures described above were only some of the events that were newsworthy and were reported in the media. The events resulted in many generating units being unavailable for weeks, months and years—significantly contributing to rolling blackouts. With all these setbacks over the preceding years, by year 2023 long-term plant breakdowns significantly contributed to more than a quarter of the utility's generation capacity being unavailable (i.e., unavailability not only due to scheduled maintenance). Figure 8.1 below illustrates the decline in the energy availability factor for the coal fleet.

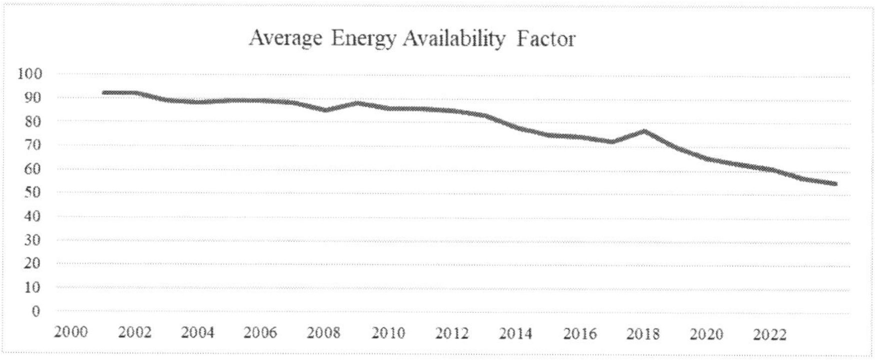

Figure 8.1 Eskom Average Annual Energy Availably Factor Trend

As described above, many factors contributed to the decline in company performance. This decline in operational performance in turn had a negative impact on financial performance. The poor financial performance meant that fewer resources were available to arrest the poor operational performance. Unable or unwilling to institute drastic changes that could arrest the downward spiral, Eskom's performance continued to decline.

Government policies on SOE operations continued to impact negatively on Eskom's performance trajectory and the performance trend demonstrated how damaging such policies could be on Eskom, as well as on other state-owned enterprises. Guided in part by inept policy preferences coupled with poor policy implementation—and to some extent immune to actual policy outcomes—the experiences suggest that policy feedback effects were not sufficiently felt by ruling elites, nor were they not considered sufficiently important to bring about meaningful and improved policy adjustments.

Despite the higher than inflation tariff increases and the government bailouts, by October 2023, when Eskom tabled its annual results ending March 2023, the company posted its largest financial loss—roughly R 24 billion—in its operating history. It also posted the worst Energy Availability Factor for the coal fleet—56 percent—during the reporting period. In addition, South Africa registered the highest intensity of loadshedding during the 2023 financial and calendar year.

CHAPTER 9

ESKOM – THE SMELL OF THE PLACE

Organisational culture can be a strong enabler or inhibitor of performance. This chapter provides insights on how increasing state involvement influenced the utility's culture and its reward and incentive systems, as well as how its people and performance management practices influenced the overall decline of the utility. It explains how employee behaviour and resultant company performance was shaped by organisational context, or as Sumantra Ghoshal fittingly described it, *the Smell of the Place.*

Incentives and Behaviours

Eskom's declining technical performance went hand-in-hand with a slowly deteriorating corporate culture, poor management practices, and disruptive managerial and employee behaviours—with an imperviousness to the realities of the company's performance outcomes.

Many inside the organisation tried to prevent activities associated with the state capture project, but they were largely unsuccessful.

When managers and employees attempted to shine a light on elements of organisational decline, their concerns were often met with disregard, apathy, and disdain. A culture of 'shooting-the-messenger' disincentivised employees from raising disquiet about the company's operations, whether within their respective divisions or in the organisation as a whole[182].

Those that persisted and became 'annoying' were simply moved out of their positions, to allow more 'cooperative and understanding' individuals to step in. Those with the resolve to fight back were systematically whittled away. Labelled disgruntled, problematic and a nuisance, they either threw in the towel and stopped complaining or sought greener pastures elsewhere. More often than not, the effort of raising concerns was not worth the repercussions, which often took the form of retaliation from those who had the authority to mete out punishment or make employees live to regret their decisions to speak up[183].

Corporate bullying pressured many well-intentioned and industrious executives, managers, and professionals, to look outside the organisation for better working environments. Many employees simply left because they did not want to be part of the organisational decline at the utility—wanting to leave early, on their own terms, with their integrity intact.

By 2013, there was a well-recognised indifference in monetary reward incentives for good or poor performance. Eskom became financially insolvent and could no longer offer employees monetary incentives for good performance, as in previous years. With regards to promotions, individuals with questionable performance track records and dubious moral integrity were moving up the ranks. The promotion of so many Eskom employees that were involved in corrupt business dealings speaks to the extent of the problem of not differentiating good ethical company employees from bad employees. Hundreds, if not thousands, of employees were implicated in all kinds of nefarious activities that hurt the company operationally, financially, and reputationally[184].

Years after the revelations of state capture at the institution, the difficulties of recovering from long periods of operation under company practices that were not sufficiently merit-based and offered poor incentives for individual and departmental performance improvements were still felt in the organisation. That is not to say that the way things were done prior to 2013 or before 1994 was always stellar. However, the inability to provide shock-therapy to a dying organisation and pull it out of its coma was the worst that was seen during the company's existence.

Contrary to widespread perceptions in the media about the company's employees, there were—and still are—many hardworking, dedicated, and experienced employees from all backgrounds in the company. However, these employees were often not in decision making positions—and not in sufficient numbers. There were at times sporadic attempts in the company to reverse the deteriorating performance trend, replace unethical leaders, and start addressing a culture that seemed benign to poor performance and high costs. However, there is still a critical mass of stakeholders who remain resistant to such reversal attempts—reluctant to agree to the earnest application of merit-based human resource processes required to accelerate a turnaround of the organisation and improve the performance at the utility.

When there were individuals in leadership positions that wanted to take steps to put the utility on a better financial footing, the required support was not always received from the relevant quarters. In June 2019 for instance, when Phakamane Hadebe was appointed the utility's new Group Chief Executive Officer, he needed the support of the shareholder, the Minister of Public Enterprises, to arrest the financial decline of the company. As previously stated, Hadebe offered to freeze salary increases for all Eskom workers, including those who were represented by labour unions. He was rescued by police and security guards when angry workers began protesting, throwing water bottles at him, booing him, and showing him the middle finger. While he did obtain the support from the Eskom board, his plan was torpedoed by the Minister of Public Enterprises, Pravin Gordhan, who found the situation to be politically sensitive and decided that it would be more expedient to give in to the demands of angry workers. While Hadebe thought that he had the backing of those who appointed him, he soon found out that he had overestimated the extent to which he could count on those whose support he required[185].

In February 2023, it was asserted by former CEO, Andre De Ruyter, that the ruling African National Congress used the utility as a feeding trough, as a means for corruption[186]. According to De Ruyter, there were at least four cartels operating amongst the utility's coal-fired plants in the Mpumalanga province and senior politicians were involved in protecting these cartels[187].

Although De Ruyter would not make public the intelligence to support his accusations—including the names of the senior politicians that he alleged were involved, opposition political parties criticised the ANC's alleged ties with Eskom and tabled a motion that the allegations of the former CEO be investigated by parliament. However, the ANC used their parliamentary majority to block the vote to proceed with a parliamentary inquiry. With his allegations which was disputed by the ANC, De Ruyter angered the ruling party and received an early discharge from his duties.

The following month in March 2023, the newly appointed Electricity Minister, Kgosientsho Ramokgopa, failed to acknowledge that the technical problems at Eskom's newest coal-fired power station, Kusile Power Station, was due to corruption[188]. He instead labelled the issues as purely technical problems. The labour movement disagreed and cited a litany of sources which listed cases of corruption that took place at various Eskom plants. Eventually the new Minister changed his tune after reaction from the labour unions, as well as various other civil society groups. Lack of acknowledgment that there were impediments to performance that needed to be addressed, has been at the root of the exponentially growing problems[189].

Inside the company there was a widespread inability to deal with performance and governance problems head-on, rather than evade them. This behavioural trait was pervasive throughout the company. A prime example from the top of the company was the approach taken by the company's board to manage the financial risk of reporting fruitless, wasteful, and irregular expenditure within the company at a time where corruption was rampant. In 2023, the government and the Eskom board was concerned that the cost of Eskom's debt from borrowers may increase.

Instead of improving fiscal discipline and dealing directly with the issues that contributed to the reported cases of irregular expenditure, the Eskom board instead opted to request an exemption from National Treasury on the mandatory reporting in its annual financial statements[190]. The culture of side-stepping accountability instead of addressing it, filtered down in the organisation. It often appeared as if the board and senior executives were oblivious to the behavioural examples that they exemplified to lower-level staff.

Leadership Appointments

The choices associated with company appointments can significantly impact on organisational performance. In Eskom, many questionable appointments contributed to the dire company outcomes.

Leadership Volatility

The lack of leadership stability was a significant failing in steering the company towards the achievement of company objectives. Between 2005 until 2023, the company had nine different chairmen during the 18-year period. The durations in tenure of these chairmen were in stark contrast to the seven individuals that assumed the role during the 82-year period prior to 2005.

In the same vein, since 2007—the year when loadshedding first started, the company saw thirteen Group Chief Executive Officers over the 16-year period until 2023. This is at significant variance with the three Group Chief Executive Officers that assumed the role in the 22-year period from 1985 until 2007.

The Energy ministry also saw eight different portfolio ministers over the 16-year period since loadshedding started in 2007 until 2023. This was hardly sufficient time for individual officeholders to get to grips with the sector issues, formulate well-constructed plans to resolve sectoral problems, and remain in their positions long enough to see plans executed to their fruition.

Add to this executive and ministerial volatility the constant leadership changes at regulatory institutions, government agencies, and other sectoral ministries, as well as similar changes within various executive and managerial positions within stakeholder institutions, and it becomes clear why the ability to follow through on most objectives proved elusive.

Recruitment and Promotions

While there were fewer organisational changes within the lower ranks within Eskom than in executive positions, these lower levels were not without problems of their own.

Some company employees, despite qualifications, hard work and dedication, simply did not possess the right demographic attributes to fill certain jobs in accordance with the country's employment equity laws. Since racial and gender demographics continued to be major pre-qualification criteria for promotion or appointment, some employees could not fill certain positions within the company. In other instances, despite capable candidates from designated previously disadvantaged demographic groups having applied for certain positions, they were still overlooked in favour of white applicants. It appeared that appointments largely depended on the extent to which final decision makers were committed to the racial transformation imperative. The perception of inconsistent approaches to the appointment of both white and black candidate (irrespective of the employment equity guidelines) had an impact on staff morale from *all* demographic groupings.

According to certain right-wing media reports, the assignment of a higher priority on the speed of achieving employment demographic targets than on energy availability performance objectives, in certain ways contributed to the company's woes. While political and social objectives such as correcting the wrongs of the previous political dispensation was widely accepted as a non-negotiable in the South African political landscape, the pursuit of these objectives appeared rushed within some Eskom departments.

In the absence of required checks and balances that would ensure that regrettable compromises were not made in key areas of the business where recovery would be difficult, performance objectives may have been directly and indirectly undermined. While the company carefully managed the employment equity transition of the workplace to better reflect regional and national demographics during the first 15-20 years following the introduction of democracy, the evidence of the utility's performance suggests that the implementation during the 20–30-year period after the advent of democracy, was too frequent—especially in the senior management and executive ranks[191]. The high management turnover at the company contributed to organisational instability and resulted in pipelining and succession management functions that were challenging to coordinate and achieve their desired outcomes.

It must be stressed that many employees were meritoriously promoted into positions where they played a significant role in arresting the decline and improving performances. However, in certain company departments this was often not the case. The number of questionable appointments proved too big a force to arrest declining company performance. Many factors contributed to poor appointment outcomes, not least the support provided to new managers—and the degree to which their sponsors supported or resisted the racial transformation objective in the workforce.

Corporate Processes and Management Culture

Corporate culture, including the underlying beliefs that shape employee behaviour is largely determined by how a company's employees and management interact. Certain company management processes and how they evolved, influenced the behaviour of many employees and ultimately the decline in the company's performance.

Centralised Functions and Accountability

Centralisation of some functions within the enterprise, made it hard to hold managers accountable for performances within their departments. Having functions whereby corporate office bearers held the decision-making power on the allocation of resources, made it easy for managers at remote plants to renege and avoid taking responsibility for outcomes due to the disempowerment that was associated with regimented 'corporate control without sufficient mitigation', rather than 'user control with increased accountability'.

Centralised control can be an appropriate solution in resource constrained environments where decentralised control of functions is weak. However, in Eskom, where centralised functions were instituted and unable to adequately respond to the needs of decentralised power stations, the objectives of centralised control were undermined.

Adequate resources to continue operations were often lacking, and corporate managers and executives (from head office) whose role it was to provide these resources could not—or would not—provide these. They had their hands tied due to insufficient budgets, or not being in control of other centralised departments (such as commercial and procurement) whose active input and cooperation was essential to achieving positive performance outcomes.

Under the guise of organisational changes for efficiency improvements, the centralisation of organisational functions—an organisational redesign that was required to consolidate control, and in some cases stealthily facilitate corruption—also contributed to incoherent operations between departments within the company (even in cases where there was no corruption). While there may have been a business efficiency justification for centralisation in some areas, the extensive centralisation of specific functions to head office departments contributed to lack of cohesion and the slow pace of implementing important tasks needed to ensure that the lights remain on. This practice also contributed to increased costs, contrary to the stated objectives of the organisational redesign.

Employee Differentiation

The nature of Eskom's dealings with government and Organised Labour also contributed to behaviours that constrained the organisation from operating in a fiscally efficient and economically prudent manner. Labour unions were often militant and highly politicised.

Within the company, labour unions pushed for arrangements that would increase their memberships and improve benefits for their core constituencies, which was the lower-level employees—often at the expense of employees that that were not covered under the Recognition Agreements with Organised Labour. In many cases benefits accrued to employees covered under the Labour Recognition Agreements with little measurable or recorded benefits returned to the company, its customers, or its other stakeholders.

The questionable manner in which salary increases were administered and disproportionately distributed among employees, resulted in silent resentment among some staff that missed out on salary increases—and the situation generally resulted in a decrease in morale. Not only were employee groupings (not covered the Labour Recognition Agreement) displeased with their management for freezing salary increases; some employees also harboured discontent towards their colleagues, who benefited from guaranteed pay increases negotiated under Recognition Agreements. It is not easy to measure the impact of such invidious company processes on staff morale and on subsequent performance outcomes. However, it is considered that the disproportionate salary rewards resulted in some high-performing staff members engage in quiet quitting or leaving the organisation.

Performance Incentives and Rewards

Administering financial rewards at a company group level with little differentiation to the performances of individuals, contributed to the indifference in behaviour by many employees. The inability to sharpen and bring into focus individual, department, and group performance management processes, contributed to overall outcomes at the utility[192].

While on paper Eskom had a world-class *individual* Performance Management process and system, based on the overall company outcomes there was little evidence to suggest that this system was having any impact in practice. This was largely due to the imperfect cascading of company performance objectives down to the level of each operating unit (or power station), the level of each department, the level of each section, and in turn each individual. Individual employee scores contributed so little to aggregate outcome scores that they rarely made a difference to the overall score and potential performance bonus that an individual employee would receive. The thinking was that individuals would be better incentivised to work as part of a team if their own scores closer reflected the collective score of the team, department, or company division—hence the personal contribution of employees counted little towards their overall performance scores.

While in theory, this judgement may have its merits. In practice, for many there was hardly a sufficient personal incentive to perform based on the small contribution that individual performance contributions had on their overall performance scores. The practice did limit the adverse effects of bias by managers where performance scores were not truly reflective of effort or outcomes, or when performance contracting went awry through no fault of employees or managers. However, the direct contribution of individual performance was simply too little to create meaningful incentives for individual and team performance—and the design of the Performance Management scoring system failed to sufficiently incentivise individuals (as a collective) to perform at their peak. A poorly integrated or cascading Performance Management system contributed to inadequate performance outcomes. A better optimised scoring system could have elevated the performance of accountable individuals, teams, departments, and operating units.

In 2013, when the performance bonus monetary incentive was initially removed due to the utility's poor financial state, the performance management scoring system was rendered less effective. At best, the system provided an extremely blunt incentive instrument to encourage the achievement of individual, departmental, and organisational objectives.

Even if the scoring system were optimised and better integrated across functional business units to ensure sufficient incentives existed to shape employee behaviours and commitment toward improved outcomes, many (especially new) managers were not familiar with the system. Managers saw little use for its implementation—at least in the manner that it was employed. Few disincentives existed for managers who decided not to use the system as prescribed. Often everybody within a functional team received the same scores or performance outcomes, irrespective of differentiated individual performance outputs.

Not only did the performance scoring system not incentivise desired employee behaviours, but the scoring system also masked the performance of employees that were not performing at all. Inexperienced managers were poorly equipped to deal with the problem of poor performers. In other cases, experienced managers reneged on their duties to implement the company's performance management processes. After all, this was arguably one of the worst roles of management. Why should managers put themselves through an ordeal that seemingly only had a downside, no upside, and no consequence if the ordeal was avoided by both manager and employees?

On Race Bias and Discrimination

Since colonial times, South Africa has had a chequered history punctuated with race relations issues. Energy and racism are historically intertwined into South Africa's socio-economic and political fabric as the Apartheid regime set out to provide benefits for privileged white South Africans while black South Africans were largely neglected. Under the Apartheid regime, blacks were excluded from working in the energy sector as educated professionals (as they were in many other sectors of the economy). Through racial labour laws, historically the employment of blacks was largely relegated to low and semi-skilled labour. With the advent of democracy in 1994, the ANC government, in an attempt to correct the wrongs of the past, have promoted the moral necessity for greater diversity and inclusion in the workplace. Uniting the initial racially divided labour force has not been an easy undertaking for the ruling party. In the post-democratic era, unintentional divisive race relations, mostly embedded in legislation, continued to dominate throughout the social, political, and economic landscapes. The ANC government has instituted corrective racial employment and economic inclusion policies to redress the outcomes of Apartheid. However, in the context of the country's high unemployment rate, increased foreign immigration, and low economic growth, these policies have in many cases deepened racial divisions within the labour force, rather than unify.

In 2019, after the departure of Group Chief Executive Officer, Phakamane Hadebe, the search for the next CEO failed to deliver another willing, suitable black candidate. The announcement of Andre De Ruyter as the company's next CEO was met with mixed reactions from all quarters of business, government, labour, and civil society[193].

Appointments to state owned institutions could be contentious, especially amongst black movements, who considered this as an insult to the country's history and a rolling back on the gains made for the country's democracy.

The permanent appointment of the company's first white Group Chief Executive in over two decades was met with fierce criticism from two of the three recognised Labour Unions within the company. The National Union of Mineworkers and the National Union of Metalworkers of South Africa articulated their discontent and expressed that the appointment of a white CEO was a setback to the country's racial transformation agenda. The Economic Freedom Fighters (at the time the country's third largest political party) stated that the appointment of a white CEO undermined the role that black Africans play in the economy. From the start, it was a tall order to pacify the sentiments from the many stakeholder constituencies involved in a very visible energy sector which was charged with problems of corruption, poor performance, and daily power interruptions. During and after his tenure, due to Eskom's deteriorating performance, critics of the CEO felt justified in their initial scepticism as the levels of loadshedding increased during his term.

The introduction of white individuals was not just a problem at the top of the organisation. In October 2022, Reuel Khoza, a respected African leader and the first black chairman of Eskom, was asked to assist with recommendations to address the low levels of technical and managerial skills at the company. One of his suggestions was to reverse the skills and knowledge loss at the company by recruiting trusted employees that served during his tenure as chairman—the period where Eskom was admired as the best global utility[194]. His suggestion was met with much chagrin, due to the likelihood that many of these employees would be white.

At the height of loadshedding in July 2022, Solidarity, a historically white denominated labour union, offered the Minister of Public Enterprises to provide Eskom with a list of skilled professionals to help stem the tide against human resource capacity shortages[195]. A feud ensued when traditionally black trade unions felt that the Minister of Public Enterprises did not recognise the contribution that black professionals could bring to the stabilisation of skills within the company. Many did not see this as a sincere offer to help, but rather as a stereotypical gesture that competence and experience only reside with white professionals. Majority black unions saw this as posturing—a means to advance a narrative that blacks were not good enough and that more whites were needed to resolve the issues at Eskom.

Even in the post democratic era, racial polarisation has remained a feature of South African society. The state-owned utility has unfortunately not escaped this polarisation—it was often dragged into racial narratives. Rather than working together to solve its problems in the energy sector, racial polarisation became a thwarting feature—it seemingly stripped the rainbow nation of its former ability to resolve problems and be a model for African development.

The disproportional emphasis on race in the power sector—and lesser emphasis on ethics, competence, service delivery, and compassion for the vulnerable, has taken away the focus on Eskom's performance. It became a distraction from the important issues that could have resolved the problems of loadshedding and uplift the lives of ordinary South Africans.

If stakeholders across the racial divide could be provided the assurances that there would not be exclusionary practices based on attributes that have no bearing on performance outcomes (and for which balanced equitable benefits would be ensured), perhaps there could be a way to have a more integrative and inclusive approach to race and energy in South Africa—an approach that is less antagonistic and more collaborative.

Workforce Morale

In any company, the way that employees feel about their work environment and the role that they play in that work setting, has a significant impact on their motivations, their engagement, and their productivity. For employees, taking personal responsibility is about executing their duties with integrity and caring about the outcomes. Therefore, the degree to which employees take personal responsibility remains one of the key contributors to the achievement (or non-achievement) of organisational performance objectives. But how did the incentives of a large workforce change to take it from the best utility in the world to one of the poorest performers amongst state-owned companies in South Africa?

It is often questioned how such a large company with such a large workforce could be sufficiently beholden to permit the scale of looting and corruption that took place during the years that coincided with the company's decline. Where were all the ethical leaders and what did they do to stop the rot? Were there no employees able to challenge the activities that have resulted in Eskom's fall from grace? Why were over 40 000 souls seemingly unable to mount sufficient resistance to arrest the decline? In addition to inadequate incentive systems (described in this chapter), as part of the state capture apparatus, a culture of fear and intimidation set in, deterring those who would mount forms of resistance[196].

The reporting of irregular activities within the company was met with poor or meaningless responses. Few authority figures seemed committed to investigating irregular activities and to providing reports on their findings. The Assurance and Forensic department often defended the actions of the alleged offenders. There were hardly credible processes in place to protect the identities of whistle-blowers and shield them from potential counter attacks. Thereafter, once identities were revealed, these employees were professionally isolated and socially ostracised. At times, it did not appear to matter if hard working employees no longer played active roles in their areas of expertise and whether the company was benefiting from their employ—as long as they were silenced and no longer a nuisance.

Newly recruited individuals were in most cases less prone to question their managers, who had just appointed them. These inexperienced recruits were new to the departments and processes. They lacked the knowledge to understand the impact of certain business decisions, let alone question the validity of these decisions and their long-term impact on personnel safety, technical performance, and financial sustainability.

Employees rarely had credible platforms to voice concerns, illuminate attention on organisational issues that were concerning, or obtain reasonable responses that they felt addressed well-founded concerns. Managers often manipulated internal reporting and governance processes to ensure that complainants did not receive the necessary support and responses to their complaints. On many fronts they were stifled as legitimate queries fell on deaf ears. Where employees did formally raise concerns on irregular activities, these reports were forwarded to the departments against which the concerns were raised. Departments where the irregular activities were taking place, were assigned the roles of investigating the issues and deciding on outcomes, thereby taking on the dual roles of alleged perpetrators and investigators. This conflict of interest significantly undermined the objective of independently investigating and preventing irregular and questionable activities.

It was believed that in some cases managers spied on their subordinates when these subordinates elevated legitimate complaints. At least two employees who had mounted complaints against Eskom senior managers stated that they had evidence that their mobile telephones were tapped. While it was confirmed that the mobile phones were being tapped, they could not prove by whom. The surveillance apparently did not stop with middle managers. So paranoid was Group Chief Executive Officer, Andre De Ruyter, that he believed he found a spying device in his car and reported it to the police. It was later reported that it was part of his vehicle's tracking system[197].

Employee Apprehension

There were no formal collective forums for concerned professionals (within the managerial and professional bands) to bring attention to and ventilate legitimate concerns. Eskom has three broad organisational levels: one band for senior managers; one band for middle managers and professionals; and one band for bargaining unit employees. While the company has a platform for bargaining unit employees, the middle and senior management ranks had no such platform.

At the middle and senior management level is where it all happens—resource decisions, technical decisions, and financial decisions. It was therefore here that interference frequently occurred in order to circumvent company processes and sway outcomes. A forum for concerned middle managers and professionals could therefore have been a useful mechanism to help deter company infringements.

The establishment of a platform for managerial and professional bands was discouraged and frustrated by the Eskom board due to concerns around the purpose of such an association of middle managers and professionals. The company did historically have a provision for managerial and professional staff to belong to the Eskom Employees Association. However, in the early 2000s when the company was preparing for possible power sector liberalisation, Eskom stopped this union. While attempts to close down the Eskom Employees Association was resisted for many years by some employees, by January 2010, Eskom was successful in driving the cancellation of the Eskom Employees Association from the registry of South African recognised trade unions[198].

Unlike workers represented by organised labour trade unions, middle managers and professionals therefore did not have the freedom of association benefits that collective bargaining structures and platforms would facilitate. While it is uncertain to what extent the establishment of collective structures amongst Eskom middle managers and professionals could have prevented or mitigated the weakening of the company, it is argued here that the deterrence of collective structures for company professionals significantly aided the goals of state capture. This weakness prevented the company's middle and senior management (as a collective) from speaking up against lapses in governance, corruption, and decisions that could adversely impact company performance.

Employment within the company became muzzled—where speaking up was not useful, encouraged, or appreciated. Even when superiors feigned interest and lent a listening ear to the concerns of employees, this demonstration of concern could not always be trusted. Lapses in confidentially often meant colleagues would soon find out who reported acts of criminality. In August 2023, an Eskom forensics manager reportedly learnt of a bounty on her life, when a contracted hitman informed her of the R 400 000 price on her head[199]. The former manager had investigated and uncovered illegal dealings that occurred within the company. It emerged that an Eskom senior manager involved in the corrupt dealings at the utility had hired an assassin to kill her. Since she was no longer in the employ of the company when she learnt that her life was in grave danger, neither Eskom nor law enforcement agencies offered her the requisite protection. These occurrences served as examples to other would-be whistle-blowers of their probable fates.

One of the worst instances that underscored the vulnerability of those who reported crimes at Eskom was the case of Thembisile Yende. In May 2017, it was reported in the media that the young Thembisile was planning to report and expose illegal dealings in copper theft to her manager. When the perpetrator learnt of her plan, he allegedly drugged her, took her to a substation where she was beaten and strangled to death. Thereafter her body was hidden for three days—then transferred to a storeroom to create the impression that she had committed suicide[200].

Many fellow employees were shocked by the events that would tragically end the life of this brave young soul. Whistleblowing consequences as experienced by Thembisile Yende served as stark warning signs to would-be informants of wrongdoing. Employees could therefore trust neither those inside nor outside the company to protect those who in good faith reported acts which conflicted with stated company policies and values.

While Eskom does have a practice of protecting senior managers and executives by offering them personal protection, the same protection was not extended to the rank and file. The condition of not adequately protecting whistle blowers meant that some were left to fend for themselves against hostile superiors and co-workers inside the company, and they were essentially powerless against Eskom managers and executives who had comparatively much more company resources at their disposal to scupper the objectives of whistle-blowers.

Fortunately for some, Eskom did have processes in place to protect the lives of some of its employees. Some of the company's senior managers and their families were continuously threatened and they used bodyguards in public spaces for their own protection. Tutuka Power Station was one of the plants worst affected by criminal activities. The Power Station Manager was issued a bulletproof vest and employed two personal bodyguards[201]. While some executives had the protection of security details to their persons and their immediate family units, for practical reasons extending the bodyguard service to lower-level employees was unfortunately not within the company's policy, practice, nor budget.

Even where honest employees were resolute in performing their jobs and following approved processes, in certain cases intimidation from outsiders with ominous interests could not be stopped. In March 2023, an Eskom employee was kidnapped and later released. The employee's vehicle was shot at multiple times and the employee was abducted by seven assailants[202]. After the ordeal, the employee was dumped in the south of Johannesburg. Once released, the employee had to be admitted to a hospital to treat injuries from the attackers. It was alleged that employees responsible for evaluating tender bids within the company had become targets for criminal syndicates.

In 2018, employees at Eskom power stations reported that when Group Chief Executive Officer, Phakamani Hadebe, visited their sites, he was not permitted to eat food that his bodyguards had not first tested by eating, presumably out of concerns that he could be poisoned. In December 2022, Andre De Ruyter, reported that he was poisoned, allegedly for getting too close to criminal cartels operating at Eskom's coal-fired power stations[203].

At the company's head office, De Ruyter's coffee mug was reportedly laced with cyanide. The Eskom Group Chief Executive Officer was rushed to hospital and later recovered. After De Ruyter's ordeal, speculation surfaced around the resignation of his predecessor, Phakamani Hadebe, who cited health problems as the reason for his early departure. Prior to Hadebe's resignation from Eskom, it was reported that he had fainted at work on two separate occasions and had to be taken to hospital by an ambulance[204]—hardly the symptoms of a healthy individual who had just stepped into the role months earlier.

If two consecutive Chief Executive Officers presumably could not cope with the demands of dealing with the problems at the utility and their lives were at risk, it is hardly surprising that ordinary employees without the bullet proof vests and security detail, failed to see themselves being successful in taking on the challenge of combating ill-contrived activities within the company.

The security conditions were no better for people from outside the company that came to investigate and deal with the criminal elements. The media reported of the appointment of a forensic coal procurement specialist who was brought in to investigate alleged fraud in coal contracts and review the validity of coal contracts in Eskom. Following a drive-by shooting at his home, the individual resigned shortly after his brief appointment.

Even law enforcement agencies appeared reluctant to expose agents of criminal networks. In June 2023, a senior Police Investigative Directorate official investigating corruption was summonsed to appear before Parliament's finance watchdog, the Standing Committee on Public Accounts. It was intended for the senior official to make presentations on allegations that senior government politicians were aware of the criminal activities at Eskom but failed to act upon intelligence reports. The Brigadier was scheduled to appear with the Police Commissioner but failed to appear because he reportedly feared for his life[205]. The Police Commissioner explained to the committee that the issue for the Brigadier was that after he had testified, it was uncertain what would be the implications to himself and to his life. In September 2023, when the Brigadier was again scheduled to appear before the Standing Committee on Public Accounts, the committee learnt that he had retired from public service.

If the country's most senior police officials were concerned about their own security in dealing with day-to-day operations at Eskom, what chance did normal employees stand against the evil and nefarious forces?

In November 2023, the retired Brigadier eventually did make presentations to the Standing Committee on Public Accounts, but he would not name any of the alleged government officials involved in the crimes at Eskom. He confirmed that the government was complicit in the crimes at Eskom, that State Capture continued under the Ramaphosa administration, and that there was a reluctance for state security agencies to address the criminality at the utility[206].

From his testimony, he also expressed grave doubts about the motives of former Group Chief Executive Officer, Andre de Ruyter, who reportedly with the help of former Apartheid operatives, launch a private investigation into the issues at Eskom. He suggested that unvalidated intelligence reports appeared to be psychological warfare tactics employed by De Ruyter to buttress his version of events. The Brigadier further revealed that De Ruyter failed to ensure that certain Eskom officials were vetted for their posts, and that the former CEO himself was not vetted by state security agencies, as required. This further muddied the already murky governance at Eskom and presented doubts about the self-portrayed 'clean image' that De Ruyter often projected.

◈ ◈ ◈

The notion of *culture* remains elusive. Something sensed, but not seen; felt, but not touched. Intangible. It is for this reason that culture is not immediately acted upon once hazards are sensed and precariousness awaits—and the future threat is always hoped to dissipate. Eskom's performance was slowly influenced by various factors from outside the company, as well as inside the company, as a putrefying culture took root. Something was rotten. As the company's deterioration began to sprout, the smell came early enough, but it was acknowledged far too late.

PART IV

INDEPENDENT POWER PRODUCERS

CHAPTER 10

PRIVATE INVESTMENT IN GENERATION INFRASTRUCTURE

Second to state owned utilities, Independent Power Producers (IPPs) are major players in the African electricity generation sector. Called, in part, to plug the shortages in capacity, they also assist in relieving governments of their obligations for financing investment. As previously stated in Chapter 3, the standard reform prescription saw the introduction of IPPs as a step forward towards wholesale competition amongst a number of generators, since private producers could eventually compete in the generation power market. This chapter examines some of the obstacles to IPPs entering emerging power markets as they contribute to the problem of insufficient capacity. The text considers ways to promote private investment in generation and improve its outcomes.

Attracting Private Investment in Generation

While many stakeholders are involved in private infrastructure development projects, the concerns of international—and to a lesser extent, domestic—investors have been prominent in emerging power sectors. To ensure that the sector remains sustainable, governments have to be in tune to their needs and interests in order to continue attracting investment from this limited source. The broader country investment climate that would attract total direct infrastructure investment and capital investment in general is a strong determinant for attracting private investment in generation infrastructure.

The progress of market-oriented reforms and the attraction of Foreign Direct Investment (FDI) are afforded by policy formulation and implementation, domestic financial systems, international trade and financial markets, the labour market, public infrastructure, tax systems, legal and regulatory frameworks, and governance[207]. In general, a good investment climate with sound regulatory governance and reliable infrastructure bodes well for attracting investment since it reduces the cost of doing business in that country[208]. Where important public interests are at stake and market forces are weak, government institutions that are strong and competent are an essential prerequisite for successful private sector participation[209].

The African region, however, generally has been unable to achieve the conditions that would facilitate and attract sufficient amounts of private investment in generation infrastructure. Africa has relatively poor investment attractiveness compared to other developing regions. Roughly two thirds of countries on the African continent are rated for their investment attractiveness. While eight African countries have managed to achieved investment grade ratings, in 2022 only three countries in the region (Botswana, Mauritius, and Morocco) have managed to maintain their sovereign investment grade ratings according to the three major ratings agencies, Fitch, Moody's and Standard & Poor's. Poor investment climates, in general, have contributed to the lack of investment, specifically in infrastructure where costs are sunk and returns are amortised over a long period of time.

Since the 1990s, when there was a flurry of interest in developing regions from investor utilities in industrialised countries, the interest from investors in developed countries has been on the decrease. By the end of that decade, the majority of investor utilities in the United States and Europe retreated from investments in developing countries and tended to remain focussed in their home regions[210]. This retreat was largely triggered by the 1998 Asian financial crisis, which devastated Asian developing economies, with the effects extending to the regions of Latin America, Eastern Europe, and Africa.

Investors faced many obstacles in realising satisfactory returns on their investments and disappointing investment experiences in some emerging markets led many investors to retreat from IPP investments in developing countries, including in Africa. The decline in private investment in generation infrastructure over the decade from 1998 to 2008 was driven by a number of contributing factors. These include the spill-over effects of economic crises and unfinished power sector reforms, as well as incomplete reforms in other domestic sectors, which has meant that infrastructure sectors have not been placed on a commercial footing as intended by reform objectives[211]. Underdeveloped local capital markets in most developing countries have also contributed to the lack of sufficient funds for infrastructure investment. Since 2008, the global economic crisis further spurred the retreat from investment in infrastructure as financial institutions worldwide suffered severe damage and triggered a subsequent international banking crisis.

The absence of domestic capital markets for infrastructure in most African states has also resulted in increased risk premiums by way of higher interest charges to offset inflation and volatility in domestic currencies[212]. Furthermore, the deteriorating financial position of many sponsors, growing concerns over re-nationalisation and disappointing returns on some projects due to renegotiations have contributed to a retreat in foreign private investment.

There was also recognition that ways in which project risks were allocated left stakeholders such as governments, investors and consumers, unnecessarily exposed. Most governments continued to face challenges in dealing with fundamental policy problems and creating an environment in which private investment can flourish while the development needs of countries were achieved.

By 2008, around forty IPPs were developed in Africa. Mostly complementing state-owned generators in providing electricity, they provided less than 9 percent of generation capacity. Despite being an important source of new generation in many African countries, this modest contribution was concentrated in a few countries on the continent with Côte d'Ivoire, Egypt, Ghana, Kenya, Morocco, Nigeria, Tanzania and Tunisia accounting for roughly 80 percent of installed IPP capacity. This small percentage of IPP capacity was indicative of the challenges that most African countries (along with less endowed developing nations) faced in bringing in investment, even though there was such a huge demand for power.

Since 2010, with the increase in renewable electricity generation projects, the presence of IPPs in Sub-Saharan African countries was again on the rise. More recent climate change imperatives which, along with decentralized, distributed, and renewable generation technologies, have fundamentally altered the type and scale of generation investment. These new technologies have challenged traditional thinking about the design of large traditional networked power systems and how they are operated to accommodate large utility scale generation investments.

Key IPP Risks

While certain risks in developing IPPs may have been well managed through traditional means, it is clear that traditional risk management mechanisms were inadequate to cater for all risks in reforming emerging power markets—and experience suggests that some risks may have been overlooked.

Below is a brief overview of three key risks that investors view as the most significant deterrents in investing in electricity infrastructure in developing countries. These are also key risks and causes behind many of the renegotiations in IPPs. Presented are brief descriptions of the risks, the traditional ways in which they were managed, and prospects for improved risk management of these investor concerns.

Expropriation Risk

Infrastructure investments are sunk costs—investors cannot use their assets in other locations and investments are irreversible. Not only are the costs sunk, but it also takes a long time for investors to recoup their investment outlays. Over such long time periods investors face numerous risks, one which is having their assets expropriated. Once investors are committed to their projects and the only exit strategies involve huge losses, governments can be tempted not to honour commitments as previously agreed and investors risk becoming victims of expropriation, or what is called 'obsolescent bargains' (a phrase coined by American economist Raymond Vernon in his book entitled, *Sovereignty at Bay*)[213]. Since outright expropriation, i.e., nationalisation of assets, is less common today, investors have been more concerned with creeping expropriation such as mandatory renegotiation of PPAs.

Robust contracts have generally been used by investors and project sponsors to give themselves legal recourse in the event of expropriation. Government guarantees have traditionally been called on to manage the risk of creeping or outright expropriation. As a way to appease investors, the use of government guarantees to attract investors to finance new infrastructure may appear appealing to host governments and investors alike. This is because sovereign guarantees are without any immediate cost to the government, who can almost immediately benefit from the investment. However, the real costs of guarantees are hard to estimate; the costs are often not reflected in the government's accounts; and the practice of issuing guarantees can become the norm—providing host governments with few incentives to resolve the underlying problems which necessitated the guarantees at the outset. Conversely, government guarantees can make projects more acceptable to private investors by protecting sponsors and lenders from risks that they are not willing to bear or have little control over.

Experiences in developing countries have shown that despite these legal measures, contracts have often been insufficient in keeping expropriation at bay. A 2005 study initiated by Stanford University's

Program on Energy and Sustainable Development (PESD) analysed the outcomes of private investment in generation infrastructure[214]. The investigation found that contracts which evaluated risk *ex-ante* and made provision for it through the legal conventions fared poorly in anticipating risks and specifying solutions. The study closely examined 33 greenfield independent power projects of varying sizes, fuel sources, and technologies, in twelve different countries in various geographic regions with varying power sector and country contexts. Out of the sample of independently contracted plants, a third of the project contracts between governments and IPPs had undergone mutual renegotiation. Roughly a quarter of the contracts faced unilateral renegotiation or non-payment—amongst these slightly more than a tenth of the sample ended in litigation or arbitration.

Even where agreements contained government guarantees, the above study found no evidence of outcomes having a bias toward the guaranteed risk provision. In many cases governments issued guarantees but failed to manage the risks they had guaranteed. They did not allow generation costs to be passed through in the tariffs; they manage the country's macroeconomics in ways that undermine off-taker's ability to service PPA charges; and they institute changes that lead to significant decreases in the value of domestic currencies.

A classic example was the case of the Dabhol IPP in India. The project received overlapping guarantees from central and provincial governments, as well as a guarantee for part of the project from the federal government—along with a series of letters of credit and escrow arrangements[215]. Despite these seemingly robust measures, the security arrangements still proved insufficient. Evidence from the Stanford PESD study showed that while contractual measures were necessary conditions to defend the financial and operational terms of the projects, they were not sufficient in themselves. Not all risks could be mitigated through contracts and there was often little certainty regarding the ability of contracting parties to uphold their end of the contractual provision. Depending on the intensity of the issues that were stressing the agreements, guarantees and other contracting provisions did not play their intended roles in resolving problems that arose, despite the intent of their legal provisions.

Reneging on contractual agreements and guarantees has also dented the image of governments and, in many cases, has deterred investors from making future investments. Some public-private infrastructure policy analysts have cautioned on the use of guarantees by governments[216]. They advocate that good outcomes with respect to guarantee decisions are more likely under the following conditions: when an effective framework for judging when a government guarantee is employed to justify the use of a guarantee; governments or their advisors know how to estimate the guaranteed cost; and when decision makers in governments follow conventions that encourage careful reflection of the guarantee's costs and benefits. As an alternative to government guarantees, although mainly used in the oil sector, securitisations or asset-backed securities in electricity sectors could be considered due to the interest reducing benefits that it has on debt in countries that are rich in fuel or mineral exports[217].

Currency Risk

Currency risk remains a key consideration for investors and governments in IPP development. While foreign investors are notionally shielded from currency risk when PPAs are denominated in hard currency, in reality they share a large part of the risk when local currencies in developing countries undergo significant devaluations. Currency risk could easily be compounded by political risk leading to creeping expropriation when governments find it politically difficult to pass on the increased costs and decide to renegotiate IPP contracts. IPP contracts extend over many years, sometimes up to 30 years, leaving stakeholders open to lengthy periods of exposure.

In a report entitled *'Exchange Rate Risk: Reviewing the Record for Private Infrastructure'* the World Bank observed that in the 25 years prior to 2003, developing country currencies lost on average 72 percent of their value relative to the US dollar[218]. Roughly a fifth of developing countries' currencies lost more than 99 percent of their value. The Brazilian real and the Argentinean peso lost almost all value between 1985 and 1990, and the Indonesian rupiah lost roughly 80 percent of its value in 1997 and 1998, which impacted on utilities' abilities to pay charges.

It is for this reason that the development and strengthening of local financial systems should not be underestimated for exchange rate risk mitigation where banking systems become independent of government and gain experience in long-term and structured finance.

A gradual devaluation in local currency over a number of years could be managed successfully in most cases. Nevertheless, serious problems are created when the decline is precipitous as IPP investors found in South Asia and in Latin America during the financial crises that gripped markets in these regions in the 1990s. In the Philippines widely publicised renegotiations followed the devaluations in currency. In Malaysia and Thailand, the dozen plus IPPs faced some pressure during the Asian financial crisis. Local capital sourced almost entirely from domestic markets was supported by long-term local currency denominated contracts that IPPs entered into with the national utility. These arrangements helped reduce financial strain on the power sector and continued to ensure healthy profits for IPP investors[219].

Currency devaluations are normally coupled with higher interest rates which affect economic growth and subsequent demand for contracted power, which could lead to power planning problems due to a reduction in anticipated power. It could also stall other projects in the pipeline—projects that must be re-evaluated to incorporate increasing costs as a result of both devaluations and higher interest rates.

Since the majority of investments were made in foreign currency and exposed shareholders and creditors to currency risk, creditors in particular often sought out ways to shape the contractual arrangements to pass this risk onto governments or consumers. The state's presumed influence over currency risk was underlined when arguing for allocating this risk to governments.

Interestingly, differing views have also been proposed whereby investors take on all the financing related exchange rate risk even though it may translate into higher tariffs for consumers as a premium for bearing such risk[220]. The proposition is supported by arguing that government's financial positions are affected in complex ways and by many factors unrelated to infrastructure projects, and because governments' responses to financial incentives differ from those of firms and individuals. Yet it is recognised that the problem could be foregrounded in the longer term when too much foreign currency debt is taken on—as experienced in the Philippines where more than forty long-term contracts were signed[221].

The disruption by the Asian financial crisis in the late 1990s had a significant impact on IPP power purchase agreements in the Philippines, making the take-or-pay contracts unsustainable. During and after the crisis, the government continued to honour the contracts until new legal requirements mandated the review of PPAs—leading to contract renegotiation efforts in the IPP sector. In cases where competitively priced plants have kept power charges low and privately contracted power represented a smaller percentage of the country's generation, currency devaluations were less of a problem, as in the case of Egypt where significant currency devaluation occurred in 2002 and 2003[222].

Regulatory and Political Risk

Another major barrier to investment in developing countries is the perceived threat of regulatory risk[223]. Changes to an initially agreed legal framework that governs investment in electricity infrastructure could spell a potential loss of income to investors. If regulatory capacity is weak or the framework is viewed as unpredictable, foreign and domestic investors are deterred. Firms with international equity investments in power sectors in developing countries often stress that the conditions essential to success are the rule of law, respect for investor's rights, as well as legal and regulatory processes free from government interference[224].

Power plants, because they sell an important and highly visible commodity that is viewed as a public good, are particularly exposed to social and political risk. Because many developing countries have a long history of subsidised tariffs, PPA charges are often highly politicised in poorer settings where consumers are expected to pay the full cost of service provision. While effective regulation is able to have an important impact on sector performance and the economy, no perfect regulatory reform models exist—indicating potential problems especially for investors finding themselves in nascent regulatory environments[225].

Even with independent regulation, objectives can conflict as regulators have to consider the socio-political impact (increased tariffs and potential political instability) of attempting to make the sector attractive to investors[226]. Regulatory and political risk insurance has been employed in many cases as means to isolate private investors from this risk. The Multilateral Investment Guarantee Agency (MIGA) provides political risk insurance cover for most types of political risk. The World Bank's Partial Risk Guarantee (PRG) is extended to cover many of the legal regulatory and contractual risks[227].

Power sector reform, in itself, can contribute to regulatory and political risk. Power sector reforms can address underlying policy problems—and reform should be an ideal to be achieved by governments. However, as reforms evolve, reform implementation in search of improved sector performances, could impact investment negatively. Power sector reform can therefore be an evolving process. Changes instituted as part of reforms could hinder and slow down the reform which was intended to encourage further investment[228].

Necessary reform steps which can stifle reform momentum are ever present. This could be the case as power sectors move toward the 'standard prescription end-state'. As part of the reform process, IPPs have to be incorporated into wholesale power markets and existing contracts have to be integrated into evolving market arrangements. In most cases, original take-or-pay contracts (in the form of long-term PPAs) do not have transfer provisions for moving towards trading electricity in competitive wholesale power markets[229]. Impediments to integrating IPPs into markets delay the scope for competition. Entry into competitive wholesale power markets could also result in large resource costs for countries if plants are dispatched out of merit order. Under market principles the costs to individual generators are optimised by bidding in the market, rather than overall systems costs being optimised through central planning by the system operator. Often the problem of integration has been a key reason why power sectors were unable to continue reforms until full retail competition, and why these power sectors have stagnated at hybrid markets.

The abovementioned risks are generally viewed by project sponsors as the most applicable in investing in reforming developing regions. There are, however, additional risks that have also contributed to stalled negotiations, delayed construction times, or cancelled private projects. Table 10.1 below gives an overview of some of the risks that both investors and governments face during the development of power generation projects and some proposed mitigation techniques which could be employed to moderate the possibility of adverse outcomes. In the empirical case of South Africa, many of the risks mentioned will re-emerge, along with the varied experiences of how the government and power sector fared in managing them.

Table 10.1 Independent Power Project Risks

Phase	Risk	Proposed Mitigation Mechanism
Project Preparation	Conflicting or lack of decision-making authority, changes in authorities (elections)	Develop a strong institutional and implementation framework
	Delays in approvals or failure to obtain approvals, permits and licences	Develop a strong institutional and implementation framework
	Inadequate or inappropriate legal structure for project finance	Legal reform
	Resistance and protests by interest groups such as NGOs and labour unions	Cooperation and integration of stakeholder concerns
	Bidding risks	Interest in project bidding should be maximised
	Legal challenges to the awarding of project	Develop and use transparent award procedures
	Environmental risk	Perform comprehensive Environmental Impact Assessment (EIA), comply with lender guidelines such as the World Bank, external monitoring
	Technological risk	Preference for proven technology and a reputable constructor. New technology should be allowed on the basis that technological guarantees and assurances are provided
	Delays in financial closure	Deadline should be realistic

Project Construction	Cost overruns and completion delays	Preference should be given to fixed-price turnkey contracts. Penalty clauses and performance incentives should be used to prevent delays
	Failure to meet performance specifications	Make provision for clauses in contracts
	Changes to approvals, permits and licences	Negotiation with relevant authorities or arbitration
	Failure to complete supporting infrastructure (transmission links, roads, fuel delivery)	Strong coordination with counterparties
	Unforeseen delays	Make provision in project agreements
	Force majeure	Make provision in project agreements, multilateral guarantees
	Default by contractors or equity holders	Invoke shareholders' agreements or step-in rights
	Liability risks	Take out private insurance
	Strikes and demonstrations	Take out private or multilateral insurance
	Expropriation or nationalisation	Compensation clauses and multilateral insurance
Project Operation	Demand risk	Perform independent and accurate demand forecast, use take-or-pay contract
	Supply risk	Robust fuel supply contract with a number of credible suppliers
	Payment risk	Make escrow facilities, letters of credit and other credit enhancers a requirement
	Breach of contract by off-taker	Government guarantees, litigation and arbitration
	Government guarantee withdrawal	International arbitration
	Inadequate price adjustment mechanisms, changes to contract, creeping expropriation	Independent regulation, international arbitration
	Change of law	Government guarantees
	Exchange rates, interest rates and inflation movements	Use hedging, user charge indexation and contract extension mechanisms
	Foreign exchange availability and convertibility	Arrange for agreements with Ministry of Finance or government guarantees

As far as possible, project risks (including construction and operational risks) should be identified, and risk management strategies agreed upon at the project preparation stage. This is due to the difficulties involved in altering agreements once all the stakeholders agree with the terms—especially when the change involves certain parties shouldering more risk that originally agreed on. Generally, risks during project construction have been relatively better managed in *turnkey* IPP projects. This is partly attributed to the short construction periods (relative to the operation phase) and the intense negotiations which precede this phase, with a strong focus on project construction and commissioning. The use of reputable, experienced project developers generally reduces construction risk. Risks during the project operation stage, due to the long duration of this phase of the project, can however vary over time—and it is here that a number of eventualities (internal or external to the project) can threaten the sustainability of the IPP.

Managing IPP Risks

As described in this chapter, the problem of attracting investment into power sectors is strongly linked to the real risks as well as the risk perceptions of investors. There are many risks in developing infrastructure projects in general. With private generation projects, the intricacies and complexities of the arrangements required to achieve the success of projects can easily become more complex.

The continuous search for optimal risk management techniques has contributed to shaping the risk management strategies employed by stakeholders in private generation infrastructure investments. Continued difficulties in dealing with risks often result in projects being distressed. This can be in the form of delays in contracting the much-needed new capacity, or even outright cancellation of planned projects[230]. Certain risks are particularly tricky to manage due to insufficient market instruments and related mechanisms to cater for risks in developing country settings[231].

Due to the relative undeveloped power pools, power markets have not developed as in industrialised countries[232]. With relatively few players and with a regional shortage of capacity in these pools markets, Contracts-For-Differences, and other derivative instruments, for example, do not exist. The scope of uncertainties on exchange rates and weather-related effects (such as droughts) would make insurances for electricity supply difficult to quantify and underwrite. Although there are insurances offered by multilateral agencies for certain risks (as in certain categories of political, regulatory and force majeure) many governments do not want to be saddled with contingent liabilities. Without such guarantees there are few similar offerings on the market to hedge against these kinds of risk.

Privately sponsored power plants are usually developed and financed through special purpose vehicles on a limited recourse basis, a structure that is exposed and sensitive to many uncertainties. The means to cater for these uncertainties are woven into a complex web of contracts and agreements. Once a project sponsor has reached an agreement with a government that specifies the details of the project, the sponsor needs to obtain all relevant licences, approvals and clearances from other national, provincial and local government entities. These include the power purchase agreement, land titles and environmental clearances, construction permits, tax agreements, import permits, fuel supply agreements, foreign exchange convertibility and transferability agreements, immigration permits, and specific government guarantees[233]. Figure 10.1 provides an example of key stakeholders with whom various agreements have to be reached.

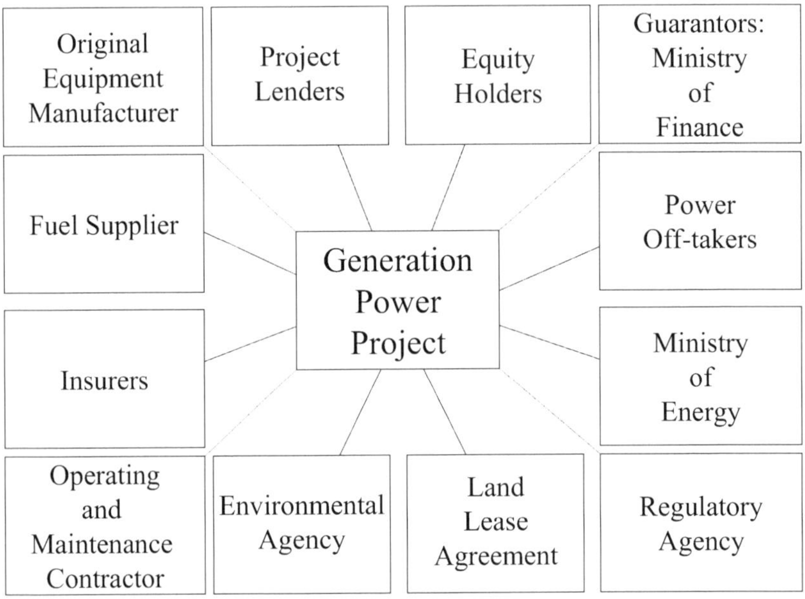

Figure 10.1 Example of Key Power Project Stakeholders

The project sponsor has to finalise agreements with other private parties that would support the construction and operation of the project such as Engineering Procurement and Construction (EPC) contractors (normally on a turnkey basis) as well as Operating and Maintenance (O&M) contractors, before the project can reach financial closure involving contractual arrangements with other investors, multilateral, bilateral or commercial lenders, insurers, and export credit agencies. These multifaceted contractual structures engage many different players whose collective expectations require conceiving an arrangement that is acceptable to all parties by meeting different objectives and incentives. The interaction and nature of the contracts motivate the financing choices and inform governance arrangements for these investments, as the project allocates contracted and non-contracted risk between different stakeholders[234].

Efficient risk allocation means allocating corresponding risk factors to the party that is best suited to exercise the associated real options to manage the risk[235]. Where returns on investments can be adjusted to cover underlying risks or the risks can be reduced to meet lower returns, attracting private capital becomes possible. Often, however, investors deem returns to be insufficient for the risks that they assume. Consequently, projects may be stalled or cancelled outright if stakeholders feel uncomfortable with the risks that they are expected to bear, especially if these risks are better borne by other parties.

Alternative Approaches to Attracting Investment into Generation

While the challenge is for investor firms and governments to find mechanisms that reduce risk and manage them in ways that are cost-effective and relatively trouble-free, the complication is that each country is different and that varying country contexts set their unique backdrops for how risks present themselves and, ultimately, the outcomes of projects. Broad conclusions about risks and how they relate to project outcomes are, therefore, often difficult to apply in specific settings. Although surveys among large sample sizes of private infrastructure projects generate broad conclusions about risks and indicators of IPP experiences, they are often tricky to quantify and compare systematically. Hence, there has been a need for alternatives to traditional risk management in improving IPP outcomes for investors and host countries. Three alternatives are discussed below.

Risk Compensation and Risk Reduction

Governments can attract private investment in infrastructure in two broad ways. Firstly, they can offer financial support to investors in the form of grants, low-interest loans and guarantees in order to compensate for risks involving low tariffs, insolvent SOEs, unstable macro-economic conditions, and other problems[236]. Secondly, they can address the underlying policy problems that trigger investors' concerns by ensuring macro-economic stability, raising tariffs to more viable economic levels, and establishing sound policy and regulatory frameworks[237]. Although both methods can attract investment, the former tends not to reduce overall costs but to allocate them to captive taxpayers, while policy reforms aspire to improve project fundamentals and make them attractive to investors without unnecessarily imposing costs on taxpayers[238]. The latter approach is more sustainable. Hence it has been the path considered by most governments, albeit with varying outcomes, due to the unique challenges that have been encountered with reforms.

Flexibility and Strategic Partnerships

Setting out to draw specific conclusions on IPP investments in specific contexts, in 2004 Stanford University's Program on Energy and Sustainable Development assessed a range of independent variables that would explain the variation in private investment outcomes for greenfield IPPs[239]. The Stanford study identified the universe of countries that had IPPs and selected a sample of countries that have a variation in the factors that may explain success or failure of projects and a variation in the role that IPPs play in the power sector.

The study closely examined the same population of 33 greenfield independent power projects of varying sizes, fuel sources and technologies in twelve different countries in various geographic regions, with varying power sector and country contexts. This Stanford IPP study, however, focussed on IPP outcomes from two perspectives: an investment perspective to assess the extent that investors' expectations were met by the project; and a development perspective to determine the degree to which projects met the expectations of the host country. In addition to strategic risk management practices helping to structure projects in ways that reduced their vulnerability to risks, the study linked future successes to more flexible contract parties or stakeholders. Goodwill *and* legal contracts sometimes go further in resolving problems when deals come unstuck than do contracts on their own. In this way, the willingness of stakeholders to make concessions generally could lead to more beneficial outcomes in the longer term[240].

The ability to manage counterparty risk, especially during politically sensitive periods which may lead to renegotiation, is also considered indispensable to preserve successful outcomes. Here, local partnerships prove to increase substantially the likelihood of successfully mitigating the political risks which are often inherent in foreign-owned investments[241]. With local partnerships, the ability to manage fuel supply, dispatch, non-payment, and renegotiation were increased and were often proximate determinants of project outcomes when these stresses threatened operations and the sustainability of the projects. In the case of one of Morocco's IPPs, where the national utility was the local partner with the largest shareholding in the plant, the project enjoyed government support to the extent where the state assisted in arranging local financing from local Moroccan banks to manage the currency risk on the project[242].

Balancing Investment and Development Outcomes

In a study of African IPPs by the University of Cape Town's Management Programme for Infrastructure and Regulatory Reform (MIR), the investment and development successes of IPPs was found to be attributed to *project level factors* as well as *factors related to the host country.* Drawing from the methodology and research framework of the previously mentioned Stanford PESD IPP study and using project and country level factors as independent determinants of outcomes, the study made a departure from the Stanford PESD IPP study. The MIR investigation sought to determine the extent to which *project* and *country related* factors made projects sustainable and created a direct link between these factors and the investment and development outcomes.

The study's hypothesis was that balanced investment and development outcomes lead to more sustainable projects. The assumption was that if investment and development outcomes were in balance and both investors and off-takers were satisfied with the project arrangements and their investment and development outcomes respectively, private investment would continue to grow. The investigation found that indeed a balance between investment and development outcomes leads to the sustainability of projects within the context of the conditions that existed when the projects were developed—even if the balance was achieved with time and, in some cases, only after renegotiation, as evidenced in the case of Kenya.

After the end of the PPA terms for Iberafrica (an initial stopgap IPP) and OrPower4, both privately owned plants agreed to reduce capacity charges in order to secure PPAs for a second term. Prices became more competitive with that of the state-owned generator, KenGen, which contributed to more positive development outcomes for Kenya[243]. The inference is that perceived imbalances often intensified by exogenous stresses lead to contracts becoming unstable and even renegotiated—despite security arrangements which could prove insufficient to sustain the contracts. In most cases, the incidences of contractual problems did not necessarily imply the end of the project but lead to a search for a new equilibrium in balancing outcomes that proved more sustainable.

From the MIR analysis, Table 10.2 details the project level factors that were cited as contributing to the outcomes of IPPs[244]. Control of these factors are largely considered to be within the purview of the project sponsor and contain elements such as favourable equity partners, debt arrangements, the means to secure revenue, credit enhancements, strategic risk management measures, good technical performance, and strategic management and relationship building. Like the Stanford study, the MIR investigation established a link between favourable equity partners and the development and investment outcomes for African IPPs.

Table 10.2 Project Level Elements Contributing to IPP Outcomes

Contributing Elements	Details
Favourable equity partners	- Local capital/partner contribution, where possible - Risk appetite for project - Experience with developing country project risk - Involvement of a DFI partner (and/or host country government) - Reasonable, fair ROE - Development-minded firms
Favourable debt arrangements	- Low-cost financing - Local capital/markets mitigate foreign exchange risk - Risk premium demanded by financiers or capped by off-taker matches country/project risk - Some flexibility in terms and conditions (possible refinancing)
Secure and adequate revenue stream	- Commercially sound metering, billing, and collections by the utility - Robust PPA (stipulates capacity and payment as well as dispatch, fuel metering, interconnection, insurance, *force majeure*, transfer, termination, change of law provisions, refinancing arrangements, dispute resolution, etc.) - Security arrangements where necessary (escrow accounts, letters of credit, stand-by debt facilities, hedging and other derivative instruments, committed public budget and/or taxes/levies, targeted subsidies and output-based aid, hard currency contracts, indexation in contracts)
Credit enhancements and other risk management and mitigation measures	- Sovereign guarantees - Political risk insurance - Partial risk guarantees - International arbitration
Positive technical performance	- Technical performance high (availability) - Sponsors anticipate potential conflicts (especially related to O&M, and budgeting) and mitigate them
Strategic management and relationship building	Sponsors work to create good image in country through political relationships, development funds, effective communications and strategically manage their contracts, particularly in the face of exogenous shocks and other stresses

Links were established between favourable debt arrangements and project successes since the financing mix and type could have implications for the financial sustainability of the projects, especially when local currencies devaluate. Closely related to financing, the means to secure a revenue stream for investors (mainly through the financial viability of the off-taker) also impacted on the successes of projects. Since revenue payments are contractually linked to plant technical performance, plant availability and dispatching was also linked to project outcomes. Lastly, ongoing strategic management and relationship building proved to be helpful when projects faced obstacles for which no provisions were made contractually. Some of these elements that contribute to the success or failure of IPP projects are themes that will feature in South African IPPs.

From the MIR analysis, Table 10.3 presents the country level factors considered to contribute to the outcomes of IPPs. Control of these factors is largely within the purview of the host government and includes elements such as a favourable investment climate; a clear electricity policy framework; impartial, transparent and consistent regulatory oversight; coherent power sector planning; competitive bidding practices; secure contracts; and the availability of low-cost fuel.

Again, similar to the Stanford study, the MIR investigation considered the role of a favourable investment climate in attracting IPPs. It established a link between clear policy and credible regulatory frameworks, and positive IPP outcomes. Since regulatory and policy risks are concerns for investors, it is beneficial for these frameworks to be enshrined in legislation, i.e., policy is clearly spelled out and regulatory decisions are transparent to command investor confidence.

The MIR study also considered the extent to which power sector planning had impacted on IPPs, i.e., has the planning (or lack thereof) facilitated or obstructed the entry of IPPs.

Lastly, it found that in the case of thermal plants, the presence of domestic fuel plays a part in reducing IPP costs and reduces the chances of renegotiations due to high prices when conditions change. Thermal IPPs are highly exposed to fuel market conditions, and plants that have been able to secure a fuel supply that was cost competitive and reliable have been able to minimise fuel risks. In Africa, countries with their own source of fuel have traditionally been more successful in maintaining lower charges for power from IPPs such as Egypt, Côte d'Ivoire, and Tunisia.

Table 10.3 Country Level Elements Contributing to IPP Outcomes

Contributing Elements	**Details**
Favourable investment climate	- Stable macro-economic policies - Legal system allows contracts to be enforced, laws to be upheld, arbitration - Good repayment record and investment grade rating - Requires less (costly) risk mitigation techniques to be employed which translate into lower cost of capital and hence lower projects costs and more competitive prices - Potentially more than one investment opportunity
Clear policy framework	- Policy framework enshrined in legislation - Framework clearly specifies market structure and roles and terms for private and public sector investments (generally for single buyer model, not yet wholesale competition in African context) - Reform-minded 'champions', concerned with long-run, lead and implement framework

Clear, consistent and fair regulatory oversight	- Transparent and predictable licensing and tariff framework improves investor confidence - Improves general performance of private and public sector assets - Cost-reflective tariffs ensure revenue sufficiency - Consumers protected – improves development outcomes
Coherent power sector planning	- Energy security standard in place; planning roles and functions clarified - Power planning vested with lead, appropriate (skilled, resourced and empowered) agency - Power sector planning takes into consideration the hybrid market (public and private stakeholders and their respective real costs of capital) and fairly allocates new build opportunities among stakeholders - Planning has built-in contingencies to avoid 'emergency power' or blackouts
Competitive bidding practices	- Procurement process is transparent, and competition ultimately drives down prices
Abundant low cost fuel and secure contracts	- Cost-competitive with other fuels - Contract safeguards affordable and reliable fuel supply for duration of contract

The MIR study made an important contribution by identifying various factors that contributed to IPP outcomes for investors and off-takers and appear to make investment in independent power projects more sustainable.

◈ ◈ ◈

African countries have not been able to adequately allay the concerns of investors, and this has contributed to insufficient investment and a shortage of capacity in African power sectors. The challenge is to find improved mechanisms to deal with the risks faced by investors and governments or be prepared to pay higher risk premiums for the higher perceived risks. Failing this, the problem of insufficient investment will persist.

CHAPTER 11

SOUTH AFRICAN EXPERIENCES WITH INDEPENDENT POWER PRODUCERS

As previously outlined in Chapter 4, the introduction of private sector participation in the South African power sector was proposed as far back as 1998, in the country's Energy White Paper[245]. The objective for private sector participation was primarily to increase investment in generation infrastructure. Private investment would create the fiscal headroom for government to focus efforts and direct limited funds to other sectors of the economy. These include achieving the social objectives of addressing energy access and energy inequality. It also included broader socio-political objectives like employment creation, housing provision, and increasing access to health. It was also believed that private investment in electricity generation would facilitate greater state of the art power generation technology and fuel diversity in addition to flexibility of supply. The introduction of private generators in the South African power sector eventually occurred. However, despite the intentions of the government, their entry was stifled by various challenges and for various reasons.

Factors Affecting Investment in the South African Power Sector

In Chapter 10, risks assumed by IPP investors and host countries were highlighted. These risks must be balanced by assigning them to the party that is best placed to manage each of the risks. Risks that cannot be effectively managed or transferred by IPPs are likely to stifle investment of private funds in generation infrastructure. In the South African case, the introduction of Renewable Energy Independent Power Producers (REIPPs) into the Generation sector was considered relatively successful for projects that were commissioned. However, private investment was not without problems. To the extent that individual project and host country contexts shaped the speed and outcomes of private sector investment, such contexts (described below) ultimately also played a role in the degree to which the country was left without adequate electricity generation.

Policy Indecision

The intent of the 1998 Energy White Paper was that the government would encourage competition amongst private and state-owned generators. The vision was for some of Eskom's coal-fired generation assets to be sold to the private sector to allow for a comparable basis for electricity price determination between state-owned and private sector generators. It was believed that competition within a generation power market would allow for efficient bulk electricity price discovery and the realisation of affordable tariffs for consumers. Increased private investment and price competition would also stimulate national economic growth and be a catalyst for employment creation and further investment in other sectors of the economy.

The 'reversal' that the government made on its policy of 1998 was one of the key factors that stalled private investment in new generation capacity. Not only did the government initially fail to follow through with its own proposed policy to invite private sector participation; the moratorium on Eskom to develop new generation capacity was not lifted—at least not until it was too late.

The prohibition on Eskom to development new capacity between 1998 and 2004 was predicated on an assumption that Eskom still had excess capacity at the time. In addition, Eskom had generation plants that were not in operation (Komati, Grootvlei and Camden) but mothballed to preserve important plant components for later reactivation.

Regulation and Tariffs

In the late 1990s when the policy was first tabled, there were concerns that the regulated price of electricity would not encourage investment. To incentivise private sector investment, electricity tariffs needed to be adjusted upward to reflect the Long Run Marginal Cost of additional investment.

However, electricity tariffs never caught up with the revenue required to make new large-scale generation investment projects bankable. As a result, it was unlikely that there could be financial closure on projects whereby private investors would sell their electricity into a power market. Instead, IPPs would have to secure Power Purchase

Agreements (PPAs) to ensure that lenders and equity holders were adequately compensated for their investments. A number of provisions had to be fulfilled, including the enactment of relevant legislation, regulations for including new IPPs into the transmission network, the licensing requirements for these new entrants, and a procurement framework for IPP investment.

Off-taker Reluctance

In August 2011, South Africa launched its Renewable Energy Independent Power Producer Procurement (REIPPP) programme[246]. The REIPPP followed a competitive bidding process designed to enable private sector investment to promote renewable energy generation in the power sector. The programme followed the publishing of the country's Integrated Resource Plan (IRP 2010), earlier in the same year, where the Minister of Energy, Dipuo Peters, signalled the start of increased private sector participation at the Generation level. Since its inception, the REIPPP programme was managed by the Department of Energy in various bid windows (i.e., the time between bid request and the deadline for bid submissions). Private investors would bid to develop solar, wind, small hydro, landfill gas, biomass and biogas utility-scale generation projects to sell onto the national grid, with Eskom as the off-taker.

The REIPPP programme implemented an auction system, whereby potential suppliers would compete to obtain the winning bids. Given the competitive auctions, the tariff setting role of NERSA was practically eliminated and Eskom would buy all the electricity generated as the single buyer. The main regulatory role that NERSA assumed, was to licence new renewable energy IPPs. The Department of Minerals and Energy assumed custodianship of the process and the REIPPP programme received sufficient policy support from other government departments and state institutions. In line with the country's Integrated Resource Plans, the determination for REIPPs were made by the Ministry of Minerals and Energy. The cost associated with REIPP Power Purchase Agreements was provided for in the Eskom multi-year tariff determination.

There were some teething issues with the REIPPP programme, such as delays in receiving cost-estimates from Eskom for providing grid access, as well as the accuracy of said cost estimates (which was a risk to financiers). The programme was, however, largely positive, with its oversubscription only one of the outcomes that highlighted its success. Between bidding rounds, adjustments were made to the programme to respond to programme design issues and to address challenges for project investors and developers. With transparent and clear criteria, bidders had to demonstrate how they would meet specific REIPPP requirements from the Ministry of Minerals and Energy, such as local content, domestic ownership, employment creation and preferential procurement.

At the time, Eskom finances were deteriorating and prospective IPPs were concerned about some of the risks associated with their proposed renewable energy generation investments. In addition to the credit risk of the off-taker, Eskom would also be the single buyer of power sold. There was no independent system operator, and the off-taker arrangements did not adequately guard against the possible restructuring of the Electricity Supply Industry that could increase risks for investors and developers. The National Treasury was therefore obligated to provide government payment guarantees. This provided financiers security in case Eskom defaulted on the PPA terms.

On top of the troubles of its own to provide sufficient generation as detailed in the previous chapters, Eskom also stifled the increase in private investment in generation. After being appointed as the Group Chief Executive Officer in 2015, Brian Molefe refused to sign any further contracts with IPPs beyond bid window 3[247]. The CEO stopped issuing budget quotes for IPP connections to the grid, citing that the utility could not afford the additional energy purchases. The status quo continued until the end of Matshela Koko's tenure as Interim Group Chief Executive Officer in 2019. The suspension of the REIPPP programme between 2015 and 2019 contributed to the mismatch between electricity supply and demand in subsequent years and deepened the loadshedding crisis in South Africa due to the absence of investment during those years.

The refusal to sign the additional PPAs of successful bidders did not have an impact on the 43 projects that had already reached financial closure under previous bid windows. However, it did appear the financiers and developers of projects that had seen financial closure were justified in their insistence on state-backed guarantees. If, in the face of government policy to sign-on REIPPs the utility backs off from the policy prescription, is it conceivable that the individuals at the helm of the utility could also have reneged on PPAs that were already signed?

Ministerial Averseness to Municipal-contracted IPPs

In South Africa, municipalities are constitutionally empowered to provide electricity and related services to its citizens. While the signing of IPPs were blocked by Eskom (between 2015 and 2019), the metropolitan municipality of Cape Town tried to use this constitutional provision to procure its own electricity from IPPs and shield its customers from the electricity crisis. However, the Electricity Act contained a clause whereby only the Minister of Minerals and Energy could decide on what generation capacity will be contracted.

Municipalities such the City of Cape Town seemed powerless against the political economy to enter into PPAs with more IPPs. In the context of insufficient electrical generation supplied by Eskom, which supplied most of the city's electricity, the City of Cape Town wanted to enter into agreements with IPPs to reduce its dependence on Eskom and address its energy security risks.

In 2015, the City of Cape Town applied to the Minister of Minerals and Energy to grant it permission to do so. However, the Minister of Minerals and Energy would not approve the determination whereby the city would be able to procure power from IPPs. The City then applied to the National Energy Regulator of South Africa (NERSA) for an interpretation on whether the minister's approval was indeed required. NERSA responded that it may not issue a licence for a new power plant unless the Minister of Minerals and Energy had first determined that a new electricity generation facility was indeed needed, and that it may be established as provided for in section 34 of the Electricity Regulation Act[248].

By 2020, the City of Cape Town proceeded in a court bid to seek an order declaring that a ministerial determination was not required to establish new generation plants for electricity supply to the municipality. The City sought an order declaring the need for a ministerial determination irrational and invalid because it undermined the constitutional powers and responsibilities of local government to provide electricity. NERSA was unable to adjudicate the matter and was subordinate to the Ministry of Minerals and Energy. It lacked the authority and independence to compel the minister to allow the City of Cape Town to meet its constitutional obligations[249].

Therefore, both the SOE and the relevant government ministry played a part in stalling private investment in generation. Eskom as the SOE off-taker prevented more IPPs from timeously accessing its transmission network through the Group Chief Executive Officers' reluctance to sign further PPA contracts. In addition, the government prevented municipalities from entering into contracts with IPPs—at least until July 2022, when the country's president overruled the Minister of Minerals and Energy by pronouncing far-reaching changes to the power sector.

Large Complex Infrastructure Projects

Although renewable energy generation projects were developed and connected to the country's power grid, a number of non-renewable projects suffered many headwinds. While not exhaustive, the projects listed below were stopped for various reasons.

New Coal-fired Power Generation – Abortions, Miscarriages and Stillbirths

After the country's first rolling blackouts in 2007, many mines were anticipating the opening of the generation sector to private capital. Although some mines planned to supply power for their own consumption, they also considered selling excess power to the national grid.

Boikarabelo Power Station

The Boikarabelo coal-fired power plant would be one of the plants that would generate power for its own consumption and sell the excess electricity to Eskom. Situated next to the Boikarabelo Mine in the Waterberg region in Limpopo province, it was envisaged that the plant would be built in multiple phases. The first phase would see the construction of a 45 MW plant to supply the adjacent Boikarabelo coal mine, which was scheduled for development in 2012. The power plant would later be expanded by 260 MW and the excess power would be sold onto the national grid. The third phase would see the addition of a further 300 MW, when demand for electricity on the national grid was expected to increase[250].

Mining at the coal facility was initially scheduled to start in 2013, but the project was hampered with logistical and financial constraints. By 2017, there were serious doubts whether the project would continue since the development of the mine had seen numerous setbacks and the Australian Export Credit Agencies were advised not to fund the project due to poor environmental assessments[251]. In April 2021, the funding for the project was halted. In July that year, the project's Australian parent company was put under administration[252].

Khanyisa Power Station

In 2011, the proposed Khanyisa Power Station was initially planned to be 300 MW coal-fired plant situated close to the Kleinkopje colliery, near Standerton in Mpumalanga. The IPP was set to use discard coal from the colliery and would supply the electrical power to Anglo Coal. By 2013, the project had still not been financed due to low platinum demand as well as poor market conditions for Anglo American Platinum[253].

In 2015, as South Africa was preparing for baseload coal-fired independent power producers under the guidance of the country's Integrated Resource Plan, Saudi Arabia's ACWA expressed interest in the project. Anglo agreed to transfer the project to ACWA and ACWA proceeded to submit a bid for the 300 MW Khanyisa project. By this time, South Africa had not yet committed to the Paris agreement and the project was still able to secure all the required site environmental permits and authorisations.

In October 2016, former Minister of Energy, Tina Joemat-Pettersson, announced that Khanyisa was amongst the two successful bidders for the country's first round of coal baseload independent power producers. With a tariff of 79 cents per kWh and increasing to over 110 cents per kWh when including the grid connection charges, the project was planned to start commercial operations in December 2020[254].

The elation for the winning bidders was short-lived. Almost immediately thereafter the project started experiencing challenges head-on. South Africa had just signed the Paris Agreement on Climate Change a few months earlier (in April 2016) and the expectation from environmental groups was that the project should not continue without a more comprehensive assessment of climate change impacts, as required by the Paris Agreement on Climate Change and the legislation on natural resources and the environment in South Africa. A court challenge to the project was launched later that year.

By March 2017, after a lengthy clarification of requirements, the Northern Gauteng High Court confirmed that a detailed climate change assessment was indeed required to assess the longer-term environmental impacts of the development. Under South Arica's Water Act of 1998, climate change assessments were required for projects that have long tenures to determine their longer-term impact.

By September 2017, two new court challenges were brought against the Department of Environmental Affairs in the Pretoria High Court. The request to the court from environmental lobby groups was to set aside the environmental authorisation that was received as part of the bid submission and to compel the project developers to perform a comprehensive climate change assessment, as confirmed by the Northern Gauteng High Court. Soon thereafter, the project was eventually shelved as developers were inundated with court challenges from environmental lobby groups[255].

Thabametsi Power Station

The proposal for the Thabametsi Power Station was for a 630 MW coal-fired plant to be installed at the Grootgeluk mine next to Eskom's Matimba and Medupi Power Stations in the Limpopo province. The development was led by resources company, Exxaro, and French energy company, Engie. The initial environmental approval was obtained in March 2015 and commercial operations were planned to commence six years later[256].

In May 2015, six months before France was set to host the 21st United Nations Climate Change Conference that would see the adoption of the International Treaty on Climate Change, supporters of Earthlife Africa marched to the French Consulate in Johannesburg,

South Africa. They demanded that the French government put pressure on Engie to divest from coal, starting with the Thabametsi project. After a sustained and successful campaign by Earthlife Africa and their supporters, Engie walked away from the project a few months before the Paris Agreement was adopted in France in December 2015[257].

After Engie's withdrawal from the project, Japan's Marubeni took over as the project's technical lead with a bid to develop the plant as part of South Africa's Integrated Resource Plan for developing coal IPPs. Like the Khanyisa project, the Thabametsi venture failed to initially perform a climate change impact assessment. By June 2017, additional climate impact assessments were completed.

However, environmental groups were still not satisfied. They mounted a legal challenge to the project citing that the greenhouse gas emissions would be the same as existing coal power stations and that the impact assessment did not adequately consider the water scarcity. The assessments also did not fully account for the social and health impacts that the project would impose on communities. The assessment proposed no mitigation for adverse impacts.

Despite Marubeni's preparedness to perform the required climate impact assessment, the aggressive court challenges and the determination by environmental groups to halt the project swayed the ambitions of Japan's Marubeni. By October 2020, the company announced it will no longer be investing in coal projects abroad, including the Thabametsi project[258].

One month later, South Africa's Industrial Development Corporation and the Public Investment Corporation, South Africa's largest pension fund manager, announced that they too would no longer be investing in coal projects. Despite the country's IRP directing the development of new baseload coal generation, the appetite for coal-fired generation projects waned amongst project developers, sponsors, and loan financiers alike.

Musina Makhado Project

In 2014, the Limpopo provincial government was in talks with Chinese Investment firms to develop a coal-fired power station in the Waterberg area in South Africa. The China Power International Energy Project was conceived as a plant that would provide capacity between 1 320 and 3 300 MW. The project was known as the Musina Makhado Project since it would be in the Musina-Makhado Special Economic Zone in Limpopo province[259].

In July 2018, media reports confirmed that a Memorandum of Understanding was signed between the South African government and the developers consisting of Chinese state-owned companies. Indicating that all the power generated would be for metallurgical processing consumption, conceptual work started to increase the plant capacity to 4 600 MW.

By September 2020, despite concerns raised about water scarcity and the impact on communities (and notwithstanding the limited extent of public participation on the proposed project), it was still hoped that mitigation actions for the water issues could save the project—and that construction could start the following year.

By September 2021, however, China announced that it would no longer continue to finance coal-fired investment overseas and further conceptual work on the project was stopped. In March 2022, it was announced that the project would be significantly downsized to a capacity of 1 000 MW and that solar energy would be used to generate the electricity[260].

The four projects briefly described above were only some of the coal-fired generation projects conceived. Despite the country's official version of its Integrated Resource Plan (2019 edition) providing for 900 MW of coal-fired generation, all large-scale coal-fired baseload IPPs had been stopped. The likelihood of future traditional coal-fired greenfield projects being approved remained sufficiently low to deter investors and developers.

Along with financing and legal challenges, environmental groups have vowed to oppose future coal-fired projects. The project, financing, and reputational risks associated with coal-fired generation resulted in suppressed interest for these types of projects amongst project developers, funders of equity, loan financiers, and many other stakeholders.

Gas Plants

Since the doors on the development of coal-fired generation were closed on practically all fronts, the expectation was that gas was the fossil-fuelled generation technology that would be viable for IPPs to pursue due to the key role that gas plays in complementing the intermittent electricity outputs of renewable generation plants.

In March 2021, the Karpowership IPP won a bid to produce roughly 1 200 MW of emergency power to mitigate the impact of national power outages. With a 51 percent shareholding by the Turkish energy company Karadeniz Holdings and 49 percent by South African company Powergroup, the PPA was intended to be for 20 years. The tenure of the 20-year PPA as well as the potential future cost was questioned by many consumer stakeholders in South Africa, since the tender was to limit *interim* power outages, and the costs were indexed to the international oil price in hard currency[261].

Although the company won the tender to produce emergency power, it initially failed to secure the permissions to moor the vessels in the national ports and harbours from where the power would be dispatched. Obtaining the required environmental approval from the Department of Forestry Fisheries and the Environment also initially proved problematic, with the department withholding the environmental authorization. The environmental ministry stated that at the outset the company did not abide by the minimum requirements for public participation under the country's environmental legislation.

The Karpowership developer appealed the ruling. However, in August 2022, the Minister of Forestry, Fisheries and the Environment, Barbara Creecy, dismissed the appeal, citing that the noise impacts on marine life (and the mitigation thereof) were not adequately addressed. She also cited there were not enough studies performed on the potential mortality rates on the various types of marine species resulting from the long operating period. Overall, the conclusion was that the Environmental Impact Assessment (EIA) lacked sufficient information to make a conclusive ruling on the environmental consequences of the project. The EIA was therefore referred to the Competent Authority to address alleged gaps in the environmental submission[262].

On the last day of public comment, the National Energy Regulator of South Africa granted the licenses sought by the project developers. This upset various civil society and environmental groups, who in turn filed court appeals for granting the licenses on the last day that interested groups who opposed the project were permitted to object to the award.

Opposition to the awarding of the project did not only come from environmental groups. One of the losing competing bidders, DNG Holdings, filed a lawsuit and accused Karpowership of colluding with government officials, excessively influencing them to award the tender[263].

After the awarding of the project, Eskom as the off-taker, also sent the company a notice requesting to be indemnified from any alleged corruption risks that the project may hold[264]. At the time many civil society organisations questioned the technical, economic, and environmental validity of the project. They argued that it was not clear what the implications were for South Africa's objective to achieve net-zero emissions by 2050. Furthermore, it was also not clear why the powership company had obtained a PPA of such long duration when the technology was generally used globally as a short-term stop-gap measure. Lastly, from an energy planning perspective the concern raised was based on the possibility that future lower cost alternatives could become available—while South Africa could be locked into a costly PPA, indexed to hard currency, ultimately presenting significant currency risk for consumers for twenty years.

Renewable Energy Independent Power Producers

By far, the most IPPs that were developed in South Africa were renewable generation projects administered under the Ministry of Minerals and Energy's REIPPP programme. While this programme was widely supported by environmental groups, it was not without obstacles.

Stalling of Renewable IPPs (2015 to 2019)

As discussed earlier in the Chapter, from bid window 4, Eskom stopped the signing of additional IPPs, stating that the utility can provide power cheaper. For a period of approximately four years therefore, the renewable energy IPP procurement programme was stalled, contributing to insufficient capacity coming online when the power was later needed.

A report by Meridian Economics released in June 2022 publicised that more than 96.5 percent of the 2021 loadshedding could have been averted if the programme had not been stalled. In addition, Meridian reported that Eskom could have saved more than R 2.5 billion in fuel and related costs during this period, by avoiding the operation of its costly open-cycle gas turbine units. Overall, the Meridian study, which assumed that at least 5 GW of renewable capacity could have been commissioned by the renewable energy IPP procurement programme, claimed that *most* of South Africa's loadshedding could have been averted—and that with additional demand response mechanisms and energy storage, loadshedding could have been eliminated altogether for some of the years[265].

Stalled Small IPP Programme

In addition to large grid-scale renewable energy projects under the REIPPP programme, smaller scale projects were also keen to sell electricity to the grid. The Smalls Renewable Energy Independent Power Producers Programme was conceived to allow smaller generation capacities of less than five megawatts to enter the power market. In 2013, generation projects between one and five megawatts were opened to permit smaller-scale PV, wind, biomass, and landfill generation technologies—projects that could not compete within the procurement framework for larger grid-scale bid windows[266].

In 2013 and 2015, a total of twenty projects were selected after two rounds of bidding. With the Eskom decision to stall the signing of new IPPs, this programme was left to the same fate as the larger utility grid-scale REIPPs. When the larger grid-scale REIPPP programme was resumed in 2020, most of the budget quotations for the smaller projects had expired. Given that the price per kWh for renewable energy had been steadily decreasing since the projects' bids were initially concluded, Eskom was no longer certain about the competitiveness of the bids and the long-term risk obligations of locked-in PPAs.

Project developers for these smaller projects were frustrated that they had to keep their budget quotes updated and incur the associated costs, without any certainty that PPAs would be signed by Eskom. Eskom and the Ministry of Minerals and Energy eventually stopped the programme. While there potentially still remained limited alternate opportunities for small-scale renewable IPPs to sell their energy to municipalities and Eskom under different programme arrangements, certain project developers felt that they were treated unfairly and unlawfully[267].

Issues for Utility Scale Renewable IPPs

Renewable Energy IPPs have done relatively well in South Africa due to their comparatively lower carbon footprint and the associated risks that projects face from a project finance perspective. Lower cost volatility has also been a boon due to the absence of fuel costs that are exposed to availability constraints and international market prices—in contrast to the Karpowerships deal described earlier in this chapter.

Up until 2022, REIPPs also saw declining bid prices, which indicated that project development costs were continuing a downward trajectory as wind, solar, and battery storage technologies continued to mature. By July 2022, 87 of the 92 utility-scale projects with a combined generation capacity of roughly 6 000 MW had been contracted via the REIPPP programme. These projects were commissioned at a cumulative investment of nearly R 200 billion[268]. In 2022, the REIPPP programme delivered of the lowest energy prices in the region and in the world. In Bid Window 5, one of the wind farms bid at a price of 34 South African cents per kWh. With over one hundred bid offers, the bid window was oversubscribed by 9 644 MW[269]. In April 2023, this positive outcome (the previous year from bid window 5) contributed to the doubling of generation capacity auctioned in bid window 6 from 2 600 to 5 200 MW[270].

Despite the positive outcomes, REIPPs still experienced certain challenges, as described below.

Equipment and Financing Cost Escalations

Even though renewable IPPs were free of long-term primary energy charges, the capital and loan charges on imported equipment still faced exposure to currency risks. And fluctuating prices of capital equipment for power generation components meant that some finance risks still existed for project developers and sponsors. As renewable generation technologies matured over the last two decades (2003 – 2023), the associated equipment costs followed a downward trajectory, gradually resulting in lower energy charges. Bidders were expecting the downward development costs trajectory to continue.

With global supply chain bottlenecks, increased commodity prices, and increasing costs of production due to upward pressure on energy costs (sparked mainly by a global post-COVID recovery and the war between Ukraine and Russia), renewable generation project costs saw an increase from the time when the bids were initially formulated. Since 2022, after the Russian invasion of Ukraine, inflationary pressures on global markets also led to a significant increase in financing costs, as central banks wrestled to curb inflationary pressures. This effect would also influence future bids and resultant PPA charges[271].

Unlike other projects, due to the short period between project bidding, financial closure, and commercial operation, REIPPs in South Africa did not make sufficient provision for cost escalations once the bidding had closed. In addition, in a burgeoning renewable energy generation sector, project developers were also believed to be too aggressive as they competed for market share. The low offerings in many of the bids in previous bidding rounds were to enter the market and obtain greater market share, rather than maximise profits.

Renegotiation of PPAs and REIPP Exposure

The initial projects from the first bid windows were contracted at prices higher than the average tariff that Eskom was able to generate. In 2019, the IPP Office in the Department of Minerals and Energy requested contracted operational plants to determine whether they could lower their charges. For the projects that have benefited from decreased costs and lower risks, IPPs were able to lower their initial charges.

As the REIPP programme gained familiarity and maturity, there was a decrease in related IPP risks especially for operational projects. Furthermore, the projects continued to be underwritten by the government. By 2022, thirteen of the projects that signed up under bid window 1 to bid window 3, applied for refinancing. The refinancing of the thirteen projects was estimated to amount to approximate R 3.5 billion in savings to consumers[272]. Although renegotiations were possible for the thirteen projects, under difference contexts renegotiations could be less favourable for investors.

Internationally, banks are increasing their exposures to renewable energy generation projects[273]. With more than R250 billion cumulatively invested in various REIPP bid windows, at least one of the local South African banks expressed concern on their exposure to renewable generation projects.

Although the renegotiation of the IPP charges was done in a manner that was mutually beneficial to IPPs and the off-taker, the requests for IPPs to lower their charges did question the likelihood of the government putting further renegotiation requests to existing or future IPPs. This trend could become worrisome for IPP sponsors amidst a growing, albeit partly subjective, sentiment that energy costs are increasing due to IPPs. Already public sentiment is that Eskom does not have sufficient funds due to disproportionately larger guaranteed payments to private generators than the 'unsecured' revenues for its own generation.

Winning the Bid, but Losing the Sale

A further issue for renewables in South Africa was the uncoordinated grid planning which was not synchronised with the country's stated energy transition. Even where there were financially bankable projects in areas where the natural solar and wind resources were abundant, insufficient grid connections were available for renewables to connect to the national transmission grid. In December 2022, as the country was experiencing a shortage of at least 6 000 MW of electricity, wind renewable energy developers with winning bids watched in disbelief, as their projects could not be approved due to insufficient grid connections.

At the signing ceremony for the projects in bid window six, only 860 MW of the 4 200 MW of bids that were expected could be accommodated[274]. This would effectively prolong the country's loadshedding woes and delay the procurement of additional electricity generation to meet the country's power needs.

This constraint on available transmission grid connections further raised the question of how long a transition to low-carbon energy generation sources would realistically take? In addition, how does this compare to the ambitious carbon reduction targets and timelines to which South Africa has committed in its Nationally Determined Contributions? Data released by Eskom in March 2023 indicated that there were over 20 GW of renewable generation projects that could be developed but were waiting for grid allocations.

Changing the Rules during the Game

In June 2023, it was found that REIPPs that won their bids and were allowed to develop their projects would not necessarily connect their renewable projects in the shortest time considered reasonable. Bid winners with allocated grid connections were slow to develop their projects and the delays in bringing capacity online could prolong the country's power crisis. Eskom subsequently announced that it would revise the rules by which grid access would be allocated amongst potential IPPs to favour those projects who were indeed ready for implementation. Investors opposed the proposed new rules stating that they were uncompetitive and that investors would be saddled with greater costs preparing their projects, without any guarantees that they would be selected[275].

In this case, to deal with the power crisis faster, the rules were changed by looking at ways to fast-track projects that were ready for implementation. A developer of two wind farms approached the court to stop the implementation, fearing that its grid allocations may be rescinded. Eskom eventually eased the rules to allay the fears of IPP developers, while still trying to ensure that projects were developed as fast as reasonably possible[276]. This compromise paved a way for the developers to drop the court case.

Transmission Readiness for IPPs and the Energy Transition

The transition to low carbon sources requires a significant reconfiguration, redesign, and extensive altering of electricity flows in the national electricity grid. Renewable energy generation plants cannot always be sited close to existing transmission interconnections, which in South Africa are typically close to coal-fired plants. Neither can renewable generation plants always be sited close to load centres, where the energy is consumed.

Renewable energy plants have to be situated where the renewable resources are located, and electricity transported to the areas where the electricity is consumed. The transition is therefore limited to what the grid can realistically accommodate, rather than just the amount of wind and solar resources that are available for conversion to electrical energy.

Given the amount of time and capital required to build additional transmission grid capacity to accommodate renewables, the pace of the energy transition could be significantly hampered. Without significant investment in transmission infrastructure, already the connection of renewables cannot be executed at a pace whereby the impact of loadshedding could be minimised in the short-term—at least not by wind and solar generation alone. IPPs can therefore only compete at a pace that the transmission expansion will allow.

The lack of readiness of the transmission grid to accommodate new IPPs therefore stifled the entry of renewable energy IPPs from entering the generation sector. This situation did not help to reduce the loadshedding impact.

IPPs in the Distribution Sector

In the Distribution sector, where the number of smaller scale generators were on the increase, there were reports from communities that Eskom was frustrating the development of distributed generation by private investors.

Despite the President's announcement in July 2022 that generators less than 100 MW no longer required generation licenses, smaller generators of less than 100 MW also faced hurdles entering the generation market within the distribution sub-sector. Where Eskom was facing competition in the Distribution sector it allegedly blocked the entry of distributed generation[277].

In April 2022, Greenstone Energy reportedly asked NERSA to allow it to supply electricity to the residents of a suburb in Sandton, Johannesburg. The residents wanted an alternate power supply. They claimed that in addition to the scheduled rolling blackouts, that they experienced an additional 66 days of power interruptions. Eskom opposed the application, claiming that the suburb had only experienced 29 days of additional power interruptions, instead of the 66 days they had claimed[278].

Without an approved regulatory framework for adding generators to Eskom distribution grids, Eskom was within its rights to oppose the application. When the community proposed that it would roll out its own distribution reticulation infrastructure to decrease its dependence on Eskom, the utility again opposed the application, stating that NERSA does not allow more than one distributor to service an area and the installation of more than one set of distribution cables would constitute a dangerous or unsafe condition. Instead of determining how the two entities (Eskom Distribution and the private generator) could work together in order to shield certain customers from extensive rolling blackouts, the issue was ventilated in the courts. One year later, Eskom won the court case.

Given the low collection rates and number of non-paying customers, Eskom would be acutely aware of losing sales from good paying customers to distributed generators, and cognizant of the need to retain these customers. These well-paying customers may never return, leaving the utility only with communities and consumers that have poor collection rates and high incidents of illegal connections (including non-metering and theft).

Where intermittent renewable self-generation was contracted without any coexisting dispatchable back-up power (such as energy storage options), loadshedding could still be experienced by these communities when energy demand outstripped supply. In August 2022, Eskom indicated that it could not increase the supply of electricity to some municipalities. As a result, many local farmers and businesses developed their own plans for additional electricity generation from solar resources. A local community then proceeded to limit the amount of loadshedding, but Eskom allegedly objected to this[279]. This caused much frustration for some communities. In April 2023, in the Free State province, the Mafube Municipality's private power distributor, Rural Maintenance, as well as the business forum approached the court to intervene until the dispute could be resolved with the National Energy Regulator of South Africa.

Communities could not see the benefit of investing in their own generation capacity when they were still 'held to ramson' and remained dependent on Eskom's transmission and distribution services for back-up power, which was not available during loadshedding[280].

◈ ◈ ◈

Despite the late introduction of private participation in the generation sector, the REIPPP programme delivered the most privately sponsored projects in South Africa. Administered from inside the Ministry of Minerals and Energy, by early 2023 the IPP Office had concluded roughly 90 contracts with IPPs, thereby bringing onboard over 6 000 MW of renewable energy capacity.

The introduction of non-renewable IPPs were however thwarted by project factors, such as those experienced by fossil fuelled IPP developers. Not a single utility-scale coal-fired IPP was developed in South Africa, in contrast to the indicative provisions in the country's IRP. Gas-fired private generation continued to face significant headwinds, as evidenced by the Karpowerships project.

Eskom stalled the REIPPP programme for many years, despite the decision by the Ministry of Minerals and Energy indicating that REIPPs should be procured in line with the country's increasing demand for electricity in accordance with the country's Integrated Resource Plan. It appears that in the Distribution sector, Eskom also resisted poorly formulated but well-intentioned attempts by communities to bring onboard their own private generation capacity and decrease its dependence on the utility.

Largely, due to the National Energy Regulator being subordinate to the Ministry of Minerals and Energy, potential IPPs and municipalities could not take their complaints to NERSA if it involved the determinations for additional generation capacity by the Minister of Minerals and Energy. The energy regulator did not have a mandate to intervene in the domain of the ministry that it reported into. In this sense, regulatory independence and authority was inadequate to meaningfully bring projects online and mitigate the effects on loadshedding.

Both Eskom and municipalities failed to sufficiently incentivise IPPs to connect and sell their energy onto transmission and distribution grids. Eskom did not adequately consider the expansion required on the transmission network to accommodate increasing utility-scale REIPPs in transmission—an oversight from the transmission planning function. Notwithstanding that financially solvent municipalities could not initially obtain approvals from the Minister of Minerals and Energy for contracting with large IPPs, in most cases municipalities were not considered financially credible off-takers.

Regardless of the entry of private generation, the programme for introducing private sector participation to plug the investment gaps in electricity production failed to propitiously shield South Africans from the scourge of insufficient electricity generation.

PART V

ELECTRICITY PLANNING

CHAPTER 12

ELECTRICITY PLANNING, CONTRACTING AND PROCUREMENT

The importance of electricity planning lies in its role in helping governments and utilities to recognise opportunities and avoid costly mistakes. Electricity planning enables planners to grasp more clearly what they want to achieve, as well as when and how they can achieve it. With power sector reforms, a rearrangement of institutional functions often resulted in the planning function being taken away from state-owned utilities and assumed by sector ministries or related agencies. Reformers often assumed that new generation investments would eventually be taken care of by *the market,* and during the reform transition did not explicitly focus on the issue of planning. The necessity of planning under hybrid market and various single buyer arrangements remained even more obscure. Planning often turned out to be inadequate leading to delays in building power plants and consequently insufficient generation capacity.

In the past, the national state-owned utility assumed sole responsibility for generation expansion planning. But with the entry of IPPs, it was often not clear whether the SOE remained the supplier of last resort. Planning functions were often neglected or were transferred to the Energy Ministry which often had insufficient capacity to plan effectively. Weak or absent regulatory and governance frameworks for generation planning and procurement undermine the credibility of investment and contracting decisions and there are often no clear linkages between generation planning, the timely initiation and implementation of tender processes, and commercial operations of new generation plants.

In reviewing the works and experiences on electricity planning as it relates to the problem of insufficient generation capacity, this chapter evaluates why reform efforts have largely ignored these issues. This discussion explores the links between planning, procurement and contracting and how the emergence of hybrid markets creates new challenges in terms of allocating institutional responsibility and capacity for these functions[281].

Electricity Planning

The purpose of generation planning is to determine the amount and type of generation capacity to be constructed, and the time in which it needs to be constructed and commissioned—while the total cost to the utility is minimised[282]. Energy security is important in the modern age due to its links to economic and social development. Energy security is reduced when countries hold inefficient generation portfolios that are unnecessarily exposed to fossil fuel price volatility or drought[283], suggesting that generation planning should not be performed in isolation.

Reliable planning scenarios for the electricity industry are often dependent on upstream fuel industries that have different drivers and constraints for quantity, price, and quality of supply to that of the electricity supply industry. Effective resource allocation, as well as co-ordination and supply projections, are therefore necessary between electricity and upstream industries[284]. If electricity planning fails to adequately consider the links to upstream supply industries, such as fuel markets and equipment suppliers to support power plants, or to downstream links, such as transmission expansions required to evacuate the power generated, and to demand patterns, it could result in undesirable consequences. It is therefore essential for planning to encompass an *integrated approach* to supply and demand-side additions, constraints, and requirements.

From Conventional Electricity Planning to Integrated Resource Planning

Traditional electricity planning focussed on supply side additions to generation infrastructure to meet the anticipated demand and minimise economic costs of expansion[285]. Until the 1970s, the supply of low-priced energy and resources helped sustain world economic growth and the traditional approach to energy planning was developed against this background[286]. Traditional planning often relied on increased economies of scale in generation capacity with little consideration of the need for greater energy efficiency. Consumers generally absorbed the costs of expansion and the holding of large reserve capacities, often with little choice[287].

One of the primary reasons for energy planning having a one-sided supply focus was because energy planning was not extensive—planning objectives evolved separately within the various energy sub-sectors and individual enterprises[288]. The energy sector was generally dominated by engineers who had a supply focus. However, after the oil shocks of the 1970s, increased supply costs led to a greater focus on least-cost utility planning. Least-cost expansion has evolved toward Integrated Resource Planning (IRP), which allows for broader economic, environmental, and social objectives to be integrated in electricity planning. Electricity costs normally exclude the external costs imposed by society. These costs can be in the form of air and water pollution, climate change, exposure to volatile fuel markets and worsening trade balances that increase debt to other countries[289].

Studies on electricity costs and externalities in South Africa and elsewhere have estimated the external costs of electricity (based on quantitative analysis of air pollution impacts of human health, damages from greenhouse gas emissions, and the avoided health costs from electrification) at significantly higher values than the industrial and residential tariffs[290]. In this regard, plant location, technology and fuel choices have become ever more important in generation investment decisions. IRP therefore goes beyond supply side technologies to include energy efficiency and Demand Side Management (DSM) technologies, amongst others, to ensure a balance between supply and demand in future planning scenarios. Put differently, the goal of IRP is to match the supply of energy service to the demand of energy services while trying to minimise the quantities and the costs of both.

Thus, if building additional generation capacity is more expensive than meeting the demand for energy by improving energy efficiency, then energy efficiency improvements should be selected as the resource to achieve the objective of least-cost. Through IRP therefore the difference between supply and demand could be reduced and, more importantly, it could be reduced more cost-effectively. Energy planning boundaries are therefore no longer fixed by the energy sector alone but by the *energy system as a whole*—by the linkages between related sectors, and by the broader economic and social environment.

Within integrated resource planning, demand-side options are just as important as supply-side options. Various studies have shown that in some cases DSM can cut average demand substantially. Further studies have also shown how peak electricity demand could be shaved by investing in cost-effective DSM programmes.

Why the Promise of Integrated Planning Fell Short of its Potential

Before power sector reforms were initiated in developing countries few African countries included IRP in a rigorous way in power sector planning or even used it as a means to compare supply and demand side options. Although many developing countries have legislated and mustered organisational support for energy conservation, these have generally not been fully integrated into power sector planning. Why is it then that, despite IRP holding so much potential to postpone or negate the need for additional generation capacity, it did not play a more central role in energy policy and power sector planning in developing countries? The reasons are numerous.

Path Dependence

Traditional rigid master plans developed by utilities and/or energy ministries were infrequently updated and lacked the flexibility required for the modern-day contexts in which power sectors were evolving. Cost estimates were often outdated and timelines for project development unrealistic. With private funding and ownership, long-term economic returns needed to make way for shorter-term financial returns[291]. While the cost of capital is a key factor that shapes investment choices, technologies that can be installed quickly and operated flexibly in response to market demands are increasingly attractive to power markets.

In many cases, however, planning failed to contemplate the *evolving needs* of power sectors in developing countries, including those in Africa. Instead, utilities reacted to energy shortages by contracting stop-gap measures rather than focussing on systematic planning. The electricity crises in certain countries were so acute that, understandably, utilities were more concerned with dealing with immediate crises rather than long-term planning. However, even when power crises were less prevalent, the concept of the traditional one-sided approach was dominant and hard to shake off. Decision-making was based on a supply paradigm that largely side-lined DSM initiatives. Little real consideration was given to energy efficiency as a means to manage the effects of increasing electricity demand and diminishing reserve margins.

Preoccupation with Power Sector Reforms

With power sector liberalisation, it was believed that additional generation capacity would be 'left to the market'[292]. Generation planning therefore became a casualty of market reforms. However, wholesale competition was not reached, and private investment did not take care of capacity expansions, as expected. Power sector reforms aimed to transform vertically integrated monopolies into wholesale and retail power markets—planning was often neglected in the process.

Although many electricity wholesale markets in industrialised countries which were opened to competition have managed to maintain adequate investment in generation, the same cannot be said of developing countries where reform has stopped short of competitive wholesale markets. The emphasis in power sector reforms in many developing countries was on unbundling and advancing regulatory frameworks in preparation for the new market. Dealing with difficult ownership transfers, complaints from agitated consumers and objections from discontented labour unions consumed the focus of those in authority, to the exclusion of what were considered longer term issues, including planning.

It would also appear that corporatisation and privatisation would lessen the need for IRP for utilities since strategic plans of utilities would be more inclined to deal with narrow shareholder-informed objectives than with the overall benefits of the energy system—or even society. Investors would therefore have been unlikely to consider externalities and other benefits that accrue to society if it potentially decreased their own profits.

Poor Institutional Co-ordination

Poor institutional arrangements have also inhibited an integrated planning approach to electricity. Often commitment from senior government officials was lacking and there were rarely institutional vehicles well-resourced to take the lead in IRP. Ministry departments or agencies able to influence demand-side factors often operated in isolation from those responsible for supply side capacity planning. In India, for example, it was noted that historically the Ministry of Power was distinct from the Ministry of Non-conventional Sources of Energy and that these two entities did not draw up integrated energy plans[293].

Thus, programmes were planned and implemented independent of each other and there was little co-ordination between supply and demand programmes. In many developing country power sectors caught in the reformation transition, the planning function was either neglected or shifted from the national power utility to the Energy Ministry, which often did not have the capacity to undertake the function adequately. Confusion set in as to who was finally responsible for ensuring that the lights stay on—the old state-owned utility, government, or IPPs? Without explicit allocation of planning responsibilities and functions, there was no proper co-ordination. Each entity was generally more concerned with its own narrow objectives than integration for overall development of the power sector.

Questionable Suitability and Lack of Resources

A belief that was widely held was that IRP would only be useful for developed energy systems in the most industrialised countries where the data, finance, management, and skills existed to use it properly. It was often claimed that developing countries have political, financial, social, and economic conditions that are distinct from those in industrial countries and, therefore, need different methods of energy planning. It was further contended that developing countries have heterogeneous societies (in comparison to industrialised countries with more homogenous societies) which make patterns of energy consumption difficult to link to groups of consumers. In addition, energy systems are in many ways still under construction in developing countries, making forecasting trickier.

Demand forecasting due to access expansion and demand growth investment decisions is often more uncertain than supply-side investment uncertainty. Planners and policy makers often did not have a firm handle on the factors that impact on growth and patterns in energy demand in order to make credible demand projections and respond to these with appropriate demand and supply-side management policies.

In more recent times and as electricity customers struggled to cope with the effects of persistent power outages, the rapid increase in 'behind the meter' private small-scale embedded electricity generators make projections for future electricity demand difficult to forecast—and challenging to accurately verify. Traditional correlations between Gross Domestic Product growth and electricity demand growth no longer proved reliable as the divergence between these two metrics was distorted by energy efficiency, related DSM initiatives, and embedded self-generation. Even standard capacity expansion models used in industrialised countries were considered ill-equipped to model and compare developing country risks between various projects and generating technologies[294]. As a result, demand forecasts in developing countries could be out by far. During the development of India's Dabhol IPP, for example, growth projections for electricity demand was three to four times higher than was the actual demand[295].

Moreover, many developing countries lacked the skills, management and finance to use complex computer-simulated generation planning programmes and techniques properly. In many cases, utilities continued to face severe financial pressure leading to inadequate resources being available for energy efficiency and generation planning—let alone IRP, which was seen as elaborate and optional. Integrated resource planning is information intensive. Energy ministries in many developing countries rarely had the required information to use as inputs to make quality IRP decisions. IRP is resource intensive because the process is dynamic. This is not only because changes in demand and supply are evolutionary, but also because DSM programmes and supply side alternatives have feedback effects which impact on the process of selecting future planning strategies[296].

Planning was often limited to high-level—or indicative—planning and failed to include financial, legal, and environmental aspects of generation development. In these cases, although planning appeared adequate on paper, in reality it failed to anticipate the challenges experienced in securing financial resources, equitably allocating project risk and contingent liabilities, evaluating environmental constraints to project development, and assessing the security of fuel supply.

Renewables — Planning Challenges

The introduction of increased renewable energy electricity generation has also presented several challenges to traditional methods of integrated resource planning. Planning models for dispatchable power generation have traditionally not been affected by the uncertainties associated with small amounts of renewable generation. However, with increasing renewable generation penetration, this situation has changed significantly.

Transmission and Distribution Planning

Historically, generation supply side additions were typical for incremental power system planning. The introduction of increasing energy from renewable generation technologies has highlighted the increasing importance of transmission planning. Transmission expansion and the provision of adequate interconnections have become progressively important for solar and wind generators. In South Africa, insufficient transmission connections, partly due to poor planning and implementation, resulted in many renewable IPPs not being signed on despite a shortage of power supply to the national grid.

Transmission planning is also important when deciding on criteria for IPP grid allocations on the transmission network. In the case of South Africa, two separate routes for developing generation projects were ongoing at the same time: one administered by the Ministry of Minerals and Energy for generators greater than 100 MW, which required the full licensing processes to be followed; the other was for generators less than 100 MW, which did not require licensing to the same extent by the country's electricity regulator. While the Ministry of Minerals and Energy was administering the bid window for adjudicating bids for generators greater than 100 MW, the country's President announced that prospective generators could apply directly to the off-taker utility for project connections less than 100 MW. By the time that the projects greater than 100 MW approached closure, there were insufficient connections left to accommodate the full bid window capacity that the Ministry of Minerals and Energy had envisaged under its programme for generators greater than 100 MW.

Geographic Location

Transmission grids also requires upgrades to accommodate the generation of electricity further from load centres. Planning often failed to adequately consider the impact of these geographical changes to power systems and the transmission economics to support renewable generation. Not only did the geographic location of renewable energy generation impact the amount of power generated due to the availability of hydro, wind, and solar resources during the day, the week, and the year—but simplified models for baseload and peaking generation had to be swapped with variability models to cater for the inherent variability of wind and solar generation.

Traditionally under a generation supply-side planning paradigm, excess generation resource adequacy was targeted at roughly 10-15 percent—to cater for unplanned generation losses. Traditional acceptable loss-of-load frequencies used as inputs in integrated resource planning models were often challenged due to the poor predictability of weather-related renewable generation output. While it was acknowledged that new trade-offs were required between transmission system reliability, weather variability, and generation investment costs (especially with increasing amounts of renewable capacity), it could not easily be determined what the new acceptable loss-of-load frequency/probability should be for increasing penetration of renewable generation.

System reliability is not free. The question of who should cover the cost of services to make up for reduced system reliability due to increased variable renewable technology, was not always clear from the start of the energy transition towards a low-carbon power sector. Responsibilities for generation resource adequacy therefore needed to be redefined and reallocated in evolving power systems that were increasing their share of non-dispatchable renewable generation.

In certain cases, modelling curtailment of wind output was not only needed in the event of windless days, but planning models also needed to be adjusted for short periods when excessive wind speeds could damage generation equipment. The economics of energy storage as a generation investment decision and for day-to-day system operations, also became a tricky issue. Excess capacity storage requirements in traditional pumped-storage schemes increased according to the new system generation intermittency and variability. While these issues were eventually better understood as experience was gained with increasing penetration of renewable generation, they initially posed as challenges for energy planners that required urgent investment decisions in power grids with dwindling dispatchable generation reserves.

The transition to low-carbon generation itself presented unexpected challenges to energy planners. Traditional integrated electricity planning computational models needed revision to accommodate new constant and variable inputs, as well as new enabling assumptions to better reflect the reality of energy supply and demand in an evolving power sector.

Power Plant Procurement in Hybrid Markets

Following on from the difficulties associated with planning, delays in procuring new generation capacity also aggravate problems of insufficient capacity. As part of power sector reforms, responsibilities for procurement have also shifted from utilities to ministries (or related agencies) with little or no prior experience in this area. Many governments face serious deficits in the institutional expertise and capacity necessary to implement private generation infrastructure projects. While they may be proficient in technical aspects of infrastructure projects, civil servants often lack familiarity with transactions in project finance and in the complex legalities of elaborate Build-Own-Operate-Transfer investments. Generation infrastructure procurement touches on various aspects which, if not optimally implemented, can lead to problems and delays in contracting additional capacity. A number of these aspects are described below.

Contracting Governance

The introduction of IPPs raises questions such as: How should the process of adding generation capacity be arranged? Should competitive bidding processes grant IPPs the right to compete for *all* future generation? What decision-making processes or price signals for procuring generation capacity should be used in the long run?

In Africa, there is little evidence of clear and transparent criteria for the allocation of new-build opportunities amongst state-owned utilities and IPPs, and contracting decisions and policies often lack sufficient governance mechanisms. The absence of certainty and transparency results in lengthy, confusing negotiations that delay project development. In addition, many countries in Africa lack independent monitoring bodies to provide oversight on procurement activities. In Ghana, for example, while an independent procurement agency existed specifically for this purpose, the urgency of getting power generation facilities developed in an environment of chronic electricity shortages appeared to have exempted the power sector from adhering to the national procurement policies of the country's Public Procurement Authority[297].

Procurement Weaknesses

Major weaknesses often seen in state procurement systems, contribute to delays in awarding contracts and non-compliance with rules and regulations. Vague guidelines, poor monitoring, weak institutional support, and inadequate knowledge and skills have exacerbated these delays. Due to time and cost overruns, the procurement system is often viewed as an obstacle to ensuring the timely contracting of generation capacity.

Figure 12.1 provides an example of the timelines for renewable energy or gas IPP contracting from project conceptualisation until closure of the deal[298]. As illustrated, with optimal contracting processes, it can take between 18 and 24 months for the contracting parties to reach agreement. With weak or vague contracting processes, each phase holds the potential for delay. When the authority over the electricity investment is shared by so many constituencies and government departments, regulatory systems often fail to secure public consent early enough for siting power plants[299]. Agencies often operate in isolation which means that good regulatory intentions often translate to ill-timed or delayed decisions. When processes are not widely agreed on by various stakeholders in the contracting process *ex ante,* delays may be experienced during the procurement process. In addition, the longer contracting takes, the costlier it becomes.

Figure 12.1: Typical Timeline of an IPP Contracting Process

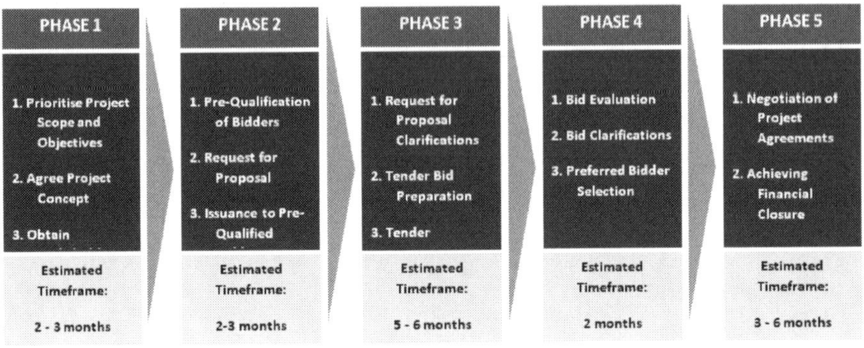

Even with surplus capacity, the long lead times before commissioning takes place make timely decisions essential. Most large power markets in the world are approaching, or are in, a major investment cycle as surplus capacity has been depleted and some fossil-fuelled plants are retired. This puts pressure on the supply of power generation equipment with some Original Equipment Manufacturers' waiting lists extending to a number of years before the required equipment can be supplied. During the years of surplus capacity, many manufacturers of equipment scaled down or closed down production facilities to focus on maintenance and consulting activities. Often, procurement planning fails to anticipate delays in the global power equipment supply market thereby leading to delays in bringing on additional generation capacity[300]. Where governments have localisation requirements and not enough preparatory work has been done to accommodate this in the procurement framework, delays in developing and commissioning generation plants may result.

Non-transparent Procurement Processes

Most power sectors in developing countries started reforms and the introduction of IPPs under a single buyer purchasing framework due to its ease of implementation and the minimal structural changes required. Although single buyer models have advantages, such as the ability to attract private capital under long-term PPAs, they also have potential pitfalls. The single buyer framework centralises many of the planning and procurement functions (in itself, a positive move), but without adequate governance or transparency. Moreover, procurement and purchasing arrangements are often open to political interference, leading to corruption[301].

Africa is not unfamiliar with controversies around government spending and many projects have been distressed due to inadequate and non-transparent procurement processes employed by government departments and utilities. In the case of South Africa, political interference by the ruling party in procurement was considered a key reason for the subsequent delays in the completion of the Medupi and Kusile coal-fired power plants.

Although there are well-known guidelines for ensuring efficient public procurement—developed by organisations such as the World Trade Organisation (WTO), the World Bank, and other multilateral organisations—many developing countries do not subject their procurement policies to multilateral surveillance or international disciplines[302].

Reasons for this may include intent to discriminate against certain firms; unfamiliarity with the multilateral endorsed governance procurement rules; a perception that the potential benefits of adhering to these rules are small; or successful opposition from groups that benefit from current practices. Non-transparent procurement processes allow for bribery of procurement officials and corruption which could increase project costs.

The lack of transparency and risk of corruption are thus significant impediments to efficient and timely procurement of infrastructure. In Nigeria, with the development of the Enron/AES Barge IPP, competitive bidding was overlooked for a directly negotiated deal. Later, the deal came unstuck, and renegotiations carried on for considerably longer. Major objections were raised regarding the lack of transparency in procurement; the fact that the plant would not be penalised for poor performance; claims that the project company would receive excessive contract termination payments; and that these payments could bankrupt national utilities[303].

For Nigeria's Okpai IPP, which was also developed from a direct negotiation, investment costs rose substantially between the time of initial negotiations and final commissioning of the plant. Among the reasons cited for increased costs was the underestimation of the cost for transmission infrastructure. Although the parties sought to settle the dispute around increased costs, the off-taker refused to make full payments for the power produced.

Unsolicited Proposals

In many cases electricity is procured from unsolicited IPP proposals. Proponents often cite their possession of intellectual property rights on aspects of project technology as a reason for sole source contracting. Others claim that special circumstances around the lack of private sector interest, cost efficiency due to the scale, risk profile or location, or uniqueness of projects, warrant direct contracting from an unsolicited bid. Still others assert that the shortage of power, especially during emergencies, dictates the need to speed up project development and bypass lengthy competitive procurement processes. While under certain conditions governments may justify direct negotiations on unsolicited proposals, the experiences in several countries have shown that sole-source negotiations usually take longer to reach closure than originally intended and could delay projects by several years.

Note that it is not advocated here that all procurement should be processed through competitive bidding since this may not be in the best interests of governments or developers when projects are complex and there are few available bidders. In the case of complex projects, competitive bidding processes may stifle communication between parties involved in procurement leading to the buyer missing out on innovative opportunities to save on costs, time, and effort[304]. However, where projects use standard technology and development is, by and large, customary, tender specifications can be simplified, and generally, more bidders will drive down prices in accordance with competition theory.

In the main, competitively contracted generating plants have found their costs to be lower than directly negotiated plants. And irrespective of the contract terms, on the whole, competitively contracted plants were found to be less likely to attract adverse renegotiations (and delays in reaching closure) than directly negotiated plants[305].

Prices also escalate as private sponsors adjust their offering to the required specifications. This could be the case when the purchaser knows little about the technology at the start of the project, or little is known about the government's requirements by the project sponsor. In Indonesia, for example, the negotiations of many unsolicited proposals spanned several years with negotiating parties not being able to reach financial closure. Negotiations for the Dabhol plant in India continued for nearly a decade when a new government cancelled the initial agreement and restructured the deal under different terms. Excessive costs and alleged corruption were cited as the main reasons for the Indian government's cancellation of the original Dabhol IPP agreements and restarting negotiations which led to a delay of sixteen months at a significant cost.

In retrospect, many government officials in India questioned the decision to use direct negotiation with the objective of speeding up the development of the project. The PPA terms were unbalanced in favour of investors and the host country payment obligations were viewed as exploitative by the public—and therefore not sustainable. Unsolicited proposals, which are not channelled through a transparent and competitive process, often increase perceptions of corruption. Some projects that have led to directly negotiated deals resulted in contracts for power projects which were not needed. In addition to attractive terms and high prices for investors, the deals shifted major risks to the buyer—the host utility government.

Public-private infrastructure advisors generally advocate that, as a minimum, all unsolicited proposals should be channelled through a process where competitors can challenge each other's proposal on pre-determined criteria, such as price—with the possibility of winning the tender. Several countries have adopted systems to establish broader sector support for projects by guiding unsolicited proposals through a process where competitors have a fair chance of winning the tender.

One such system is the 'bonus system'. A bonus is awarded to the original proponent of the project when the project subsequently goes out on open tender[306]. If, for example, the bonus allocated to the original proponent is 5 percent, the tender will only go to this proponent if his offer is less than 5 percent above the lowest price tendered for the project. The bonus is, therefore, a reward for the preparatory work done in the original project proposal.

Another popular system for treating unsolicited proposals is the 'Swiss challenge' which allows third parties to make counter proposals to that of the original promoter. If a third-party challenger's bid is found to be more favourable, then the original promoter is given another chance to match this. The idea behind the process is to discourage opportunism and avoid exaggerated project development costs[307]. Another similar system is known as the 'best and final offer'. Here, the initial promoter does not enjoy the advantage of matching the lowest bid, since only one round of tendering is allowed.

Allocation of New Build Opportunities

In many cases, new build opportunities for the public and private sectors are not based on equitable and transparent criteria. While SOEs often maintain that they can build new plants cheaper than can the private sector, they often do not provide any financial bases for their claims or explain how conditional risks will be allocated. With public investment, the cost of power is frequently assessed without considering contingent liabilities that are saddled on governments, consumers, and taxpayers.

Single buyers are often the incumbent SOEs who can block potential private investments in generation by discriminating against them with respect to transmission access. With only one wholesale buyer, the creation of flexible off-taker agreements has proved to be difficult when SOE utilities have not allowed potential IPPs to supply power to existing customers. Rules for the dispatching of power stations are developed by SOE utilities, which are also the transmission system operators. Under single buyer arrangements, therefore, SOE utilities have a conflict of interest. This concerns investors contemplating entering the market. Given the flexibility required for progressing future market development, investors have also been concerned about the certainty of their long-term PPAs[308].

◈ ◈ ◈

Integrated Resource Planning was often crowded out by power sector reform agendas, leading to meticulous, detailed, and deliberate planning being largely neglected as a means to avoid the problems of insufficient electricity. This oversight exacerbates the problem of insufficient electricity generation in hybrid markets, despite IRP aiming to mitigate the impacts. During power sector reforms, handover of responsibilities to new planning functionaries can further aggravate the situation when new planning institutions are not suitably equipped to take over these functions.

Delays in contracting new generation infrastructure due to inadequate planning increase the risk of insufficient capacity and prolong the inconvenience of rolling blackouts. Similarly, deficient procurement frameworks often lead to delays—and in an environment of non-transparency they are subject to corruption. Prospective investors and lenders are wary of making investments in countries where such problems exist, or they add significant premiums to compensate for the increase in the perceived risks. Experiences or perceptions of corruption make it more difficult for countries to attract investment for future generation projects, thereby exacerbating the challenges of dealing with shortages in generation capacity. Furthermore, in many cases, purchasing arrangements have allowed state-owned utilities to frustrate investment by the private sector.

CHAPTER 13

ELECTRICITY PLANNING, PROCUREMENT, AND CONTRACTING IN THE SOUTH AFRICAN POWER SECTOR

The ushering in of intended reforms in the power sector in 1998 signalled a reduced role for Eskom in future power sector planning and the development of generation projects. With responsibilities for energy planning being transferred from state-owned utilities to government ministries, the transfer of responsibilities played a part in slowing down the process of timely planning, procurement, and contracting of electricity generation plants. South Africa has experienced many of the general problems discussed in the previous chapter. The specific experience in the South African context is briefly described in this chapter.

Transmission Planning Challenges

Chapter 11 has illuminated some of the problems experienced by renewable energy IPPs in South Africa and how the national transmission network was ill-prepared to allow timely grid connections of new generation capacity when the projects were ready to have their bids accepted by the IPP office in the Ministry of Minerals and Energy.

Unlike many developed countries that have well-balanced interconnected grids with sufficient dispatchable generators and consumer loads evenly spread across its geographic jurisdictions, South Africa's national transmission grid was found wanting. South Africa's baseload plants are mostly sited close to coal mines (in the north of the country) and high-voltage transmission lines transport electrical energy to inland and coastal areas where the electricity is consumed. However, good renewable energy resources are not always situated near consumers of electricity, or close to existing transmission interconnections for baseload plants. This presented a challenge for the transmission system to evolve fast enough to cater for the integration of renewables.

Where generation projects were ready to be fast tracked, the funding for future grid expansions were delayed. Eskom did not always have resources to execute grid strengthening and upgrade projects[309]. The national grid had limited capacity for new connections and new generation grid connections required significant investment in transmission infrastructure.

South Africa's Transmission Development Plan is an indicative plan that reflects the national grid requirements to satisfy the country's future electricity supply and demand. It directs the transmission investments for the country's rollout of national grid infrastructure.

The plan provides a 10-year look-ahead and is updated to reflect changes in policy, regulatory and planning assumptions. There was a considerable delay before the Transmission Development Plan was eventually aligned to the country's generation plan (IRP 2019 edition) for the rollout of renewable energy generation. Despite the late alignment in scope, experience has shown that (in 2023) there was still considerable misalignment when it came to the timelines for the rollout of the grid infrastructure required for future stated renewable electricity generation sources.

Furthermore, although the Integrated Resource Plan considered *least-cost* electricity generation options, national electricity planning functions initially failed to consider the required increases in transmission investment. There were significant costs associated with the transmission expansion required to accommodate increasing renewable generation capacity in locations that have favourable wind and solar resources. Other hidden costs of renewable generation were additional grid services for voltage regulation, frequency control, reactive power control, as well as other ancillary services required to maintain grid stability for a number of grid configurations and grid incident scenarios.

With increasing penetration of renewable generation sources, greater amounts of spinning reserves (standby generation required to maintain a stable grid frequency) are required to operate in concert with the variation in renewable generation supply. These are costs that will have to be catered for through investment. In the case of South Africa, it is still not clear who in the future will be responsible for these services (public or private), and ultimately who will pay for the associated investment cost.

It will best serve electricity planners and South Africans if all costs associated with the energy transition are taken into consideration in the country's integrated electricity plan, not just the cost of generation expansion. Without considering *all* costs, it becomes difficult to estimate the true costs associated with various generation technologies—to understand where investment efficiencies can best be optimised to reduce the wholesale cost of electricity and to evaluate whether (and how much) limited investment funding should be best spent in the generation sector, the transmission sector, the distribution sector, or on demand side management initiatives.

In 2023, the Centre for Sustainability Transitions at Stellenbosch University, the Centre for Renewable and Sustainable Energy Studies, and the Blended Finance Task Force published a paper indicating that the speed at which grid capacity must be expanded is seven to eight times faster than what was the case in that same year[310]. This is despite South Africa's Integrated Resource Plan indicating the rollout of renewable generation sources in 2019, and South Africa's commitment to prepare for a low carbon economy as far back as 2016.

Nevertheless, going forward, if South Africa hopes to achieve net zero with mostly wind and solar additional generation sources, the most significant obstacle to ensuring sufficient electricity could be Transmission, and not Generation, as previously thought. Transmission expansion under state-ownership in South Africa could be encumbered with the same obstacles that has weighed down Generation expansion under the current government's state-dominant model, where the function is saddled with too many other competing objectives as requested by the government.

The negotiation process for obtaining transmission servitudes can be a lengthy process and it involves the agreement on the exact location of the servitudes, access and access road arrangements, agreement on the residual rights of landowners, and maintenance responsibilities. Environmental Impact Assessment processes have also evolved in complexity, with more stringent environmental requirements being placed on large projects that traverse sensitive ecological areas.

In South Africa, the slow pace of transmission infrastructure expansion has even led to prospective IPP developers offering to pay for grid expansion if they could be equitably compensated. This would however create other problems with the independence of the grid owner and the system operator. While this is not an insurmountable challenge it nonetheless presents a potential problem that would have to be adequately catered for under the legislative frameworks and long-term contracting arrangements between IPPs and off-takers.

As the windiest and sunniest places with grid access has already been taken by project developers, future projects are left with poorer resources and fewer grid access points. These factors put increasing pressures on consumer wholesale electricity costs in two ways. The remaining locations with lower natural renewal resource availability means that less wind or sunlight is available to generate electricity, thereby prompting an increase in the price per kWh. Then, the construction of longer transmission lines to transport the energy from the locations where the electricity is generated to where the energy is consumed, results in larger transmission line losses and ultimately increased transmission charges. Although generation curtailment can be offered as a solution to this problem, it also comes with increased (hidden) costs to either investors or off-takers.

On the road towards decarbonisation, insufficient transmission readiness can arguably become the greatest obstacle to increasing investment in generation. Increased focus must be given to this sub-sector in future versions of the country's Integrated Resource Plan.

Generation Planning, Contracting, and Procurement Challenges

In South Africa, the genesis of electricity planning failures was the 1998 Energy White Paper. Since Eskom was prohibited from building new plants, key planning functions which historically featured centre-stage on the company's long-term performance metrics, were relegated to dwindling support functions. Comprehensive planning for future technical, financial, human resource, and supply chain functions, was significantly reduced. By the time that Eskom was allowed to continue with new-builds in 2005, the departments that were historically responsible for these functions were either under-resourced or no longer in existence. This dereliction had profound consequences for Eskom and South Africa's future proficiency to get electricity planning right—or woefully wrong.

Shutdown and Decommissioning of Aged Plants

In 2017, during the period that Eskom suspended signing on more REIPPs, the utility announced that it would close six of its oldest coal-fired power stations by 2029. These plants included the Arnot, Camden, Grootvlei, Hendrina, Komati, and Kriel Power Stations[311]. Located within a 200 km radius of each other, all of these plants were situated in the Mpumalanga province. Combined, their capacity contribution to the national grid was about 11 000MW, at the time representing nearly one quarter of Eskom's generation capacity.

The planning for the shutdown of these plants was patently out of step with the demand trajectory for electricity in the country. In October 2022, despite persistent bouts of rolling blackouts, the utility proceeded with the permanent shutdown of Komati Power Station. Although the shutdown of the plant was scheduled and anticipated, there appeared to be no flexibility in the decision to do so. By deferring the scheduled shutdown and decommissioning, Eskom could have reduced the intensity of the power cuts nationwide. It angered some critics inside and outside the company, that Eskom was not flexible enough in its decommissioning planning and was, in this instance, contributing to the power crisis—rather than resolving it. The last unit of Komati was one of the better performing units in the Eskom coal-fleet, and the timing of its decommissioning caused further resentment amongst those battling to keep the lights on.

It was alleged that in preparation for the 27th United Nations Climate Change Conference in Sharm El Sheikh, Egypt the following month, former Eskom Group Chief Executive Officer, Andre de Ruyter, needed a 'good-news' story to share and demonstrate Eskom's commitment to cutting greenhouse gas emissions. Sharp criticism toward the utility therefore also came from the Minister of Minerals and Energy, suggesting that Eskom was 'actively agitating for the overthrow of the state' due to the manner in which the utility was dealing with the energy crisis.

In the wake of South Arica's 2022 announcement that it will adopt more ambitious Nationally Determined Carbon Contributions, the decision to continue decommissioning some older power stations was celebrated by champions of the energy transition who wanted to see a faster transition to net zero. However, more pragmatic observers of the energy transition supported a more flexible transition arrangement whereby generating units would only be decommissioned based on energy security considerations.

Delays in Planning, Contracting and Commissioning New State Sponsored Generation

In the early 2000s, South Africa was behind schedule with bringing online new generation units. Due to the fast-diminishing margin between electricity demand and supply—and despite a policy favouring private new investment—by 2004 the government decided that Eskom would be permitted to build new generation plants.

The Medupi, Kusile, and Ingula projects were given the green light by government after long delays in lifting the moratorium on state sponsored investment in large coal-fired generation. The work on the Medupi and Kusile coal-fired plants started immediately thereafter. The rush to get the concept designs finalised and contracts placed, meant that many of the required technical and procurement governance processes were neglected and overruled in order to swiftly register and execute the projects.

Medupi Power Station

Medupi is a 4 800 MW designed coal-fired plant constructed in the Waterberg region of the Limpopo province. The site selection was due to the proximity to the Grootgeluk coal mine, the availability of land in the area, and existing transmission infrastructure. The plant featured Eskom's first supercritical boiler, and the design boasts among the largest dry-cooled power station units in the Eskom fleet—and of its kind in the world.

By 2007, the Medupi project reached financial closure and ground clearing construction work began. The initial schedule indicated that the first unit would commence commercial operations in 2012 and the last unit would be commissioned by 2015[312].

The Medupi project was initially costed at R 69 billion. However, these costs soon escalated when Eskom decided to act as project and contracts manager for the project, rather than award the project to a credible power-construction consortium on a turnkey basis. The completed project more than doubled in cost when incompatible plant systems, defective components, and poor-quality workmanship, were accepted by Eskom on various contracting manufacturing, installation, and services work scopes. The consequences of these adverse outcomes fell on Eskom, the main project contractor and sponsor.

The ANC's investment arm, Chancellor House, obtained US$10 million in payments from Hitachi, the Japanese Multinational company that secured the contract to build the boilers for the Medupi and the Kusile coal-fired plants[313]. At the time, former cabinet member and minister, Valli Moosa, was elected to the chairmanship of Eskom. As a senior appointed member of the ruling party, he also sat on the ANC's Finance Committee, presenting a conflict of interest when considering the payments made indirectly to the ANC for Eskom contracts.

Such conflicts of interests were not sufficiently probed by financiers, notably the World Bank, a major lender to the project. Opponents of the loan in South Africa lobbied against the debt. These included journalist and media houses, opposition parties, environmentalists, as well as business and labour communities. The debt played no small part in the subsequent strain on public finances, since Eskom could not shoulder all its debt obligations and the government frequently had to step in to bail out Eskom.

Although Hitachi was fined by the United States Securities and Exchange Commission for the bribes paid to Chancellor House, due to state capture of law enforcement agencies in South Africa, these institutions were defanged and therefore lacked the political independence and support to hold the ANC, or its investment holding company, to account.

The first completed Medupi generation unit was synchronized to the national grid in March 2015 and the last unit in July 2021. Despite the plant being handed over by its contractors to commence commercial operations, Eskom announced that it would still take many years longer to fix plant defects amounting to an estimated R8 billion.

Therefore, although the units were late in their completion, when they were contractually completed, they still did not operate efficiently according to their specifications and nameplate generation capacities. Despite alleviating some of the load-shedding, the required redesign and retrofits to the generating units required more funding, tapping much needed finances intended for older Eskom units that were also in dire need of refurbishment and maintenance.

In June 2022, the African Development Bank (a lender to the project) announced that the Medupi project would never realise a positive financial return on investment. At a final cost of R 145 billion, significant cost overruns contributed to Eskom's unsustainable debt burden which meant that the future cash flows from the project would never cover the capital costs, the interest payments from the loans on the project, and the continued Operating and Maintenance expenses[314].

Instead of plugging the gap for the much-needed electricity in the country, the project was plagued with technical defects, and the debt on the Medupi project, including the large amounts of interest during construction that the project incurred, remained a millstone for Eskom to bear for many years. The African Development Bank report also stated that, despite a fifty-year projected life, it was expected that in its current form, the project would come under increasing climate change and environmental pressures due to its use of coal, and that the plant was unlikely to see its full projected life until the year 2071.

Kusile Power Station

Like Medupi, the Kusile plant was also beset with large-scale corruption and the project experienced significant cost overruns and completion delays. The knock-on effects of the corruption in the Medupi and Kusile projects therefore had devasting effects on the existing coal fleet. To begin with, less funding was available for operating and maintenance on other power stations. Even when there were funds available to effect repairs at the other older Eskom plants, the low energy availability factors at Medupi and Kusile, meant that fewer opportunities were presented for these older plants to be taken off-line to perform the maintenance and repairs. The lack of sufficient maintenance at these older plants further reduced the performance of these units resulting in lower energy availability factors, and more extensive national power rationing.

Construction at the 4 800 MW Kusile plant started in August 2008 and the first unit was scheduled to reach commercial operations in

2015, with the last of the six units planned to be completed by 2019[315]. By March 2023, due to additional construction delays, it was projected that the last unit would only reach commercial operations in 2025.

The delays in the completion of the units significantly contributed to generation capacity shortages—and subsequently to daily power supply interruptions in South Africa.

Ingula Pumped Storage Hydro Power Station

Construction on the Ingula Pumped Storage Scheme started in 2005. Located between the Free State and Kwa Zulu Natal provinces, the facility comprises of four hydro turbines, each delivering 333 MW. The plant was planned to be operational by 2013 at an initial cost of roughly R 9 billion. However, like other Eskom plants (Medupi and Kusile) constructed at the time, the Ingula plant would run into serious delays and incur huge cost overruns.

In October 2013, during construction of the first unit, six workers died when a working platform failed. A lengthy investigation ensued to determine the causes of the accident and prevent further fatalities at the construction site, contributing to delays in completing unit construction. In 2016, while a contractor was performing commissioning tests, the same unit (where the platform had failed) experienced a fault on the generator. The repairs caused further delays to the completion of the unit.

The unit, scheduled to be operational in 2014, only went operational in August 2016 and the entire facility entered commercial operations in 2017. Eskom weathered much criticism on the project for not managing its contractors' safety practices and the project experienced a number of labour strikes, mainly by the project contractors and their own sub-contractors.

Akin to the Medupi and Kusile plants, the project also had serious allegations of corruption, overspending and irregular expenditure. The final price tag on the project was R 36 billion—four times the initial projected cost—and the project was completed four years after the original scheduled commercial operation date. In 2019, following the plant's completion, it surfaced that the plant was unable to operate at full capacity. It therefore had to be returned to the contractor to resolve the defects. The defects were eventually resolved during the contractual defects period.

The multiple delays incurred on the Ingula project meant that the available energy storage capacity was not available to mitigate the country's power cuts, especially during peak times when electricity demand on the grid was highest.

Nuclear Procurement

In addition to new coal and hydro projects that experienced significant delays due to inadequate linkages between generation planning and plant commercial operations, Eskom also had plans to build more nuclear capacity.

Nuclear 1

In 2007, after Eskom was given the green light for the development of additional generation capacity, the Eskom board approved a plan to double electricity output by 2025. This included the development of 20 000 MW of new nuclear capacity, which would be developed over twenty years[316]. The nuclear expansion plan would start with roughly 4 000 MW of Pressurized Water Reactor technology. Five coastal sites were initially assessed for siting the first new-build plant. In the end, it came down to two potential sites. The Koeberg site was a strong contender, where Eskom already had 1 800 MW of operating nuclear generation. The Koeberg site had also been earmarked for the demonstration modular reactor that South Africa was developing at the time. The other potential location was the Thyspunt site in the Eastern Cape province.

In January 2008, nuclear contractors Areva and Westinghouse submitted bids for the new-build project. Later that year, citing financial constraints, Eskom announced that it would no longer follow through with the stated nuclear procurement 'due to the magnitude of the investment'[317]. While the costs associated with the bids remain undisclosed, it is noteworthy that at the time similar international construction projects by Areva and Westinghouse were delayed and experienced cost overruns in the countries where they were developed.

Without the financial support from its shareholder (i.e., the government), and with the company's balance sheet faltering from the financial debt impacts of the Medupi, Kusile, and Ingula new builds, the utility had little fiscal headroom for any new large-scale generation investments. Also, the effects of the global financial crisis were starting to be felt all over the world as capital markets were tightening their criteria on debt instruments. In addition, the country and Eskom was preparing for hosting the 2010 Soccer World Cup and a new generation project would be another distraction to hosting a successful event. Lastly, the ruling ANC was dealing with intense internal party factions, which along with other collateral damage saw ousted president, Thabo Mbeki, becoming a casualty of political squabbles. Against this backdrop, and with the country's general elections set for the following year, politicians were more focused on these developments than the proposition of a contentious investment in nuclear.

Russian Procurement?

After successful elections for the ANC in 2009, the ambitions of investment in new nuclear capacity persisted. About a year after the country's fourth national democratic elections, the prospects of investment in nuclear generation assets were revived with the country's Integrated Resource Plan (edition 2010), which made provision for more nuclear capacity. In November 2011, a National Nuclear Energy Executive Coordination Committee was established for decision-making, monitoring, and oversight of the nuclear programme. In 2012, Minister of Energy, Dipuo Peters, announced that South Africa would procure 9 600 MW of new nuclear capacity. The minister's ambitions were to increase local manufacturing of specialised nuclear components, to re-establish the country as a nuclear fuel manufacturer and usher in a new era of nuclear industrialisation in South Africa[318]. This announcement was followed by an Integrated Nuclear Infrastructure Review by the International Atomic Energy Agency in 2013[319].

Russia's State Nuclear Energy Corporation, Rosatom, signalled its interest in bidding for the new nuclear build programme. In September 2014, Rosatom signed an agreement with the Nuclear Energy Company of South Africa (another state-owned company) to develop a strategic partnership with financial assistance from Russia. The strategic partnership would cover nuclear power plants and waste management, including the construction of Russian VVER reactors totalling 9 600 MW. Up to eight nuclear power generation units would be constructed on a Build-Own-Operate Basis[320].

With affirmed new state sponsored domestic interest in nuclear expansion, French, Chinese and South Korean contractors were positioning themselves for what would be the largest nuclear procurement in South African history. In February 2015, in his state of the nation address, former President Jacob Zuma, announced that the Request for Proposal would be issued later that year and that the strategic partner would be announced by the following year. Many delays were experienced by the nuclear procurement effort, not least the difficulty of finding a finance minister that would financially commit South Africa to a nuclear procurement agreement.

Over four days in December 2015, President Jacob Zuma went through no less than three Ministers of Finance reportedly to keep the nuclear deal on track. The president's actions, purportedly signalling his preference to enter into nuclear procurement with the Russian government, led to significantly increased scrutiny from public watchdogs and resulted in mounting opposition to the nuclear transaction. Opposition to the nuclear procurement was due to two main features. The first was that the deal was rumoured to be more than one trillion rand, which if true, could have made the deal prohibitively costly (depending on how the transaction would be structured). Second were allegations of corruption, as it appeared that the Russians were favoured due to their close ties to the ruling ANC, and President Jacob Zuma[321].

In April 2017, in a highly contested court battle between non-governmental organisations, Southern African Faith Communities' Environmental Institute and Earthlife Africa, and the Ministry of

Energy, the Western Cape High Court set aside agreements with contesting countries, including Russia, South Korea, and the USA. The court also declared invalid the approvals by the National Energy Regulator of South Africa (NERSA) for the ministerial determinations concerning the procurement of 9 600 MW of nuclear capacity[322].

The court found evidence of favouring Russian suppliers—unlike the relatively vague agreements concluded with the other supplier countries, the Russian agreement contained more detail. The Russian agreement specifically committed South Africa to build nuclear plants using Russian VVER technology and set out a timeframe for the execution of the nuclear expansion programme. It also indemnified Russian suppliers of adverse outcomes. The court further found that former Energy Minister, Tina Joemat-Petterston, had committed an error in approving the go-ahead for the procurement deal. The terms of the deal would place incommensurate liabilities on South Africa and very little on the supplier country.

The court ruled that NERSA failed to allow public participation, in accordance with its legislative mandate, and the ministerial determination for the 9 6000 MW new-build program in South Africa was therefore set aside. The court case raised pertinent issues concerning the role of government as policy maker; the powers of the energy minister in approving determinations for additional electricity capacity; the separation of powers between the executive, the energy regulator, parliament, and the judiciary; and the processes followed in energy planning, procurement, and contracting.

In February 2018 Jacob Zuma resigned, replaced by Cyril Ramaphosa. By August of that year the government announced that it had abandoned its plans for the 9 600 MW of nuclear generation. In the updated Integrated Resource Plan issued in 2019, the government did however make provision for the 20-year life extension of Koeberg Nuclear Power Station, as well 2 500 MW of new nuclear generation. In 2021, taking the lessons from the previous round of failed procurement, the government announced that it would contract a professional service provider to help craft a framework for the procurement of the 2 500 MW of nuclear capacity catered for in the Integrated Resource Plan (edition 2019)[323].

Careful not to have too big ambitions as it did with the previous two failed attempts of nuclear procurement, the government assured South Africans that nuclear generation would continue 'only on a scale and pace the country can afford'. The government did not clarify what this statement meant. With the concurrence from NERSA received in 2023, the Minister of Minerals and Energy was closer to the announcement of the Request for Proposal for the 2 500 MW of new nuclear capacity.

New Gas Generation

In January 2022, Eskom followed through on a provision, in accordance with the Integrated Resource Plan (edition 2019), for the development of a 3 000 MW gas plant in Richards Bay, in the province of Kwa Zulu Natal. Civil society groups opposed the project, citing inadequate gas supply and infrastructure. The project was further opposed by environmental groups, who stated that there was important and relevant information missing from the application, and that there had been insufficient public engagement[324].

A controversial clause in the IRP provision for the plant mandated Eskom to buy the gas from another state-owned entity. Eskom's view was that it should be able to purchase the gas at the correct quality and at the least cost from any supplier if Eskom's conditions are met—and therefore the clause should not be an unnecessary obligation.

In addition to the stalling of the project due to civil society opposition and controversial gas provision clauses, during the time that lapsed between the ministerial determination and the NERSA approval, the finance minister agreed to take on a substantial portion of Eskom's debt. This agreement was subject to the utility taking on no further loans for generation investment for three years.

Due to this prohibition from the National Treasury, Eskom subsequently reported that it would no longer be permitted to finance the project off its own balance sheet. This would mean that the project would have to assume a different ownership model, or the National Treasury would have to reconsider the conditions placed on the Eskom debt bill. Although the development of gas generation was allocated to Eskom, bailout conditions imposed by the Finance Ministry effectively torpedoed Eskom's chances of developing the project.

This stalled the project planning beyond any delays envisioned by the IRP (2019 edition). In accordance with the country Integrated Resource Plan, the first 1 000 MW of gas generation should have been commissioned in 2023. However, in 2023 the license approval to develop a gas plant was still pending.

New Independent Power Producer Connection Delays

Delays in getting state-owned generators supplying power to the grid significantly contributed to the country's power crisis. Preceding chapters have provided insights on the difficulties experienced by IPPs. When sufficient generation is not available, often countries revert to stop gap measures to temporarily deal with droughts or other emergent issues which may have an adverse impact on available generation reserves. The case of the Karpowerships previously discussed was a good example of a risk mitigation power procurement measure that experienced more delays than was initially estimated.

In July 2020, as the country was experiencing severe energy shortages, the Ministry of Minerals and Energy announced that it would procure 2 000 MW of electricity from various generation technologies under the Risk Mitigation programme. Due to the *urgent nature* of the procurement, this special programme would only permit projects that were *near-ready*. For this reason, only projects that could deliver electricity output *as soon as possible*, were permitted to bid.

The projects were earmarked to start producing electricity by June 2023. While many bids were accepted, there was significant controversy around the bid from Karpowerships, as described in Chapter 11. Despite an expedited emergency procurement round to rapidly deal with acute problems of insufficient generation, this project was stalled for much longer than some projects that were not considered as emergency risk mitigation procurement. The example of the risk mitigation gas IPP involving Karpowerships illustrates how *urgent* procurement can also be significantly delayed, despite its relative higher priority and importance.

In South Africa, many other privately sponsored power projects also experienced significant delays before the final approvals were obtained for their implementation. Many applications never received approvals—and were outright cancelled. Often, where private electricity generation could readily be developed to feed into the national grid, approvals from government departments were slow to allow Eskom to follow through on decisions to buy more power from private power producers.

In 2022, a National Electricity Crisis Committee was established in the Office of the Presidency to represent all affected government departments (including Eskom) to develop and implement a plan to resolve the persistent power cuts. The high-level committee had representation from the Minister in the Office of the Presidency, the department of Mineral Resources and Energy, the department of Public Enterprises, the department of Finance, the department of Forestry, Fisheries and the Environment and the department of Trade, Industry and Competition, amongst others[325].

One of the committee's first tasks was to determine whether the contracting of generation projects in the planning phases could in any way be accelerated. The bureaucratic process of licensing was cited as a significant obstacle to timely connection of generation capacity to the grid. The National Electricity Crisis Committee determined the extent to which the registration process could be streamlined and the delays in licensing of renewable IPPs could be reduced. The Committee found that it could take up to 1 000 days to obtain the necessary permits before renewable energy construction could be started[326].

While many of these plants eventually came online, there were often problems with various aspects of their development, as described previously. This translated into significant time lags between the initial planned operations dates and the actual date when the plants eventually entered commercial operations. While the aphorism 'better late than never' was often the sentiment, worse were the situations where the plants never came online, since it meant that there was no relief from the rolling blackouts.

Existing Coal Plant – Emissions

As detailed in previous Chapters, even when there was installed generation capacity, Eskom coal-fired units were prohibited from operating because they did not adhere to national emissions requirements. A study conducted by the Centre for Research on Energy and Clean Air, concluded that approximately 80 000 people risk dying prematurely from related air pollution illnesses if Eskom continued to operate its coal-fired fleet without meeting emissions standards[327].

In 2022, in a suit filed by environmental justice groups, a High Court ruled that the air quality in the Mpumalanga Highveld Priority area (which included many of Eskom's coal-fired power plants, Sasol's coal-to-liquid fuel refinery, and other coal mining operations) was so poor that it breached the threshold for the constitutional right to an environment that was not damaging to health and well-being. The court had found that there was an unreasonable delay in giving effect to the emissions regulations[328].

In accordance with the country's National Environmental Management Air Quality Act, Eskom's coal and liquid fuel-fired power stations must meet specified Minimum Emission Standards. Over the years, Eskom submitted various applications to the Department of Fisheries, Forestry, and the Environment to have these minimum emission standards relaxed for some of its units, to have the limits suspended for other units, and still for other units to have the emission limits waived until their decommissioning.

Even with these concessions, Eskom often found itself in the situation where it could not meet the relaxed requirements and units were shut down. This further worsened the power shortages. In many cases the units were simply too old to financially justify the capital costs associated with meeting the minimum emissions limits. Many plants were scheduled to be decommissioned—economically it made little sense to invest in costly equipment that would only operate for a few more years, especially when the company was short of financial resources.

Environmental groups argued that knowingly agreeing to allow unhealthy air quality conditions, where it was clear that affected communities would die of stochastic health effects, would be homicidal. Eskom was therefore under constant pressure to implement plans to reduce emissions. Many of the waivers were set to expire in 2025 when various coal-fired units were scheduled to be decommissioned. However, given the power shortages, it appears that the utility would have to request further exemptions or repair equipment for emissions reductions, if sufficient new generation plants are not brought online in a timely manner.

Planning for existing plants to remain operational has therefore also been shown to be problematic due to public health and environmental considerations. When plants have to be shut down for these important reasons, it hampers planning flexibility and further contributes to the problems of insufficient electricity generation.

Maintenance Planning and Scheduling of Generation Units

Even where existing capacity was readily available with no emissions constraints, the inability to execute the proper maintenance on the existing coal fleet resulted in a decrease in available electricity generation. The deterioration in the performance of these generation units could not be easily arrested. In the financial year ending March 2022, close to a third of Eskom's coal-fired units that required comprehensive maintenance could not be overhauled in accordance with their comprehensive maintenance scopes mainly due to insufficient funds and cash flow constraints[329]. The maintenance of these generation units was therefore postponed, ushering the utility into another year of unreliable coal-fired generation.

Nuclear Life Extension

While plant equipment life extensions to limit emissions were not economically feasible at some of the utility's coal-fired units, there were some generating units where life extensions could be economically justified.

Given the challenges of getting greenfield baseload projects going, where possible Eskom sought to extend the life of existing generation units. The Koeberg Nuclear Power Station, situated in the Western Cape has generally been one of Eskom's most reliable plants. It was also considered the most affordable baseload plant in the Eskom fleet. Its capital had already been depreciated—and significantly lower fuel costs, its low-carbon footprint, as well as its reasonable Operating and Maintenance costs, made this plant an ideal candidate for life extension. The two-unit Pressurised Water Reactor (PWR) plant entered commercial operations in the mid-1980s, and its design was based on the Westinghouse and Framatome 900 MW reference, with three steam generators per unit.

In 2008, it was realised that the Koeberg steam generators may not be able last for the 40-year plant design life. Many PWR plants worldwide had started to replace their steam generators before the end of their projected design lives. A project feasibility study was initiated to replace the steam generators. Due to the significant cost associated with the steam generator replacement and to make the investment bankable, in 2010 the Eskom board approved the investment decision to replace the steam generators and perform further work to extend the life of the plant by an additional 20 years. The steam generators would initially be replaced by the year 2015.

The American and Japanese-owned Westinghouse as well as French-owned Areva, both submitted bids for the steam generator replacement project under three separate design, manufacture, and installation, packages. Westinghouse was recommended to be awarded some of the contracts in 2011 and again in 2013. However, in a turn of events, in August 2014, Eskom announced that the entire contract suite would be awarded to Areva[330].

Westinghouse mounted a court challenge, citing irregularities in the tender process at the highest level—the Eskom Board Tender Committee. In 2022, during the Zondo Commission Inquiry into state capture, it was revealed that Board Tender Committees were established at SOEs mainly to ensure that tenders were granted to companies linked to politically connected individuals.

While Westinghouse was first in line for certain tender packages, the board tender committee, headed by Eskom (Acting) Group Chief Executive Officer, Colin Matjila, overturned the decision and awarded the entire contract to Areva[331]. The board tender committee apparently favoured a single contract, ostensibly based on Eskom's construction experience at Medupi Power Station, where the company struggled to integrate different project work scopes from multiple contractors[332].

Westinghouse Belgium challenged the contract award. It lost its challenge in the High Court but won the appeal in the Supreme Court of Appeal. The dispute was ended in the Constitutional Court, when the court found, on a technicality, that Westinghouse Belgium did not have the locus standi to bring the action to the court and that it should have been Westinghouse USA. The final court judgement was given in December 2016, a year after the project should have been completed, paving the way for the project to commence the design, manufacture, license, and installation of the six steam generators.

The date for the steam generator replacement was therefore postponed to 2018. Due to various delays in the project, steam generator replacements were finally scheduled on the first unit in 2023, a year before the plant's nuclear operating licence was set to expire. The delays in steam generator procurement had a significant impact on the time available for Eskom to prepare for the plant's life extension.

Beyond IRP 2019 and Beyond 2030

While Eskom is able to mitigate the impact of future power outages by extending the lives of the Koeberg units, many of the company's large baseload coal-fired units are scheduled for decommissioning by 2034. Given the time required to replace large dispatchable base-load plant, the future prospects for generation sufficiency are perplexing.

According to the Integrated Resource Plan (edition 2019), 22 000 MW of Eskom coal-fired fleet could be retired by 2034. Insufficient new generation projects have been comprehensively planned for the replacement of this capacity. The Integrated Resource Plan (edition 2019) assumes a low electricity growth scenario. Implicit in that assumption is the likelihood of an uncoupling between electricity growth and economic growth. If this assumption turns out to be false, the prospects for future loadshedding could be worse.

The Integrated Resource Plan (edition 2019) also has embedded assumptions of improved plant availability figures for the existing coal fleet as well as good availability factors for the newly built Medupi and Kusile plants. The energy availability factor of the coal fleet was 55 percent (in 2022) against an assumption of 71 percent (for 2022) in the Integrated Resource Plan (edition 2019). The availability of Medupi and Kusile was approximately 65 percent (in 2022) against an assumption of 83 percent (for 2022) in the Integrated Resource Plan (edition 2019). The 2022 and 2023 plant availability factors for Medupi and Kusile were extremely low when compared with the original Eskom requirement of 92 percent two years after commencing commercial operations.

Considering that the Medupi, Kusile, and Ingula new-build decisions was made in 2004—and assuming that the last of Kusile's units are operational in 2024, it would likely take Eskom approximately 20 years to connect approximately 10 GW of new generation capacity onto the national grid.

The development of these projects has come at great financial, social, and economic cost—not to mention the immense controversy. It is therefore hard to consider that the equivalent of 22 000 MW of replacement generation production capacity (required over the next decade) could be developed, unless the pace and scale of planning, procurement and contracting, is significantly intensified.

Complementing Renewables with Dispatchable Generation

While the focus has been getting more renewable energy generation online, the same intensity to getting the renewables reliably integrated in the grid by balancing these intermittent technologies with dispatchable gas has been less impressive. Also, the planning for adequate supply provisions of future primary fuels such as gas or diesel has also been slow.

Due to the addition of intermittent renewable energy, dispatchable gas plants are required to make up for the intermittency of renewable plants. There have been many independent renewable plants that have been added to the grid. However, the difficulties with getting a commensurate amount of gas generation connected could be problematic in the future if the ratio of intermittent renewable energy is not proportionately complemented with adequate generation storage capacity and dispatchable plants. The challenges with commissioning gas generation are due to certain stakeholders opposing related licensing permits for new gas plants for reasons such as high costs, increased carbon emissions, broader environmental and societal impacts, and the potential for corruption.

The Integrated Resource Plan (edition 2019) acknowledges that the unavailability of domestic gas resources poses a risk to energy security. Coupled with the lack of domestic gas is the foreign exchange risk associated with gas imports—should gas plants be built to partially replace decommissioned dispatchable coal capacity.

Development of gas infrastructure expansion in South Africa has proved to be a difficult prospect due to the guarantees required from developers and the insufficient number of long-term and creditworthy bulk off-takers. Given the uncertainty with the future technology generation mix and reform trajectory, the momentum to establish a large gas industry in South Africa has been slow. If gas demand for power generation is too low, it could potentially diminish the profitability for developers of gas infrastructure.

Significant variances in expected gas supply and actual demand could have adverse outcomes on a future gas sector and on future electricity prices. Significant over—or under—demand estimations could have adverse consequences for suppliers and developers of gas infrastructure, consequences for the profitability of gas-to-power producers, as well as consequences for electricity tariffs if gas supply risks to suppliers and developers are priced in.

In 2023, the Integrated Resource Plan (edition 2019) was still the official version even though, in many respects, it was no longer reflective of the power sector realities. New editions of the IRP have not yet been released at the frequency which could timeously consider evolving assumptions such as the tempo at which new generation plants are being implemented, or Eskom's Energy Availability Factors for its generation fleet.

Integrated Electricity Planning

With the addition of renewable generation resources, due its intermittency and its lower energy availability factors, renewable generation requires at least two to three times the electricity generation replacement volume in MWh to displace the equivalent traditional dispatchable power – assuming storage arrangements are optimal. This means that transmission grid planning iterations must become more extensive and frequent than under historical grid planning scenarios which had mostly dispatchable coal and gas fired plants.

The lack of sufficient grid capacity in transmission (in favourable renewable energy locations) has meant that many renewable energy IPPs could not be signed on due to grid constraints, as detailed in Chapter 11. The focus on increasing utility-scale renewable generation more at the high voltage transmission level and less at the low voltage distribution level (especially for solar PV) meant that fewer connections for renewables were available. This has delayed the onboarding of sufficient renewable generation, largely owing to insufficient incentives at the Distribution level for industrial, commercial, and residential generation.

Due to the potential loss of sales, few distributors or municipalities are incentivised to permit greater amounts of self-generation for industrial, commercial, and residential customers. Many municipalities have also been ill-equipped (technically and financially) to permit expansion in distributed generation. In order to meet national electricity demand, it is thus expected that in future more utility-scale generators will connect to the grid at the transmission level. The funding for future transmission grid expansions therefore must match projected future demand for renewable energy generator grid connections. In addition, funding must also be allocated for projects to stabilise the grid (such as battery storage and other ancillary services), during the transition to lower carbon electricity production technologies.

Imports from Neighbouring Countries

Regional Power Projects have been considered, such as a power offtake arrangement from the Inga Hydro project in the Democratic Republic of Congo. After South Africa signed a Treaty for its commitment to buy at least 2 500 MW from the project, the Integrated Resource Plan was updated to reflect this commitment. However, due to political instability in the region and the distance of the hydro generation from its potential off-takers, despite its low carbon feature this project has struggled to gain the kind of backing that could make it a serious contender for regional power purchases and electricity integration.

For many years Mozambique has also been keen to obtain an anchor customer for another hydro-electric project. South Africa, however, has been slow with negotiations to purchase more Mozambican hydro power, favouring domestic sources instead. The two proposed Mozambican electricity generating projects—a second hydro plant at Cahora Bassa, and a new dam at Mphanda Nkua, further downstream from Cahora Bassa—have therefore been delayed for many years on account of the lack of a firm buyer for the electricity that these generation plants would produce. While Mozambican officials felt that Eskom could be the anchor off-taker that would give the projects a boost, South Africa has displayed little interest in buying more power from Mozambique as a means to mitigate South Africa's energy crisis—presumably due to potential long-term energy security, high energy costs, and contractual concerns.

Financial Planning and Modelling

Historically, Eskom has financed large capital programmes for generation and transmission with retained earnings and the issuing of its own bonds. Eskom has since lost its investment rating and access to traditional capital markets has been reduced for both Eskom and South Africa. With the utility and the sovereign having been allocated junk bond status by the three major investment ratings agencies, traditional access to affordable sources of capital has dried up. With Eskom being technically bankrupt and partially dependent on government bailouts and government guarantees for loans, it means that the speed at which Eskom can arrange for financing and execute capital expansion projects has significantly slowed down. South African pension funds have limited their exposures to Eskom debt, leaving Eskom to deal with a host of different development financing institutions for its funding requirements.

This has meant that Eskom had to deal with far more financial institutions than it had to deal with in the past when the company issued its own bonds. Sovereign donor nations, development banks, export credit agencies, and other bilateral and multilateral financial institutions, each have their own requirements that have to be achieved before funding can be approved and accessed.

Instead of using its own consistent process of raising capital in the form of bonds (as it did decades earlier), Eskom subsequently had to use individual processes for each of the bilateral and multilateral funding institutions from which funding was sought. Coupled with the need for domestic National Treasury approvals, the increased complexity of obtaining finance has had a significant slowing down on the speed at which decisions can be made and plans can be executed. The effect on timeously bringing on board new capacity has been dealt a blow. Furthermore, the ability to shore up sufficient generation for energy security has been hampered, not least by the commitment required by some donor governments and development finance institutions to shut down old coal-fired generation plants before funding can be accessed.

Inadequate frameworks for generation planning, procurement, and contracting have been at the heart of the delays in getting existing and new capacity reliably supplying the grid. The foundations of this weakness were first laid by undecided power sector reforms, and then later by the energy transition. Delayed decisions to build new plants (Medupi, Kusile and Ingula), resulted in a deficit in generation capacity for many years when the construction and commissioning of these plants were further delayed. Thereafter, given the location of renewable energy natural resources and its remoteness to traditional electricity loads, the South African transmission network was ill-suited for rapid deployment of renewable generation.

Even though the private sector can play a significant role in alleviating the burden of providing sufficient generation, it still requires state-owned institutions to operate in tandem for the achievement of stated objectives. While South Africa has experienced a relatively successful renewable energy IPP programme, greenfield coal-fired IPPs did not register any successes in entering the generation sector and assisting with electricity generation supply, despite the country's IRP advocating for their inclusion.

The resultant delays in onboarding sufficient electricity generation underscored the shallow, haphazard, and excessively simplified assumptions that were made in the indicative electricity generation planning phases, as directed in the country's high-level Integrated Resource Plans. Before and during the energy transition, risk management and change management processes failed to adequately identify and satisfactorily manage the critical linkages that existed between high-level electricity planning and the commencement of commercial operations. These included detailed transmission and generation planning, licensing and permit authorisations, public participation, as well as procurement and construction, to ensure timely generation of electricity. This effectively exacerbated the problems of insufficient electricity generation in South Africa.

PART VI

SYNTHESIS AND CONCLUSION

UNDERSTANDING INSUFFICIENT GENERATION

CHAPTER 14

THE ANATOMY OF LOADSHEDDING IN SOUTH AFRICA – A SYNOPSIS

The performance of the power sector has significantly deteriorated, despite a well-functioning Generation sector inherited by the newly democratically elected government in 1994. Attracting adequate generation investment on competitive and sustainable terms has progressively grown into a formidable challenge. Notwithstanding the 1998 policy document signalling the move towards competitive power markets in accordance with the standard model of power sector reform, private investment did not immediately materialise. Reform momentum was inhibited by policy hesitation on the part of the government, electricity tariffs that were well-below the investment cost for new generation, and a strong belief by the ruling party that dominant state-led development was important for the achievement of national socio-economic objectives.

Many years after the government's initial policy decision on power sector liberalisation in 1998, the introduction of private sector participation in Generation started in earnest in 2011. This was spurred more by the proponents of the imperative to decarbonise through renewable energy than any deep impulse to privatise the power sector. Private sector investment in generation, however, has not kept up with consumer electricity demand. The decline in the operational performance of the state-owned utility has contributed to insufficient electricity being available to satisfy consumer demand. Despite plans in 1998 to put the power sector on a sustainable reform trajectory, more than 25 years after the policy reform prescription, there have been insufficient reform steps taken to move the power sector towards the intended and desired policy outcomes. Competition amongst state-owned and private generators in a wholesale competitive power market, as described in Chapter 3 of this book, has not materialised.

Instead, what has emerged in South Africa—and elsewhere on the continent—is a hybrid arrangement where the incumbent SOE has retained a dominant market position while IPPs have been introduced on the fringes. How power sectors in developing countries have evolved to accommodate IPPs, as described in this book, offers an important opportunity to critically evaluate and synthesise the lessons learnt from power sector reform in South Africa and to identify the specific challenges associated with attracting new investment. Given the state of the South Africa's power sector—low tariffs, poor performance of state-owned utilities, imprudent planning regimes, poor revenue collection rates, and a weak generation investment climate buoyed only by government guarantees—the transition towards a competitive power market continues to pose a challenge.

This book has sought to appraise the hurdles and pitfalls utility SOEs and IPPs face in meeting the objective of providing adequate electricity generation. The main issues addressed have been as follows: the extent to which the emergence of hybrid electricity markets have created new challenges in attracting investment into generation capacity; how policy, regulatory, and institutional frameworks have frustrated investment in generation; and how planning and contracting challenges have contributed to the problem of insufficient generation capacity. The book has further considered how to respond more effectively to these challenges faced by hybrid electricity generation markets.

This chapter has three primary goals. Firstly, it gives a brief recap of generation investments in South Africa. Secondly, it integrates the analysis of power sector reform, the management of state-owned generators, the emergence of IPPs, and the challenges of attracting new investment, in South Africa. By revisiting and summarising key aspects of the experiences in the South African power sector, general conclusions are drawn around the specific challenges that arise from the hybrid power market arrangements in relation to attracting new investment. Additional conclusions are drawn about how these challenges might be overcome. Lastly, this chapter returns to the overall theoretical framework for the book outline first introduced at the end of Chapter 2 and aims to extend the frontiers of our understanding of the nature of hybrid markets in relation to the conundrum of insufficient generation capacity.

An Analysis of Factors Contributing to Insufficient Generation

A common theme that emerges from the analyses of African power sectors is the failure of hybrid power markets to deal effectively with timely and efficient procurement of new power. A number of functions which used to be undertaken by state-owned utilities have fallen between the cracks and are either neglected or performed inadequately. This section summarises the generation planning, procurement, and contracting challenges for hybrid markets.

Generation Planning in Hybrid Markets

The purpose of explicit, comprehensive, and detailed electricity planning in the power sector is to develop clear strategies to guard against both over-capacity and under-capacity. Over-capacity can result in consumers paying for generation capacity they do not need, whereas under-capacity can result in consumers not being supplied with adequate electricity when needed. There are a multitude of forecast inputs required for generation planning. Coupled with the number of hurdles that have to be successfully negotiated even before a power station is constructed, the potential for getting the planning wrong is significant.

Many who operate at the decision-making level are often confronted with optimal generation plant mix decisions, as well as problems related to securing adequate financial resources for investment, realigning tariff structures to accommodate generation expansions, and negative consumer reaction to the upward adjustment of tariffs. Despite these challenges, generation expansion planning remains essential, especially during power sector transitions.

In the past, incumbent state-owned power utilities generally assumed near-complete responsibility for generation expansion planning. Because Eskom was generally run by engineers, the tendency was to plan conservatively—to build more capacity than was needed to ensure that the lights never went out. This was in part informed by previous experience when Eskom was not sufficiently conservative, which resulted in insufficient electricity generation to meet consumer demand.

In some periods during its more than 100-year existence, Eskom also got it wrong when its conservatism resulted in excess generation capacity. Eskom subsequently ran into financial difficulties. Investment costs were high, and tariffs had to be increased substantially to offset the required new investment.

Not learning from the past, the ANC government made some of the same mistakes that was made by the previous government in the 1970s. The year 2007 saw inadequate electricity generation being available and the government eventually allowed Eskom to build new plants and invited IPPs to assist Eskom with providing more generation capacity. Power sector policy reforms paved the way for IPPs to enter the generation market so that private investment could supplement Eskom's efforts.

However, under this hybrid market arrangement, it often became unclear who should be responsible for future generation expansion planning and project development. Would the private sector, or 'the market', simply respond to needs for more power? What would be the role of planning if market forces would be the determinants for future investment? If a competitive market was not developed, who would step in and invest? If traditional supply-side generation planning was still necessary and important, who was responsible for this function—the utility, the electricity regulator, or the government? And if the government takes over this function, would it have the capacity and expertise to undertake timely, flexible, detailed, and relevant integrated electricity planning?

With the introduction of IPPs, planning also needed to take into consideration a host of additional legal and financial issues—for Eskom and the Ministry of Minerals and Energy. Private finance assesses risk conservatively and comprehensively, often factoring in additional security and other risk mitigation measures. In addition, with IPPs the required linkages between planning and investment call for a different approach.

Previously, Eskom undertook planning, investment, and procurement. Now, in a hybrid market, the government (and sometimes also Eskom) would undertake generation expansion planning – this combined approach requires that explicit processes are in place to procure private investment. With the generation planning that occurred to bring onboard increasing amounts of renewables for the energy transition, the specific mandates of other entities in South Africa also responsible for planning similarly evolved—and responsibilities for power sector planning became opaque. This includes mandates for entities such as the Presidential Panel on Climate Change who direct planning for the achievement of net zero emissions, and the National Planning Commission who deal with cross-sectoral economic planning. Consequently, generation planning in the power sector has been elevated to a level of complexity different to what utilities like Eskom were used to a few decades earlier before private sector involvement.

Evolving Planning Frameworks

The evolution in generation planning in South Africa resulted in planning mandates becoming unclear. In 1998, when Eskom was prohibited from adding new capacity due to the intended power sector reforms, this brought about a change in planning accountability. Eskom no longer had sole responsibility for planning and the Ministry of Minerals and Energy became the new *de jure* custodian of the country's Integrated Resource Planning function. However, while Eskom performed detailed power sector planning prior to signaled reforms, the mandate of the Ministry of Minerals and Energy was limited to high level or indicative planning. Apart from indicating the size, type and timing of generation capacity needed in the power sector in the Integrated Resource Plan (IRP), the energy ministry had no obligation, nor mandate, to take infrastructure development beyond this high-level planning phase.

The Ministry of Minerals and Energy administers the processes for IPPs to enter the power sector. However, administering Eskom Transmission expansion does not fall within the ambit of the ministry's stated functions. Consequently, planning, within the scope of the Ministry of Minerals and Energy, has not been extended to include preparations for ensuring that sufficient renewable generation IPPs could indeed be connected to the transmission grid, or ensuring that financial, legal, and environmental requirements would be achieved.

In many instances, planning within the South African context was shown to be unrealistic with timelines that did not take into consideration the real challenges of the related planning and execution functions in developing generation projects. Various examples of Eskom generation projects (such as Medupi, Kusile and Ingula) that took two to three times longer to bring to fruition, signaled the mismatch between planning and credible project execution.

Procurement of generation capacity from IPPs is significantly different to that traditionally procured by Eskom. Each entity (state-owned and private) was allowed to follow procurement routes that differed substantially. This left the door wide open to irregularities and inconsistencies in the procurement processes and impacted on the efficiency and timeliness of generation procurement. While Eskom's support was needed to connect IPPs, Eskom's reluctance to sign the PPAs over a few years (2015 to 2019), and its failure to provide for physical IPP grid connections defeated the intentions of the Ministry of Minerals and Energy to timeously bring IPPs online.

The South African planning outcomes parallels with the experiences in other African power sectors that have transferred their generation planning functions to new institutions. Many African countries have also experienced new problems in ensuring timely and effective procurement of additional capacity under hybrid arrangements. The propensity for certain aspects of planning risks being missed—or falling through the cracks—increases with extensive reforms and subsequent reshuffling of responsibilities among sectoral institutions. Such lapses occur especially where insufficient consideration is given to how the planning, procurement and contracting processes unfold under new institutional arrangements. South Africa is a prime example of how institutional frameworks and planning arrangements have failed to respond adequately to hybrid market needs.

It should be noted that the institutional frameworks and transitional planning arrangements were instituted with the intent of evolving to the standard reform model —to a fully unbundled, privatised, and competitive wholesale power market—and not necessarily to a hybrid market arrangement. However, instead of a transitional step towards the standard reform model, the hybrid model has become the reality and perhaps even the *'end state'*.

When the end state of reform is not reached, hybrid markets present very specific challenges regarding generation planning. Not only does clear institutional responsibility need to be allocated, but the linkages between planning, investment, and procurement of new generation plants need to be explicit. Strong state and political leadership are still crucial to ensure that state-owned utilities such as Eskom work positively with the state to achieve national goals and objectives—especially when the steps towards fully competitive power markets have not been realised.

Flexibility in Generation Planning

Power sector planning requires a significant degree of flexibility to make provision for unexpected issues which can emerge and delay the provision of electricity services. Contingency provisions must therefore be retained as options to assist in periods when setbacks challenge security of supply. In South Africa the number of coal, gas, nuclear, and renewable generation plants that never materialised beyond the planning stages demonstrates the difficulty in planning, procuring and contracting generation projects when there are multiple constraints.

Since the rolling blackouts started in 2007, South Africa has had more generation power projects in the planning phases than its total installed generation capacity. Put differently, South Africa would have more than doubled its installed generation capacity, if all the planned generation projects were fully developed and executed. Given its low success rate in bringing projects to completion, it is easy to appreciate the approach that the government has taken, i.e., to increase the number of planned projects in the face of high attrition.

Increasing the *shots at goal,* however, doesn't necessarily translate to *scoring the goals.* While this approach may increase the chances of adding generation capacity, the benefit of a more carefully crafted and targeted approach with fewer projects may hold greater potential for securing increased investment. This is true especially for its dispatchable generation—coal, gas, and nuclear projects. A more focused and systematic approach would serve to dislodge the 'hit-or-miss' experiences observed. The public display of its seeming inability to bring projects to completion does decidedly more harm than good to the country's reputation as an attractive destination for infrastructure investment. More planned projects were cancelled than were developed, thereby sending an unfavourable signal to the investment community.

The flexibility of having many projects that can be onboarded as a risk mitigation measure for other projects that were not materialised therefore did not work well in South Africa. A good example was the Karpowerships gas-to-power project, where in spite of the project being specifically fast-tracked under the risk mitigation bidding round, the project experienced multiple delays.

Historically, South Africa has used its excess capacity to export to neighbouring countries. The dwindling excess export capacity to South Africa's neighbours provided insufficient signals that the country was in trouble and that it would no longer have sufficient generation reserves. Even though Mozambique had domestic gas, there was insufficient progress made with the Mozambican utility to supply electricity from gas, especially when there was resistance to gas

IPPs in South Africa. A gas-to-power IPP based in Mozambique with South Africa as an off-taker may have faced similar resistance from environmental protestors. However, neighbouring countries could have benefited from supplying South Africa with electricity to stem the power crisis, albeit with fossil fuels, to create a mutually favourable energy security situation for the region and foster further regional integration. Such arrangements could have created some flexibility for South Africa to better weather the storm against loadshedding.

Flexibility can be achieved in various ways and Eskom did enter into interruptible load contracts with many large electricity consumers. These are contracts whereby large energy users (such as smelters) voluntarily reduce their power consumption when there is too little generation available, in exchange for more favourable energy charges. Furthermore, simple energy-efficiency demand side management strategies were implemented to reduce the intensity of the blackouts. However, South Africa could have done better to consider more flexible planning and contingency options as resources. Flexibility, however, only buys power sectors time, and planning frameworks cannot escape the need for sound supply-side fundamentals which will allow large-scale expansions to be timeously developed.

Project Planning and Risk Evaluation

In hybrid markets, project planning and appraisal is often left to newly formed institutions that lack the capacity to execute these functions effectively. In some cases, these institutions inherit functions for which they lack the human resource skills (financial, legal, environmental, and engineering) to conduct adequate risk assessments during the planning and appraisal phase of the projects' development. Even where the SOE institutions retain planning functions, a lack of proficiency can lead to inadequate risk assessment—especially when certain project aspects are new. Governments and off-taker utilities often leave project appraisal to consultants, private sponsors of IPPs, and negotiators, all of whom may have different incentives to close the deal. This is evidenced when upside opportunity incentives end up being significantly overshadowed by downside risks.

In South Africa's energy transition, the detailed risks of transitioning the power sector were inadequately appraised by Eskom and by government. Agreements to accept funds from institutions were accepted without a clear understanding of where, and how, these funds could be best spent. Many commentators have contended that the energy transition was pushed by wealthier countries without providing South Africa with the tools to critically appraise the potential pitfalls of transitioning to a low-carbon domestic power sector. They have also held that insufficient sharing of experiences occurred between South Africa and forerunner western states. While individual projects risks were separately appraised, the total integrated risks to energy security, influences on other sectors, energy flows through the grid, and socio-economic impacts were underestimated. In many cases, the urgency with which power was required also contributed to hurried and inadequate risk evaluations.

Even amongst Eskom's own projects—Medupi, Kusile, and Ingula—the project experiences draw attention to the importance of the capacity needed for comprehensive project appraisal in all facets of generation project development. The experiences also demonstrate the potential for lapses in risk management in critical phases of projects, and how these contribute to the problem of insufficient generation capacity.

Country specific risks need to be managed and resolved by host governments. South Africa's power sector and country risks are such that government guarantees are still required for the procurement of private generation capacity. The government has taken steps to address the lack of financial credibility of the off-taker and deal with Eskom's large debt by announcing that the country's National Treasury will take over much of Eskom's debt, including the debts of municipalities, provided that certain conditions are achieved.

With government taking over Eskom's debt, however, it is still not clear to what extent government securities will still be required for future IPPs. And if government guarantees are still required, for how long? While the debt take-over from National Treasury will be beneficial for Eskom and for municipalities, it is not yet clear whether the underlying factors, incentives, and behaviours that contributed to the significant debt within municipalities and at Eskom would be adequately addressed to persuade private investors in the absence of government guarantees. Many international investors are prohibited from partnering with utilities and investing in countries with poor credit ratings. Uncertainty therefore remains regarding the government's timeline for the power sector to be self-sufficient and no longer be dependent on state bailouts and guarantees.

Demand Side Management Planning

Institutional coordination and agreement in dealing with the problem of insufficient generation capacity has been shown to be poor in the case of South Africa. In 2023, analysis performed by Deloitte indicated that a remote geyser switching programme could save as much as 5 000 MW[333]. The same year, Electricity Minister, Kgosientsho

Ramokgopa estimated that it would cost approximately R 16 billion to install smart meters in eight million homes across the country[334]. In South Africa, it took fifteen years for the government to pilot the installation of specific DSM programmes, such as additional smart meters and expanding the geyser remote switching programme (in 2023). Earlier programme adoption could have significantly changed the electricity demand load profile and limit the amount of load-shedding that occurred. Such examples are indicative of the obstacles faced in coordinating DSM strategies to systematically deal with the problem of insufficient generation. A large portion of power demand could be shaved by commercially available control and management systems. Eskom staff estimated that 10 percent of power demand could be shaved by implementing DSM technologies nationally, and that this reduction could potentially be as much as 35 percent during peak demand periods[335].

These demand side management initiatives are often not only less expensive than traditional generation expansion projects, but they have the potential to permanently alter load demand profiles to better match renewable and dispatchable generation production, shift load-shedding to times of the day and night where the impact on consumers are less inconvenient, influence consumer electricity consumption behaviour, and lock-in energy efficiency gains.

Since Eskom is not responsible for most of the country's distribution functions the company was not properly incentivised to roll out demand side management initiatives, as its own sales and profitability would be impacted by DSM implementation. Municipalities that account for most of distribution were also not appropriately incentivised to implement DSM initiatives since such programmes ultimately reduce revenues for municipalities due to reduced consumption. This would also impact on the quality of other municipal services since electricity revenues are often used to subsidise other services. Where load shifting could have played a meaningful role in better managing the power crisis, the absence of time-of-use tariffs for most consumers meant that real-time price signals were not used to effectively influence the consumption behaviour of many electricity consumers. With time-of-use tariffs, since charges are higher during low generation reserve periods than during periods when there is ample generation, consumers are incentivised to reduce their loads when generation capacity reserves are low.

The poor state of most municipalities meant that most local government offices had neither the technical nor the financial capacity to institute programmes aimed at reshaping load profiles and consumer behaviours.

Generation Procurement

Procurement of generation infrastructure requires specific processes to minimise procurement costs and the total cost of the acquisition, to minimise opportunities for corruption, and to make plain the rules of the game to all interested stakeholders. Procurement can be a long process spanning a number of years. Hence, efficiency and transparency are key determinants in the timely acquisition of generation capacity. Delays or irregularities in the procurement process can result in delayed construction and commissioning of power plants, exacerbating the problems of insufficient electricity generation. Efficient and transparent procurement frameworks are thus pivotal in the acquisition of new capacity. The manner in which procurement is conducted has the potential to attract or discourage investment and ensure or prevent timely commissioning of generation, as is elaborated in the section below.

Procurement Procedures and Adherence

Procurement of new generation capacity generally needs to be done in accordance with established rules and regulations governing procurement opportunities, bidding, and awarding of contracts. A lack of guidelines for how funds should be spent can lead to several problems in procurement. Equally distressing is the non-adherence to policies and guidelines since this can also lead to problems, as evidenced in South Africa. Despite a policy of contracting large infrastructure projects through international competitive bidding procedures, adverse outcomes were still experienced for the Medupi, Kusile, and Ingula projects.

With state capture having the objective of intentionally circumventing good governance processes, it may be a moot exercise to underscore the importance of adhering to sound governance practices when the intention of unethical politicians, government officials, Eskom managers, and private individuals, was to undermine these good processes at the outset. The shareholding of the ruling party in power plant Engineering Procurement and Construction transactions underscores the incestuous nature of state capture and the difficulty in separating party from state.

Nevertheless, the failure to adhere to well-conceived domestic and international procurement policies resulted in a tarnished reputation for South Africa as an investment destination. Eskom and South Africa lost its investment ratings and significant investment capital dried up, compared to the era when the country benefited from investment-grade credit ratings by the three major credit ratings agencies. When credit ratings were downgraded to junk status and where capital could still be obtained, investment funds which were mainly in form of loans, came with strict lending conditions, significantly higher interest charges, and slow processes for accessing and directing the much-needed funds. The inconsistency within government departments and corruption as experienced in Eskom and in many other state-owned enterprises, prompted wary equity investors and lenders to withdraw from deals.

Non-adherence to procedures can result in problems for investors even when it is the state that does not follow its own prescriptions as evidenced in South Africa. Many of the contractors that were involved in corrupt practices were called to account for their actions in their domicile and other jurisdictions and had fines imposed. Hitachi paid to settle the charges the United States Securities Exchange Commission brought against company under the United States Foreign Corrupt Practices Act. Aware that Chancellor House was an investment and funding vehicle for the ruling African National Congress, Hitachi nonetheless partnered with Chancellor House to use its political connections to help secure contracts from Eskom. The multinational, ASEA Brown Boveri, also agreed to pay over some of its profits made through corrupt dealings with Eskom. Through its subsidiaries, the company secured many government contracts through bribes and the siphoning of illicit payments. So also did the German software giant, SAP, pay restitution damages for contracts that were irregularly obtained at Eskom, as well as at other South African SOEs.

The extent to which countries are consistent in applying their policy prescriptions can attract or deter private investment. Inconsistencies, as evidenced in the case of South Africa, should make honest investors wary of countries where procurement standards are blurred and where adherence and enforcement are arbitrary.

The Influence of Development Finance Institutions and the Energy Transition

Development finance institutions have historically embraced competitive tendering since it endorses fairness and transparency, generally attracts more affordable charges, and better promotes environmental and climate change objectives. In April 2010, the World Bank granted Eskom a US$ 3.75 billion loan in part to assist with funding for the construction of the Medupi coal-fired plant and another project, to compete a railway line to transport coal.

The World Bank came under severe criticism for its failure to execute its own governance and oversight role. This criticism came from all over the globe, including opposition political parties in South Africa, from environmental watchdogs, and from civil society organisations.

In 2019, the Belgium-based international activist network, the Committee for the Abolition of Illegitimate Debt (formerly known as the Committee for the Cancellation of the Third World Debt), called for the cancellation of the World Bank debt to Eskom. It claimed that due to the adverse environmental impacts on scarce water resources and corruption on the project, the completion of the Medupi coal-fired plant was against the interests of the population of the borrower state. It also contended that the harmful effects of coal pollution would be felt for decades to come, given the scale of the largest coal-fired plant of its kind in the world. It further argued that the debt is odious and in terms of international law, the transaction must be cancelled because it was not incurred in the best interests of the citizens of South Africa. The committee stated that this condition was known, or ought to have been known, by both borrower and lender[336]. The World Bank subsequently altered its policies on funding of fossil-fueled generation projects but did not cancel the debt.

The push by many other development finance institutions for renewable projects has also raised objections from different quarters, mostly those with interests in fossil fueled generation projects such as mining companies, local communities who often constitute the poor, and related value-chain interest groups. These constituencies argued that the energy transition failed to recognize that many local businesses and communities are disadvantaged by the transition to a low-carbon power sector. Moreover, despite the noble environmental goals of the proposed energy transition, transition frameworks—as implemented in western states—failed to acknowledge the very different conditions on the ground in the coal-rich province of Mpumalanga, South Africa. The startling conditions of poverty and inequality were indeed starkly different to the conditions in many western settings, and the proposed energy transition fails to provide adequate procedural, distributive, and restorative justice elements.

Allocation of Generation Investment Opportunities

While the Renewable Energy Independent Power Producer Procurement programme, administered by the Department of Minerals and Energy, spelled out the investment opportunities for investors in renewable generation, South Africa has not ruled out state sponsored investment in generation. SOEs therefore remain an option to expand generation capacity. However, the main driver for private investment persists—Eskom lacks sufficient finances to fund additional generation expansion. Private investment will thus continue to play a vital role in the development of additional generation infrastructure. South Africa, nonetheless, still lacks clearly stated criteria for the allocation of investment opportunities (i.e., private versus public), especially for non-renewable generation projects.

Having clear criteria for investments can help develop a more predictable environment for investors, thereby making investment processes more transparent and bringing credibility to decision-making processes. Investors are likely to react more favourably to such an environment and this, in turn, could facilitate further investment. The random allocation of generation opportunities to private sponsors and SOEs characterises the reality that credible criteria for private or public investment under a hybrid arrangement are lacking.

Had South Africa's power sector evolved to the end state of the standard reform model, such investment allocation guidelines may not have been necessary, as a different set of factors would largely have determined which entities would have been allocated investment opportunities. However, when the wave of power sector reforms swept across the globe in the 1990s, it was not foreseen that so many power sectors that embarked on the standard reform prescription would remain stalled in a transition state—especially not for three decades.

In South Africa, despite the government announcing its intention to increase private ownership in Generation, Eskom was still the allocated developer of the 3 000 MW of gas-fired generation capacity as directed in the country's Integrated Resource Plan (edition 2019). Although the national utility does not have the funds to develop the project and the Ministry of Finance has placed a moratorium on the utility taking on more loans (as a condition for taking on most of Eskom's debt), government has been unclear on who would develop and own the project—when the project eventually obtains all the approvals. Surprisingly, there have been proposals for the Central Energy Fund, to take on the project. The Central Energy Fund is another state-owned enterprise reporting to the Ministry of Minerals and Energy, responsible for contributing to the country's security of mainly primary energy supply through exploration and development activities.

The Integrated Resource Plan (edition 2019) is also not clear on who will be responsible for the tranches of future baseload generation investment. This is despite Eskom not having the financial resources to invest in additional baseload generation infrastructure or to extend the life of the existing power sector infrastructure. Private investors have stated their interest in traditional state sponsored projects if sufficient securities can be provided, but neither allocation criteria for such projects nor descriptions of the securities, are in the public domain. What might these allocation criteria be? Various possibilities exist.

Where finance is a temporary constraint, government might announce that IPPs will be sought over a specified period. The national utility will then resume responsibility after the specified period. Perhaps the national utility has expertise in hydro but not renewable plants; or IPPs could explicitly be sought to meet specific technology diversity targets. Perhaps government, or the planning authorities, might discuss the 20-year power expansion plan with the national utility and agree up front which options it would take responsibility for and which would be bid out to the private sector.

The point here is not so much the actual allocation criteria themselves, but rather that there is a transparent allocation of responsibilities that creates clear and certain investment opportunities for IPPs and SOEs. Transparency in allocation criteria also implies that the incumbent national utility is aware of its own investment responsibilities, what it needs to budget for, and what its targeted financial status needs to be in order to meet its investment and operations obligations—including those responsibilities in the transmission and distribution sectors. The split in responsibilities between the national utility and IPPs also needs to be backed by strong and consistent political leadership and state action to sustain long-term sector credibility and sustainability.

Generation Contracting

In most cases, IPP contracts extend over a long period of time and typical contracts can range for a period of approximately 20 years. The length of the contract is considered both a strength and a weakness. The length of the contract makes it possible for the sponsor to make a return on their investments and service debt with long tenors. Conversely, in an environment of increasing liberalisation or during financial shocks, both parties can encounter problems with fixed long-term Power Purchase Agreements if the conditions change under which the contracts were initially agreed upon.

All contracts between IPPs and utility off-taker in South Africa have been in the form of long-term PPAs. The legal and regulatory frameworks within which these contracts have been entered into shape the degree of predictability (and governance) in the sector, and ultimately impact on the manner and extent to which investment in generation infrastructure is facilitated. Several factors have influenced generation contracting in South Africa.

IPP Charges and Payback Periods

In general, the ability to keep power charges from IPPs competitive has an impact on a country's ability to attract more investment and is therefore linked to the problem of insufficient generation capacity. Lower IPP power charges are easier for off-takers to service and require lower consumer tariff increases. Conversely, adequate tariff increases help off-takers to stay afloat financially, making it easier to attract more investment.

Overall, the ability to attract cheaper finance and keep interest payments low are factors that play a role in making private investment in Generation more sustainable. Lower power charges resulting in lower tariffs to consumers make IPPs more acceptable to the public, especially when coupled with service improvements. By having lower power charges, the likelihood of stresses on contracts between IPPs and off-takers decreases.

In the case of South Africa, several factors contributed to the reducing costs of renewable generation IPPs. PPAs were denominated in local currency and therefore had a stabilizing effect on tariffs to consumers, not subject to fluctuations in currency exchange rates. The absence of primary energy costs, which are normally indexed and subject to market forces, also contributed to a predictable tariff trajectory. The use of competitive auctions further drove down auctioned prices, as sponsors were keen to *enter* the generation market, and then increase or maintain their IPP market share.

One concern expressed by consumers, however, is the future trajectory of electricity tariffs with increasing additions of renewable energy generation capacity from IPPs. There has been no prediction on the consumer tariff trajectory for the years until 2050. As a result, consumers are concerned that locking into a specific energy transition pathway, without understanding the impact on consumer tariffs, could cause unanticipated problems in the future. Electricity costs from IPPs have generally been calculated without adjustments for power grid upgrades (such as energy storage and ancillary services) as well as other services to ensure a reliable future power supply. These costs are often hidden from publicly cited renewable energy costs, despite being accrued to consumers.

Allocating Explicit Responsibility and Building Capacity for Contracting

Contracting with IPPs effectively and competitively can be complex. With renewable energy IPPs, due to the absence of primary energy contract provisions, the contracting arrangements are simplified to some degree. However, whichever way the government decides on allocating future investment in Generation (including energy storage and ancillary services), the immediate implication is that government and national utilities require a great deal of specialised expertise in order to negotiate robust and competitive contracts—and optimally allocate project risks. Private sponsors will often hire the best legal, financial, and technical transaction advisors. Whether responsibility for procurement and contracting of new investment will rest with the national utility or with the host government, both entities need good and knowledgeable people on their sides of the table when dealing with project developers.

Unfortunately, this is often not the case and governments underestimate the need for special assistance. In the case of Eskom, the utility lost many skilled staff, putting many projects at risk technically, contractually, legally, and financially, at new and existing plants. More recently, given the benefits of distributed generation, the need for transmission and distribution planning has been identified as a new area where novel expertise and experience is needed.

Once again, this points to an area where hybrid power markets present new challenges that have to be dealt with consciously and purposefully. Similarly, many of the challenges experienced in South Africa could have been avoided with the transition to a competitive power market in accordance with the standard reform prescription. As with planning, contracting in hybrid markets is not a trivial exercise.

Governments need to allocate clear responsibility to either the national utility or a government agency to undertake this function. If the national utility is responsible, then it is also critical that a ring-fenced contracting function is established separate from the utility's own generation operations or new-build functions—to avoid any conflicts of interest.

Perhaps the best location for the contracting function is within the independent system operator which also takes responsibility for planning. This responsibility can be integrated with the procurement function. In this case the system operator takes responsibility not only for short term balancing of the system but also long-term security of supply. The government of South Africa has committed to separate the Generation, Transmission, and Distribution sectors. However, in accordance with the government's proposal, all of these independent legal entities will still be held under the Eskom holding company for the foreseeable future.

It is therefore not yet clear whether this unbundling will provide the requisite independence if the Generation and Transmission functions (including the independent system operator) report into the same holding company. Even if there is complete separation anticipated in future, it is also not clear whether the objectives of unbundling will survive the intrusive effects of state dominance where overreaching government interference could undermine the intended independence.

Regulatory and Governance Frameworks

The end state of the standard model of reform would include an independent, transparent, and credible electricity regulator to provide oversight and to promote efficient and fair markets. It would also oversee tariff structures that cover the cost of electricity generation and provide incentives for further investment. Using private sector financing for electricity infrastructure requires good regulatory systems to protect investor and consumer interests and to ensure the long-term interests of power sector stakeholders. These requirements are equally important in hybrid power markets.

An analysis of regulatory and governance functions globally suggests that the presence or absence of formal regulatory institutions in hybrid markets does have a significant impact on the country's ability to attract sufficient generation capacity. More important, is that *de facto* or *de jure* regulatory functions create the necessary certainty and predictability to support investment. Analysis of power sector experiences outside of South Africa suggest that the extent to which de facto or de jure regulators have acted in an independent, credible, transparent, and consistent manner is important. In practical terms, it is the governance role that regulators play (whether independent, or within government) in ensuring transparency and predictability that helps attract adequate investment in generation.

In South Africa, the PPAs of independent private producers were backed by government guarantees. Therefore, apart from licensing, the National Energy Regulator of South Africa (NERSA) had less significance in bringing credibility to the generation investment market. NERSA had few powers to incentivise investment and actively narrow the gap between supply and demand.

Even when the City of Cape Town tried to obtain NERSA's concurrence with its decision to procure more power from IPPs without the approval of the Ministry of Minerals and Energy, NERSA was unable to concur with the City of Cape Town. The powers of NERSA as an electricity regulator were limited and only the energy minister could provide the longer-term relief sought from the rolling blackouts by agreeing to the determination for additional generation. The National Electricity Regulator of South Africa was subordinate and reported to the Ministry of Minerals and Energy and could therefore not compel the minister to grant the City of Cape Town the approvals to contract with more IPPs in order to relieve the city from the power crisis. In this regard, NERSA's lack of independence and authority was therefore not benign in the management of South Africa's power crisis.

During the power crisis, it has often been argued that the real cost of electricity was not adequately reflected in the tariffs approved by NERSA. This was the case since the electricity regulator was formed in 1995. According to an analysis by Power Optimal, between 1998 and 2007, when Eskom had no obligation for building new generation capacity in accordance with the government policy, electricity tariffs increased by roughly 225 percent, while inflation over this period rose at approximately 335 percent. However, NERSA did approve significant tariff increases when Eskom was given the green light to build Medupi, Kusile and Ingula power plants. From the time that the loadshedding crisis started, there were significant tariff increases that were imposed on South African consumers. Between 2007 and 2022, average tariffs increased by roughly 650 percent, while inflation over this period was at approximately 130 percent. With adjustments for inflation, by the year 2022 electricity consumers were therefore paying four times more for electricity than they did fifteen years earlier, as reported in the Power Optimal review of tariffs over the stated period[337]. For 2023, NERSA again approved an average tariff increase of more than 18 percent against an annual inflation rate of roughly 7 percent.

From 2007, during the years immediately after Eskom obtained approval to continue with new-build projects, Eskom hoodwinked NERSA into believing that the funds were allocated towards efficient spending on generation capacity expansions and prudent operating and maintenance costs at its existing power stations. It was only later, once the nature and the extent of corruption was better understood, that NERSA tried to resist significant tariff increases.

Unfortunately, the national power crisis deteriorated to a point where NERSA had to provide the tariff increases to complete new-build projects (supplementary to government bailouts). NERSA presumably had no resource capacity nor mandate for detailed oversight on the *actual* spending of the funds once the tariff increases were approved.

Eskom still budgeted for maintenance costs in their tariff applications, yet the plants were often not allowed to shut down for prolonged outages to perform the required maintenance.

Therefore, while NERSA was trying to allow only prudent costs to be passed through, there was no way of NERSA knowing or verifying that the costs were indeed for prudent expenditure, or whether it was used in corrupt and reckless spending. While NERSA approved tariffs for expenditure looking forward, looking backward it did not perform an assessment on whether the funds were indeed spent on the allocations that Eskom promised, and perhaps more importantly whether the expenditures were well-advised and sensible.

Employing an *ex-ante* and an *ex-post* tariff review approach might have assisted NERSA with avoiding the many court cases that the electricity regulator lost against Eskom, where it did not use its own tariff determination formulae for determining tariffs. Eskom has since applied to NERSA to change the tariff determination methodology to separate capacity and energy charges in the tariff structure.

Should the current multi-year price tariff setting methodology remain, and if the electricity regulator has the resource capacity to use the forward and backward approach to adjudicate Eskom's average multi-year price determinations, NERSA could consider this approach to better hold Eskom to account. However, once there is a power crisis, politically and socio-economically it becomes harder to withhold funds through the tariff, if this action will further deteriorate the utility's performance and worsen the impact to the country's economy and its citizens.

With private power producers, shareholders could be expected to act swiftly to rectify indiscretions. However, with the many divergent stakeholder interests that governments must satisfy, their responses can be sluggish. It remains to be seen whether a firm regulatory approach of only approving sensible tariff increases based on efficient expenditure could soon be achieved in South Africa. Such a regulatory approach could spur a well-considered and timely response from Eskom to achieve efficient costs—a response that results in effective management changes that are in the wider interest of stakeholders.

Regulatory risk, as first introduced in Chapter 3, does not appear to have impacted adversely on private projects that were successfully commissioned in South Africa. This is because the IPPs were regulated by their contracts and the contracts were agreed on by the Ministry of Minerals and Energy. The experience in South Africa is that notwithstanding the stated independence of the electricity regulator, the powers of NERSA were insufficient to incentivise new capacity to come onboard timeously. NERSA functions were always subordinate to the actions of its reporting ministry. In addition to its reduced authority to facilitate new capacity from being ushered in, its independence was also questioned at times when tariffs were maintained low during the years before elections. The electricity regulator also failed to adjust its tariff determination methodology and institute (and report on) effective investigations into Eskom's poor performance.

Experiences from power sector reforms globally suggest that having independent and transparent regulatory institutions is important for the sustainable functioning of the power sector. More important, it is the commitment to regulatory and governance functions that is more important to the sustainable functioning of this sector and the attraction of adequate investment—regardless of whether these are separate regulators or embedded in the state.

In South Africa the absence of strong political leadership has contributed to lacklustre regulatory outcomes. Purposeful political leadership and integrated governance is essential for achieving policy outcomes. A national utility should not only be aligned to government policy but become an effective instrument in executing government policy towards achieving the stated policy outcomes. For this to occur, regulatory incentives must be conducive and adequate for the achievement of the desired performance of state-owned and private generators.

◈ ◈ ◈

Power sector planning is no trivial task. Adequate planning policies, processes, systems, human resources, and institutional capacity must be secured and nurtured to ensure that planning delivers on its intended purpose. Hybrid power markets create additional challenges of integrating public and private options, incorporating risk management requirements, as well as maintaining some level of flexibility, to ensure security of supply.

Thus, any power sector reforms that bring in IPPs while maintaining the incumbent state-owned utility need to deal with these challenges explicitly and purposefully. In addition, to ensure allocative efficiency, there must be clear criteria whereby new-build opportunities are allocated to either the national utility or to IPPs. In hybrid power markets, the incumbent state-owned utility often continues to invest in new generation capacity in parallel to IPPs entering the generation market. Or if state-owned utilities have not built new generation for some time, they often continue to harbour ambitions for doing so. In certain instances, such as those seen in the South African context, they could discourage the entry of IPPs through delaying the signing of PPAs or delaying the expansion of grid capacity connections to accommodate private generators.

In these contexts, the planning function needs to develop transparent criteria which make clear what investments the state utility will do in the future and which projects will be bid out to the private sector. Once these criteria are clear, procurement needs its own set of rules to ensure least-cost outcomes are favored.

CHAPTER 15

THE PARADOX OF HYBRID MARKETS – IMPLICATIONS FOR FUTURE POWER SECTOR REFORMS

The standard model of power sector reform was intended to introduce unbundling, privatisation, and competition into the Electricity Supply Industry, including the Generation sector, as detailed in Chapter 3. Such competition in Generation was intended to drive down the price of electricity, which tended to be high in many state-owned utilities due to operational and financial inefficiencies. It was believed that corporate governance and investor oversight, prevalent in private generators, would encourage increased competence and efficiency and that greater discipline would be applied to operational and financial management.

In addition, it was expected that the stronger profit motive in private investment and wholesale electricity market price signals would encourage more efficient investment in Generation including in technology choices and timing of investment decisions. Private investment was expected to introduce a more efficient approach to generation planning and contracting, one based on sound market-based economic principles. State-owned generators, most of which were considered to be inefficient and lacking the financial resources for capacity expansions, would be unbundled, corporatized and set up to compete against each other. These developments would address the historically poor operational and fiscal performances that persisted in many African countries and other developing regions.

The introduction of private capital through IPPs was seen as a convenient first step towards this market and could provide almost immediate relief to power systems that were short of generation capacity, since they could be introduced before actual market trading platforms were in place. The general notion that was widely held was that the private sector could procure and develop, maintain, and operate generation assets more efficiently than the public sector. Private sector-led investment and operation, therefore, was expected to roll back the consequences of inefficient state-led development and operation.

Many developing countries in Africa and the rest of the developing world were sceptical about the appropriateness of implementing reforms where the starting conditions were different to those in more developed countries where reforms had been successfully implemented. Notwithstanding their scepticism, and with few alternatives available, many countries reluctantly proceeded in enacting reforms. Many of the early reformers in developed countries had generation capacity excesses, as well as experience with private sector participation in other infrastructure sectors. This situation differed substantially from most developing countries which had very different drivers for reform as well as little experience with private participation in public infrastructure. When power sector reforms were initiated in African countries, the most pressing driver has often been to fill the gaps with urgently procured power rather than providing benchmarks for state-owned plants and enabling long-term sector efficiency.

While a few cautionary voices had warned against the replicability of early reform accomplishments in African states—and how the successes of early reformers were strongly linked to their domestic power sector contexts, the reform message spread as it was advocated by development finance institutions, international policy consultants, and in some cases, domestic champions. Legislation was enacted to make provision for the reforms, state-owned utilities were corporatised, electricity regulators were established, and relevant institutions were revamped to closer align with the reform agenda, in order to manage performance drivers and achieve the objectives of reform. Irrespective of these actions to reform power sectors in accordance with the standard reform model, many countries abandoned further reform efforts and settled at hybrid markets, devoid of wholesale competition.

Given that the desirable conditions for advancing reforms do not generally exist in many developing countries—and that competitive wholesale electricity trading markets are unlikely to be realised anytime soon, what can governments do to orient their reform efforts towards better sector performance outcomes? What are the implications for further power sector reforms in Africa and elsewhere, and what could other developing nations learn from the experiences in South Africa? The sections below provide some guidance for power sectors where reforms have stalled at hybrid markets.

Power Sector Project Development

Especially given the propensity for delays in developing generation projects in African countries, linkages between planning and implementation would require tightening, with effective governance frameworks providing the necessary oversight. Institutions responsible for planning should be resourced with adequate expertise for project evaluation to assess potential risks in project development. Management strategies should be directed at minimising delays in developing generation infrastructure projects.

Guiding principles should be in line with the possible, feasible, and likely, generation technologies that are country—and project—specific. Not to be missed are the potential obstacles that projects could face during implementation, as well as the social, environmental, and financial aspects that may impede the development of these projects. Given that there are many specific project-related and country-related factors that have the potential to stall project development—and even to cancel projects—strategies to manage project risk would require some degree of customisation for each project in each country. Policy and planning frameworks, therefore, need to take cognisance of a range of issues—financial, environmental, social, and labour—as these frameworks are formulated and implemented.

The future generation mixes of many countries will continue to be guided by decarbonisation objectives, new fossil fuel discoveries, the future availability of primary energy, geo-political considerations, and increasing domestic societal pressures. Where feasible, regional power pools, alternative energies, and a host of other integrated electricity planning options, should continue to be promoted since they give flexibility to the planning process and allow for more options to deal with the problem of insufficient generation capacity.

A range of technologies allow for improved flexibility. Each option comes with its own advantages and disadvantages. A combined cycle gas plant, for example, is more energy efficient than contemporary generation technologies, has a lower unit capital cost, can be operated in either baseload or peaking modes and is generally easier to site than coal or hydro plants. Coal is generally a lower priced fuel but its use triggers concerns about air and water quality when expensive treatments are not factored in to meet increasingly stringent emissions standards. Even in countries like South Africa that are rich in coal resources, funding for coal plants have practically disappeared. Wind and solar plants have virtually no fuel costs, but apart from the lower capital costs, on their own they have intermittent outputs as well as low energy availability and transmission capacity utilisation factors. They can also be unsightly or impact negatively on animal life in ecologically sensitive areas.

While nuclear plants do not emit greenhouse gases and are good sources of reliable, dispatchable, baseload electricity, in some jurisdictions there are unresolved questions around their high capital costs, project completion schedules, and the long-term disposal of high-level radioactive waste.

Power Sector Reform and the Private Sector

In South Africa, power sector reforms were proposed with the objective of achieving the end state of the standard model, as was done by the early reformers, and as first described in Chapter 2 and Chapter 3.

While South Africa did make profound changes to its power sector, for more than a quarter of a century (from 1998) the country tried, but it did not achieve the end state of the standard reform model. Indeed, nowhere in Africa is a fully unbundled, private, or competitive electricity market to be found. Power sector reforms in Africa and in many other developing countries globally has resulted in what this book has defined as a hybrid model in Generation, where state-owned utilities and IPPs operate side by side with virtually no competition between generators—in contrast to what was espoused by the standard model of reform. As demonstrated in the practical examples described in this book, power sector reforms have brought in its own challenges to achieving an end state where power markets, private capital, price signals and other market mechanisms would facilitate investment in generation infrastructure—and help deal with risks related to insufficient electricity.

In her book entitled 'Making Competition Work in Electricity' Sally Hunt observes that globally, no country that had reached the end state of competitive markets has reversed its decision[338]. This suggests that the functioning of the market itself, barring imperfections, operates reasonably well and sustainably. This is not to say that if, and when, developing countries achieve the end state of competitive power markets it will be relatively easy to sustain power sector developments.

The problem for many developing countries, however, has been *how to get there.* The journey towards competitive power markets appears to have encountered a number of obstacles that have prevented many developing countries from reaching the end state. Hybrid generation markets consisting of state-owned utilities and IPPs are therefore expected to be around at least for the foreseeable future. Many countries have jettisoned the drive to reform in accordance with the standard model. And those that have not, are finding out how difficult it is to progress towards the end state.

As seen in the case of South Africa, competition in Generation (and Distribution) has not been realised as prescribed by the standard reform model, or as intended by the country's Energy White Paper, first published in 1998. Given that, in all probability, competitive generation power markets will not be realised as intended in many developing countries (at least not in the near future) a key question to be addressed is: How should power sectors reorient reform initiatives in order to nonetheless achieve the benefits of initial reform objectives? Moreover, if the de facto situation is a hybrid market, how can hybrid markets be made to function so that the original objectives of increased investment and more efficient operations are still achieved?

The analysis of experiences in the power sectors of developing countries suggests that power sector improvements should focus on improving the conditions for continued and timely generation investments in the hybrid market. In many developing countries, since the ushering in of IPPs, national utilities are no longer suppliers of last resort and pre-reform planning and procurement frameworks residing with SOE utilities have been dismantled to make provision for new frameworks that are housed elsewhere.

In the absence of price signals for attracting new generation (as would be found under the standard model of reform end state), planning needs to be more carefully co-ordinated amongst institutions in the sector, providing certainty and transparency to potential investors. The planning needs to encompass a wide range of functions (engineering, financial, legal, regulatory, environmental) to adequately assess planning and project risks.

Planning should be dynamic, transparent, frequent, and reflect latest market prices. In addition, planning should be flexible enough to accommodate setbacks in project development. The planning function should be well resourced and equipped to deal with the intricacies and challenges of public *and* private sector investment, as described in this book. Serious consideration should be given to individual project contexts and conditions in the power sector. Special attention should also be paid to the commitment of governments to the institutions that will enable power sectors to realise these improvements in planning to accomplish desired outcomes.

Procurement and contracting should preferably be conducted by an institution that is independent of SOE generators—possibly an autonomous and unbundled transmission company or system operator. The impartiality of such an arrangement would assist in minimising conflicts of interests between state-owned generators and potential IPPs. Clear and efficient bid and procurement rules should be developed for the acquisition of new capacity. Satisfactory oversight and enforcement over procurement processes is needed to ensure transparency and fairness.

Many of the above points might seem obvious—and they are. Yet, what this book has revealed is that they are often neglected. Hybrid power markets give rise to new challenges. Many functions previously undertaken within vertically integrated, state-owned national utilities have been omitted, overlooked, and neglected. The over-riding insight from the South African experience is that hybrid markets require explicit and purposeful policy actions to deal with the challenges of integrated planning, allocation of new-build opportunities, linkages to investment, competitive bidding practices, and robust contracting of IPPs. Furthermore, clear institutional responsibility needs to be assigned for these functions.

State-Owned Enterprises

To a large extent the analysis in this book has focused on the interactions between state-owned utilities and IPPs in hybrid markets and the planning, procurement and contracting challenges that have to be addressed. But the specific nature and functioning of the dominant players in these hybrid markets, namely the state-owned enterprises (SOEs), also needs to be re-examined.

The Importance of SOEs

The development role of SOEs in economic sectors of developing countries is arguably more important than the role they play in the economies of their industrialised counterparts. SOEs are useful vehicles to assist developing countries in addressing social and economic predicaments and backlogs. This is due to the influence that governments have over their existence. In many parts of the world the nationalisation of various parts of the energy and minerals sectors suggests that state control might indeed be required in times of turbulent transitions.

Take the management of the energy transition for instance. In many countries it is considered prudent and strategic to nationalise certain energy resources to guard against price shocks. In recent years, various forms of energy sector nationalisations have also been witnessed in developed countries such as Japan[339], France[340], and Germany[341], despite utilities in these countries continuing to operate in competitive markets.

Utility SOEs have remained prominent, even in many industrialized nations—and especially in strategic infrastructure sectors. This feature is indicative of the advantages that state ownership can have as governments influence the role of public enterprises in various economic sectors. The problem occurs when the development role that the SOE plays come at the expense of its operational and financial performance and threatens its own survival and sustainability.

It is for this reason that various governance mechanisms were advocated during the first round of reforms, introduced in Chapter 7. In many cases, developing country electricity utility SOEs, due to their public service nature, have continued to be organs of social and political patronage. This could be awarding contracts to politically connected elites or keeping tariffs artificially low to garner support from the voting masses, especially before election years.

It is clear that the extent of government commitment to public enterprises—through allowing tariff increases, providing adequate governance arrangements, and enforcing accountability of SOEs—plays a significant role in the ability of state-owned utilities to show positive performances. Positive operational and financial performances enable public enterprises to act as credible power off-takers to IPPs or to self-invest in generation infrastructure through raising debt in domestic and foreign bond markets.

In summary, SOEs can—and in many cases, should—serve as plausible instruments of social advancement in developing countries. However, when political interests adversely impact on the ability of

SOEs to deliver services, then their role becomes problematic. When a government expects an SOE to operate in a manner that puts the utility's own well-being at risk, the relationship between the SOE and the state becomes troublesome.

Striking the Right Balance

It is the ability to strike a balance between development interests and SOE sustainability, that determines the success of power sectors in advancing social and economic progress for African and other developing countries. If there are legitimate political interests that the SOE must cater to, it is critical that such interests are well articulated, scoped, and costed. Policy pricing of political mandates, other than what would have been the mandate for any private company, needs to be determined and articulated *before* such policies are adopted.

In the case of South Africa, despites the intended benefits the real and potential adverse implications of the country's Black Economic Empowerment policies (how these policies were first introduced and evolved over the years) were not well understood by many in South African society. Neither was the ANC's cadre deployment policy, which saw Eskom and other SOEs come under severe mismanagement by ill-equipped and unscrupulous agents of state capture—first during the Jacob Zuma presidency, and then worsening during the Cyril Ramaphosa presidency. The potential harm of the preferential procurement and ANC cadre deployment practices was camouflaged at their inception and insufficient governance mechanisms were in place to arrest their damaging effects. It was the combination of these two policies—as well as the absence of a credible implementing governance framework—that made it hard, even for honest cadres inside the ruling

ANC and amongst its alliance partners, to stop the looting once it started.

To ensure that the long-term impact on various sectors of society and the economy is not unduly compromised, objective, in-depth, comprehensive, and cross-functional quantitative and qualitative valuation of policies, as well as enacting regulations, are vital. The application of such critical evaluation tools to appraise proposed policies is especially important within the context of a rise in populism and proselytising of ideologies, not only in the power sector but also in other related sectors.

To reemphasise, the analysis of the new challenges that arise in hybrid power markets has also highlighted the important role that the national utility continues to play, and that in many cases it continues to make sense to allocate core responsibilities for national planning and the procurement and contracting of IPPs to an *independent* transmission utility SOE. Experiences have shown that government departments often do not readily have the expertise to perform detailed and inter-disciplinary power sector planning. Well-resourced national utilities can assist or take responsibility for these functions.

This means that the imperative of SOE reform and ensuring well-performing national utilities remains as important as ever. National utilities can still be effective instruments in enabling the creation and operation of an effective hybrid power market that responds to power requirements and delivers new investment. Given its performance in most of its 100-year history, Eskom can again take on this role if there is sufficient political will to shape enablers.

Still, the *de facto* situation in most developing countries is that SOEs remain important. In such contexts more careful thought needs to be given to institutional reforms. These reforms include ring-fencing or separation of the system operator function which could become the home of the integrated planning, procurement, and contracting function, necessary for the effective functioning of hybrid power markets. In assigning and designing these functions, effective governance will remain essential.

Crafting a New Reform Framework

Hybrid power markets are thus the result of stalled power sector reforms in South Africa, elsewhere on the African continent, and in many other developing regions in the world. This has profound implications not only for the way we think about power sector reform, but also where further reform efforts are directed. It would now seem inappropriate, even futile, to retain the standard reform model or to measure power sector reform progress in terms of how many of the elements of the standard model have been achieved. For many countries the standard model is no longer the normative option or end goal.

Much more productive is to recognise the reality of what power sectors actually look like in Africa and elsewhere, and to respond to the specific challenges that emerge from these hybrid markets. What the previous section has emphasised is the recognition that state-owned enterprises are probably here to stay, and thus SOE-specific reform remains of vital importance.

It is acknowledged that effective SOEs are vital to the successful functioning of hybrid markets—not only in the areas highlighted above (i.e., planning, procurement, and contracting) but also in being financially credible off-takers for IPPs. For SOEs to perform well, there needs to be credible commitment from governments to support their sustainability, and from regulatory institutions to support their continued long-term financial viability. This includes traditional sectoral SOEs and also well-functioning municipalities — Distribution utilities who can also act as credible off-takers of generated power.

In turn, there has to be accountability to the government by SOE managers and municipalities. Moreover, adequate governance mechanisms must be in place to provide oversight of their operations—including long-term planning, procurement, and contracting. In this way, SOEs can be geared for delivering developmental outcomes without eroding financial and operational performance.

While the private sector is certainly needed to assist in plugging shortages in generation capacity, efforts should be aimed at state-owned utilities being financially self-sufficient, with efficient operations and good operational performances. For SOEs to improve and achieve this level of quasi self-dependence and sustainability, each country will need to examine its policy, regulatory, and governance frameworks, and identify gaps and weaknesses. The interventions required to overhaul hybrid power sectors and create sustainability may involve broader macro-economic policy changes. The absence of such required broader policy changes invariably has adverse effects in other economic sectors also requiring infrastructure investment. Positive benefits can therefore be achieved from implementing broader policy changes in other sectors as well.

It is recognised that the political costs of such interventions may be high for certain governments. However, without these changes, neither SOE reforms nor private sector participation is likely to be successful in improving power sector performances since both require strong commitment from ruling governments to bring about transformation in earnest.

The inference drawn is analogous to the World Bank's perspective on the political economy of state enterprise reform which concluded that because privatisation has similar political costs as corporatisation, the two (privatisation and corporatisation) tend to succeed or fail together. Where reform was politically feasible, desirable, and credible, countries corporatized and privatised successfully. Whereas where countries were not politically ready to reform, substitute ownership strategies were not successful in improving performances. Earnest reforms are likely to change harmful policies, reduce subsidies to customers (directly or through bailouts), affect changes in SOE management, and allow independent tariff reviews and adjustments, regardless of the impact on government ownership[342].

EPILOGUE

This book contributes to the current understanding of power sector reforms by recognising the hybrid power market as *a new model in itself,* and not simply a *paused transition* toward the end state envisaged in the standard reform model. By investigating SOEs and IPPs, what it reveals are the elements essential to a *successful symbiosis* of state-owned and privately owned generators. To make this mutual partnership work, it also highlights the importance of policy and procedural conditions for facilitating the attraction of new investment in Generation, and thereby assisting in alleviating the problem of insufficient generation capacity.

By identifying disconnects in the nexus between planning and implementation of generation power projects, the book elucidates the factors that contribute to delays and failures in developing electricity generation plants, and how governments and power utilities can better respond to the challenges faced. Drawing on literature and experiences of power sector and SOE reforms, as well as project management, planning, procurement and contracting, these areas have been combined to provide a framework for power sector development.

A key contribution on offer here is the review of power sector reforms in South Africa. The period of loadshedding in South Africa is an important era in the country's post-democratic history not only for contextualising the evolution of power sector reforms, but also due to the extensive impact that rolling blackouts continue to have on daily life for ordinary South Africans. This book has attempted to capture some of the key revelations of the story of loadshedding in South Africa. Using the South African experience, the theory of hybrid markets has been operationalised to demonstrate its effectiveness towards the improved understanding of insufficient electricity generation.

Lastly, the theory of hybrid markets recognises the need for new planning, procurement and contracting frameworks and highlights critical areas where improvements can be made to facilitate timely investment and commissioning of electricity generation infrastructure. It is my hope that the book will help navigate the South African power sector, power sectors elsewhere on the continent, and the rest of the world, towards sustainable outcomes—where the lights stay on.

A luta continua; vitória é certa

ABBREVIATIONS

ANC	African National Congress
BOO	Build-Own- Operate
BOOT	Build-Own-Operate-Transfer
CEO	Chief Executive Officer
CFD	Contracts-For-Differences
COP	Conference of the Parties
COSATU	Congress of South African Trade Unions
COVID-19	Coronavirus Disease 2019
DSM	Demand Side Management
EAF	Energy Availability Factor
EFF	Economic Freedom Fighters
EIA	Environmental Impact Assessment
EIUG	Energy Intensive Users Group
EPC	Engineering Procurement and Construction
ESCOM	Electricity Supply Commission
ESI	Electricity Supply Industry
EVKOM	Elektrisiteits Voorsienings Kommissie
FDI	Foreign Direct Investment

FERC	Federal Energy Regulatory Commission
FIFA	Fédération Internationale de Football Association
GDP	Gross Domestic Product
GW	gigawatt
HR	Human Resources
IMF	International Monetary Fund
IPP	Independent Power Producer
IRP	Integrated Resource Plan
ISCOR	Iron and Steel Corporation (South Africa)
JET	Just Energy Transition
kWh	kilowatt hour
LCOE	Levelized Cost of Electricity
LNG	Liquefied Natural Gas
LRMC	Long Run Marginal Cost
MIR	Management Programme for Infrastructure and Regulatory Reform
MW	Megawatt
MWh	Megawatt hour
NDR	National Democratic Revolution
NERSA	National Energy Regulator of South Africa
NGO	Non-governmental Organisation
NTC	National Transmission Company
NUM	National Union of Mineworkers
NUMSA	National Union of Metalworkers of South Africa
O&M	Operating and Maintenance
OEM	Original Equipment Manufacturers
ONE	Office Nationale d'Electricité
OPEC	Organisation of Petroleum Exporting Countries

PESD	Program on Energy and Sustainable Development
PFMA	Public Finance Management Act
PPA	Power Purchase Agreement
PPI	Private Participation in Infrastructure
PRG	Partial Risk Guarantee
PURPA	Public Utility Regulatory Policies Act (PURPA) of 1978
PV	photovoltaic
PWR	Pressurized Water Reactor
R	South African Rand
REIPP	Renewable Energy Independent Power Producer
REIPPPP	Renewable Energy Independent Power Producer Procurement Programme
SACP	South African Communist Party
SADC	Southern African Development Community
SAP	Structural Adjustment Programme
SCOPA	Standing Committee on Public Accounts
SDG	Sustainable Development Goal
SENELEC	Senegal Electric Company
SOE	State Owned Enterprise
SOMELEC	Société Mauritanienne d'Electricité
SONEL	Société Nationale d'Electricité de Cameroun
SSEG	Small Scale Embedded Generator
TANESCO	Tanzania Electricity Supply Company Limited
TDP	Transmission Development Plan
UNFCCC	United Nations Framework Convention on Climate Change
US	United States
USA	United States of America
US$	United States Dollar

USSR	Union of Soviet Socialist Republics
VFTPC	Victoria Falls and Transvaal Power Company
WTO	World Trade Organisation
ZESA	Zimbabwe Electricity Supply Authority

List of Figures

List of Tables

E N D N O T E S

Chapter 1 - References:

1 Ritchie, H. et al. (2019). Access to Energy. Our World in Data.

2 Michael Boulle and Anthony Dane. (2020). The impacts of Covid-19 on the power sector in sub-Saharan Africa, and the role of the power sector in socio-economic recovery. Konrad-Adenauer-Stiftung.

3 World Energy Outlook Special Report. (2022). Africa Energy Outlook 2022. Paris: International Energy Agency.

4 Africa Infrastructure Country Diagnostic. (2008). Underpowered: The State of the Power Sector in Sub-Saharan Africa. The World Bank.

5 ESI Africa. (2021). A Snapshot of Africa's Energy and Power Sector. Issue 1-2021

6 International Finance Corporation. (2019). The Dirty Footprint of the Broken Grid - The Impacts of Fossil Fuel Back-up Generators in Developing Countries. Washington DC: The World Bank Group.

7 World Bank (2007). Enterprise Surveys. Washington D.C.

8 Statistica. (2022). Annual electrical outages in Africa by key country 2018. Statistica Research Department.

9 Shulman, H. (2018). In Sub-Saharan African Countries with Unreliable Power, Outages Cost Companies as Much as 31% in Sales. Center for Global Development.

10 World Bank Policy Paper. (1993). The World Bank's role in the electric power sector: policies for effective institutional, regulatory, and financial reform. Washington DC: The World Bank Group.

Chapter 2 - References:

11 Eskom Library. (2023). Eskom History. Retrieved from Eskom Heritage: https://www.eskom.co.za/heritage/

12 IOL. (15 December 2001). Eskom scoops top global award. Independent Online.

13 Eskom. (2001). Annual Report.

14 Department of Energy. (2011, August 31). Fact Sheet for the Media Briefing Session on the Renewable Energy.

15 Engineering News. (2015, October 20). Molefe: Eskom budget can't support new IPPs. Creamer Media.

16 Slater, D. (27 March 2020). Mantashe sustains 1 MW licence-exemption cap despite calls for higher threshold. Engineering News. Creamer News Media.

17 Maree, A. (15 June 2021). South Africa: Ramaphosa overrules Mantashe, allows private firms to generate power. The Africa Report

Chapter 3 - References:

18 Smith, V. L. (1996). "Regulatory Reform in the Electric Power Industry." Cato Review of Business & Government 19(1).

19 Estache, A. and M. Rodriguez-Pardina (1998). Light and Lightning at the End of the Public Tunnel: The Reform of the Electricity Sector in the Southern Cone. Washington D.C., The World Bank.

20 US DOE (1990). Implementing PURPA: Renewable Resource Development in the Pacific Northwest. United States Department of Energy.

21 Hirsh, R. F. (1999). "PURPA: The Spur to Competition and Utility Restructuring." The Electricity Journal 12(7): 60-72.

22 Hunt, S. (2002). Making Competition Work in Electricity. New York, Wiley Finance.

23 Joskow, P. L. (1998). Restructuring, Competition and Regulatory Reform in the US Electricity Sector. Designing Competitive Electricity Markets. H.-P. Chao and H. G. Huntington, Springer Publishing.

24 Sotkiewicz, P. (2007). Review of Selected International Experience in Electricity Reform. Frontiers in Managing Reform & Regulation of Infrastructure Utilities in Africa, Cape Town, South Africa, UCT Graduate School of Business.

25 Raineri, R. (2006). Chile: Where it all started. Electricity Market Reform: An International Perspective, Elsevier Publishing.

26 CEE (2002). Results of Electricity Sector Restructuring in Chile. New Era in Oil Gas and Power Value Creation. Center for Energy Economics, Bureau of Economic Geology, Jackson School of Geosciences, The University of Texas at Austin.

27 Fischer, R. and A. Galetovic (2000). "Regulatory Governance and Chile's 1998-1999 Electricity Shortage." World Bank Institute.

28 Pollitt, M. (2005). "Electricity Reform in Chile: Lessons for Developing Countries." Department of Applied Economics, Cambridge University and the Development Research Group, The World Bank.

29 Newberry, D. M., Ed. (2006). Electricity Liberalization in Britain and the Evolution of Market Design. Electricity Market Reform: An International Perspective, Elsevier Publishing.

30 Sioshansi, F. P. and W. Pfaffenberger (2006). Electricity Market Reform: An International Perspective, Elsevier Publishing.

31 Bacon (1995). "Lessons from Power Sector Reform in England and Wales." Public Policy for the Private Sector, The World Bank Note No.61.

32 Hjalmarsson, E. (2000). "Nord Pool: A Power Market without Market Power." Department of Economics, Göteborg University Working Paper in Economics No. 28.

33 Fehr, N.-H. M. v. d., E. S. Amundsen, et al. (2004). "The Nordic Market: Signs of Stress?" European Regulation Forum on Electricity Reforms.

34 Sweeney, J. L. (2006). California Electricity Restructuring, The Crisis and its Aftermath. Electricity Market Reform: An International Perspective. F. P. Sioshansi and W. Pfaffenberger, Elsevier Publishing.

35 World Bank (1993). The World Bank's Role in the Electric Power Sector: Policies for Effective Institutional, Regulatory, and Financial Reform. Washington D.C.

36 Hunt, S., Graham, et al. (1996). Competition and Choice in Electricity, Wiley Publishers.

37 Gros, J.-G. and O. Prokopovych (2005). When Reality Contradicts Rhetoric: World Bank Lending Practices in Developing Countries in Historical, Theoretical and Empirical Perspectives. CODESRIA Monograph Series. Senegal, Council for the Development of Social Science Research in Africa.

38 World Bank (2008b). Public Sector Reform: What Works and Why? An IEG Evaluation of World Bank Support. Washington, D.C., International Bank for Reconstruction and Development.

39 Gratwick, K. and A. Eberhard (2008). "Death of the Standard Model." MIR.

40 40 Besant-Jones, J. E. (2004). "Lessons from Experience of Power Sector Reform." ADB-JBIC-World Bank.

41 Heller, T. C. and D. G. Victor (2004). A Political Economy of Electric Power Market Restructuring: Introduction to Issues and Expectations. Programme on Energy and Sustainable Development, Stanford University.

42 Heller, T. C., H. I. Tjiong, et al. (2003). "Electricity Restructuring and the Social Contract." Program on Energy and Sustainable Development Working Paper #15.

43 Gökgür, N. and L. Jones (2006). Privatisation of Senegal Electricity. Assessing the Impact of Privatization in Africa, Norwegian Trust Fund and The World Bank.

44 Stern, J. and J. Cubbin (2005). "Regulatory Effectiveness: The Impact of Regulation and Regulatory Governance Arrangements on Electricity Industry Outcomes." World Bank Policy Research Working Paper 3536.

45 Pollitt, M. (2004). "Electricity Reform in Argentina Lessons for Developing Countries." Department of Applied Economics, Cambridge University and the Development Research Group, The World Bank.

46 Woolf, F. and J. Halpern (2001). "Integrating Independent Power Producers into Emerging Wholesale Power Markets." The World Bank Group.

47 Lovei, L. (2000). "The Single-Buyer Model: A Dangerous Path toward Competitive Electricity Markets." The World Bank Group, Private Sector and Infrastructure Network Note 225.

48 Arizu, B., D. Gencer, et al. (2006). "Centralized Purchasing Arrangements: International Practices and Lessons Learned on Variations to the Single Buyer Model." Energy and Mining Sector Board Discussion Paper, The World Bank Group(16).

Chapter 4 - References:

49 Stull et al. (2016). Environmental apartheid: Eco-health and rural marginalization in South Africa. Journal of Rural Studies, 369-380.

50 Leonard, L. (2018). Mining Corporations, Democratic Meddling, and Environmental Justice in South Africa. Social Sciences.

51 Filatova, I. (2012). The Lasting Legacy: The Soviet Theory of the National-Democratic Revolution and South Africa. South African Historical Journal, 64:3, 507-537.

52 Department of Minerals and Energy. (1998). White Paper on the Energy Policy of the Republic of South Africa. Pretoria: Department of Minerals and Energy.

Chapter 5 - References

53 Rivett-Carnac, K. (2022). Insights into the Solar Photovoltaic Manufacturing Value Chain in South Africa. WWF Trade and Industry Policy Strategies.

54 MyBroadband. (2022, August 24). How the government crushed a great renewable energy company. South Africa.

55 Creamer Media. (2023, November). Ramokgopa seeks to unlock private finance for 6 000 km of new grid in coming three years. Engineering News.

56 Eskom Press Release. (2022, October 14). Eskom signs land lease agreements with independent clean power generators. Eskom Media Desk.

57 2023 Budget Review. (2023). Government Debt and Contingent Liabilities. National Treasury.

58 Engineering News. (2022, May 26). South Africa needs $250bn to transition away from coal.

59 Parliamentary Monitoring Group. (2023, May 31). Auditor-general raises red flag on local government audit outcomes.

60 OFM. (2023, May 16). Free State municipality finally signed agreement with Eskom.

61 Moneyweb. (2022, June 15). Let Eskom take over, fed-up Nelson Mandela Bay chamber asks Nersa.

62 Maliba, A. (2022, June 22). Less than half of clients in Soweto pay for electricity. Sowetan Live.

63 Mail & Gaurdian. (2023, August 20). R63 billion municipal debt places Eskom at risk, says minister. M&G.

64 Tracy Ledger and Mahlatse Rampedi. (n.d.). Hungry for Electricity. Public Affairs Research Institute.

65 Daily Investor. (2023, June 24). Eskom lost R22 billion from illegal connections.

Chapter 6 - References:

66 Smith, S. (2017). Just Transition - A Report for the OECD. Just Transition Centre.

67 Mathew Henry, M. B. (2022). Just transitions: Histories and futures in a post-COVID world. Energy Res Soc Sci. 2020 Oct; 68: 101668.

68 Heffron, R. (2022). Applying energy justice into the energy transition. Renewable and Sustainable Energy Reviews, Volume 156.

69 Naidu, R. (2023). South Africa puts labor market at the centre of a Just Energy Transition. Development Aid.

70 Tshitereke, S. L. (2023, March 6). Will coal's demise be the making of SA's Rust Belt? Business Day.

71 Sguazzin, A. (2023, September). South Africa's coal heartland is ill-prepared for the energy transition - Mpumalanga has received no government funding to help communities find alternative livelihoods, a new study shows. Tech Central.

72 International Centre for Transitional Justice. (2022, March 10). South Africa Most Unequal Country in the World: Report.

73 Statistics South Africa. (2022). Quarterly Labour Force Survey.

74 Groenewald, Y. (2022). Komati shutdown: Future bleak for communities as people lose jobs, money - The community is beginning to understand that coal must end, but it is jobs that are top of mind. The Citizen.

75 The Star. (2022, August 4). Stop using Gordhan's name over jobs, says community.

Chapter 7 - References:

76 Appiah-Kubi, K. (2001). "State-Owned Enterprises and Privatisation in Ghana." The Journal of Modern African Studies 39(2): 197-229.

77 Haile-Mariam, Y. and B. Mengistu (1988). "Public Enterprises and the Privatisation Thesis in the Third World." Third World Quarterly 10(4): 1565-1587.

78 Akinsanya, A. (1981). "Host Governments' Responses to Foreign Economic Control: The Experiences of Selected African Countries." The International and Comparative Law Quarterly 30(4): 769-790.

79 Root, H. L. (2001). "Do Strong Governments Produce Strong Economies?" The Independent Review 5(4).

80 Ayoub-Geday, P. (2006). State Owned Enterprises. Cairo, American University in Cairo.

81 Blunt, M. E. (1970). "State Enterprise in Nigeria and Ghana: The End of an Era?" African Affairs 69(274): 27-43.

82 Ayub, M. A. and S. O. Hegstad (1987). "Management of Public Industrial Enterprises." The World Bank Research Observer 2(1): 79-101.

83 Ramamurti, R. (1987). "Performance Evaluation of State-Owned Enterprises in Theory and Practice." Management Science, 33(7): 876-893.

84 Zif, J. (1981). "Managerial Strategic Behavior in State-Owned Enterprises -- Business and Political Orientations." Management Science 27(11): 1326-1339.

85 Vernon, R. and R. J. Barnet (1974). "Does Society Also Profit?" Foreign Policy,(13): 103-122.

86 World Bank (1990). Review of Electricity Tariffs in Developing Countries in the 1980s. Industry and Energy Department Working Paper, Energy Series Paper No. 32. Washington D.C.

87 Nellis, J. (2005). "The Evolution of Enterprise Reform in Africa: From State-owned Enterprises to Private Participation in Infrastructure - and Back?" The Centre for Global Development FEEM Working Paper No. 117.05.

88 Gros, J.-G. and O. Prokopovych (2005). When Reality Contradicts Rhetoric: World Bank Lending Practices in Developing Countries in Historical, Theoretical and Empirical Perspectives. CODESRIA Monograph Series. Senegal, Council for the Development of Social Science Research in Africa.

89 Welch, C. and J. Oringer (1998). "Structural Adjustment Programs." Foreign Policy, 3(3).

90 Anastassopoulos, J.-P. (1985). "State-Owned Enterprises between Autonomy and Dependency." Journal of Public Policy 5(4): 521-539.

91 Kikeri, S., J. R. Nellis, et al. (1992). Privatization: The Lessons of Experience. Washington DC, The World Bank.

92 Tangri, R. (1991). "The Politics of State Divestiture in Ghana." African Affairs 90(361): 523-536.

93 Shirley, M. M. and L. C. Xu (1997). "Information, Incentives, and Commitment: An Empirical Analysis of Contracts between Government and State Enterprises."

Policy Research Working Paper 1769, The World Bank, Policy Research Department, Finance and Private Sector Development Division.

94 World Bank (1996). From Plan to Market, Oxford University Press.

95 Yergin, D. and J. Stanislaw (1998). The Commanding Heights: The Battle for the World Economy. New York, Simon and Schuster.

96 World Bank (1995a). Bureaucrats in Business: The Economics and Politics of Government Ownership. New York, Oxford University Press.

97 Kikeri, S., J. R. Nellis, et al. (1992). Privatization: The Lessons of Experience. Washington DC, The World Bank.

98 Malgas, I. and Gratwick, K (2008). Through the Fire: Independent Power Projects and Power Sector Reform in Cote d'Ivoire. Management Programme in Infrastructure Reform and Regulation. MIR Working Paper. University of Cape Town, Graduate School of Business.

99 Hall, D. (2007). "Energy Privatisation and Reform in East Africa." Public Services International Research Unit.

100 Ghanadan, R. and A. Eberhard (2007). "Electricity Utility Management Contracts in Africa: Lessons and Experience from the TANESCO-NETGroup Solutions Management Contract in Tanzania, 2002-2006." MIR Working Paper, Graduate School of Business, University of Cape Town.

101 Appiah-Kubi, K. (2001). "State-Owned Enterprises and Privatisation in Ghana." The Journal of Modern African Studies 39(2): 197-229.

102 UNECA (2002). "Cameroon Energy Report." United Nations Economic Commission for Africa.

103 Mangwengwende, S. E. (2002). "Tariffs and Subsidies in Zimbabwe's Reforming Electricity Industry: Steering a Utility through Turbulent Times." Energy Policy 30(11-12).

104 AEI (2002). ONE Fails in SOMELEC Grab. Africa Energy Intelligence.

105 Fall, A. (2004). Energy Reform in Sub-Saharan Africa, Global Energy.

106 Gökgür, N. and L. Jones (2006). Privatisation of Senegal Electricity. Assessing the Impact of Privatization in Africa, Norwegian Trust Fund and The World Bank.

107 Nellis, J. (2005). "The Evolution of Enterprise Reform in Africa: From State-owned Enterprises to Private Participation in Infrastructure - and Back?" The Centre for Global Development FEEM Working Paper No. 117.05.

108 Akinsanya, A. (1981). "Host Governments' Responses to Foreign Economic Control: The Experiences of Selected African Countries." The International and Comparative Law Quarterly 30(4): 769-790.

109 Malgas. I. (2008). Energy Stalemate: Independent Power Projects and Power Sector Reform in Ghana. Management Programme in Infrastructure Reform and Regulation. MIR Working Paper. University of Cape Town, Graduate School of Business.

110 Shirley, M. M. (1999). "Bureaucrats in Business: The Roles of Privatization versus Corporatization in State-owned Enterprise Reform." World Development Journal 27(1).

111 Seidman, H. (1954). "The Government Corporation: Organization and Controls." Public Administration Review 14(3): 183-192.

112 Gómez-Ibáñez, J. A. (2007). "Alternatives to Infrastructure Privatization Revisited: Public Enterprise Reform from the 1960s to the 1980s." The World Bank Sustainable Development Network (Policy Research Working Paper 4391).

113 Irwin, T. and C. Yamamoto (2004). "Some Options for Improving the Governance of State-Owned Electricity Utilities." The Energy and Mining Sector Board, The World Bank Group (Discussion Paper No. 11).

114 Vagliasindi (2008). "Governance Arrangements for State Owned Enterprises." The World Bank, Sustainable Development Network(WPS 4542).

115 Victor, D. G. and T. C. Heller (2006). The Political Economy of Power Sector Reform, Cambridge University Press.

116 Williamson, O. E. (2000). "The New Institutional Economics: Taking Stock, Looking Ahead." Journal of Economic Literature 38: 595-613.

117 Estache, A. and D. Martimort (1999). Politics, Transaction Costs, and the Design of Regulatory Institutions. Policy Research Working Paper No. 2073. Washington D.C., The World Bank.

Chapter 8 - References:

118 African National Congress. (2007, December 20). Adopted Strategy and Tactics of the ANC. 52nd National General Council.

119 ANC (2012). Economic Transformation - Policy Discussion Paper on State Owned Entities and Development Finance Institutions. African National Congress.

120 African National Congress. (2002, April 6). Consolidated Report of Commission Discussions on the NDR - Balance of Forces and Building the Alliance. Tripartite Alliance Summit.

121 NGC Discussion Documents. (2015). Reflections on the Balance of Forces: Is the National Democratic Revolution in Danger. African National Congress.

122 Tsholo, K. (2021). Do Transitions from Liberation Movements to Political Parties Guarantee Good Governance? The Case of ZANU-PF and the ANC. Strategic Review for Southern Africa, Vol 43, No 2.

123 Ukwandu, D. C. (2019). South Africa as a Developmental State - Is it a Viable Idea? African Journal of Public Affairs, Volume 11 number 2.

124 Jacobs, S. (2023, November 1). Transnet owes Eskom R503 million – with no plan to pay it back. Daily Investor.

125 Ballim, F. (2022). Eskom and the Electricity Act 42 of 1922. South African Historical Journal. Volume 4, 680-682.

126 Capazoria, B. (2017, October 18). Gigaba's man set up 'coal' meeting with Guptas, says Brian Dames. Times Live.

127 Government Communications. (2013, February 20). Minister Gigaba intervenes to end industrial action at Medupi power station. South African Government Media Statement.

128 Parliamentary Monitoring Group. (2013, September 11). Medupi Power Station issues: Updates by Eskom and the Department of Public Enterprises. National Council of Provinces.

129 News24. (2013, July 26). Name and shame Medupi culprit - DA.

130 Sehloho, M. (2028, November 13). Explosive testimony by Hogan at Zondo Commission. 702 Media.

131 Sunday Times. (2019). 27 top black execs did not want Eskom CEO job. Times.

132 Swanepoel, C. F. (2021). The slippery slope to State capture: cadre deployment as an enabler of corruption and a contributor to blurred party-State lines. Journal of Law, Democracy and Development, ISSN 2077-4907.

133 The Conversation. (2023, February 7). South Africa's ruling party has favoured loyalty over competence - now cadre deployment has come back to bite it.

134 Southall, R. (June 2008). The ANC for Sale? Money, Morality and Business in South Africa. Review of African Political Economy, Vol. 35, No. 116

135 Hogg, A. (2016, August 31). Curious case of Eskom's Mark vd Riet, suspended after blowing whistle on Gupta coal. BizNews.

136 Nyathi, M (2022, September 28). NUM clashes with Eskom over Koeberg. Mail & Guardian.

137 Public Service Commission. (June 2011). Report on Management of Precautionary Suspension in the Public Service. ISBN: 978-0-621-40303-9.

138 van Staden, M. (2023, April 10). Prolonged public service precautionary suspensions are getting out of hand. Daily Maverick.

139 Business Day. (12 June 2018). Unions to picket at Eskom offices over salary freeze.

140 Nicolaides, G. (30 July 2018). Eskom: Coal Truck Hijacked, Employees Intimidated at some Power Stations. EWN.

141 Lechman, A. (14 June 2022). Eskom offers up to 5.3% wage increase - way below workers' demands. Independent Online.

142 Eskom Media Statement. (24 June 2022). Labour protests causing operational disturbances bring more loadshedding risk. Eskom Media Desk.

143 Engineering News. (2022, June 28). Gordhan says Eskom, unions reach wage agreement; hopes second day of Stage 6 load-shedding can be avoided. Creamer Media.

144 Paton, C. (2021, November 4). Eskom falling short of cash for maintenance. Business Day.

145 Nchabeleng, A. (2023, September 13). Lack of maintenance budget at Eskom calls its leadership into question. Independent Online.

146 Reuters. (2020, January 15). South Africa's Eskom in court over tariff dispute.

147 National Business Initiative. (2021). Just Transition and Climate Pathways Study for South Africa.

148 Nzimakwe, T. I. (2023). Procurement in State-Owned Enterprises and its Implications on Service Delivery in South Africa. African Journal of Public Affairs, Volume 14, No. 1.

149 Jacobs, S. (2023, July 7). Eskom corruption and fraud worse than stated - Middlemen cause 3 stages of load-shedding. Daily Investor

150 Politics Web. (2021, May 17). Preferential procurement case gets even bigger – Sakeliga.

151 Comrie, S. (2022). The collapse of old king coal. amaBhungane, Centre for Investigative Journalism.

152 MacKay, D. (2016). Coal supply bids for Eskom's Arnot fail to hit the spot. Mining Mx

153 Business Tech. (2022, August 14). Spike in 'coal mafia' activity targeting Eskom: report.

154 Burkhardt, P. (2023). Thieves Threaten World Bank's South African Coal Rail Project. BizNews.

155 Kessides, I. N. (2020). The Decline and Fall of Eskom - A South African Tragedy. Report 45, The Global Warming Policy Foundation.

156 Creamer Media. (2023). Nine people arrested at the Kusile power station for theft of coal, fraud. Engineering News.

157 My Broadband. (2022). Syndicates stole 65 truckloads of Eskom coal in a day — Report. The Sunday Times.

158 Eskom. (2022). Eskom confirms sabotage incidents at Tutuka Power Station. Media Desk.

159 Illidge, M. (2022, April 20). How to steal a billion from Eskom – and leave SA in darkness. Biz News.

160 Smith, T. (2021, November 19). Eskom says downed electricity pylon is evidence of sabotage. ESI Africa.

161 Eskom Media Desk. (2023, June 23). Two Eskom contracted security guards and taxi driver arrested in possession of cable at an Eskom warehouse.

162 Reuters. (2022). Eskom's outgoing CEO says lack of political support made position 'untenable'. Thomsom Reuters.

163 Smit, S. (2022, December 18). Army deployed to Eskom power plants amid security threats. Mail & Guardian.

164 News24. (2022, December 30). DMRE rejects Eskom's bid for diesel licence.

165 Parliamentary Monitoring Group. (2018, August 28). Eskom update on governance challenges; coal power stations; key performance targets, with Minister.

166 World Bank. (2016). Financial Viability of Electricity Sectors in Sub-Saharan Africa: Quasi-Fiscal Deficits and Hidden Costs. Washington DC: The World Bank Group.

167 Minaar, U. (2020). Policy implications of the World Bank utility staffing analysis in South Africa. Utilities Policy Elsevier

168 Eskom Media Desk. (2021, August 9). First Update: Medupi Unit 4 generator failure.

169 Jacobs, S. (2023, March 16). Medupi unit 4 explosion repair update. Daily Investor.

170 Eskom Media Desk. (2021, September 11). Kendal Unit 1 generator transformer incident.

171 Polity. (2021, March 31). SA: Statement by Eskom, South African electricity public utility, on incident at Duvha Power Station.

172 Business Day. GE accuses Eskom of rigging tender – Claims contract favoured Chinese company; Politically connected Trillian supported bid.

173 Donnelley, L. (2011, March 18). Power plant blast threatens supply. Mail & Guardian.

174 Zwane, T. (2014, November 3). Eskom: Majuba coal silo collapse has 'significant consequences'. Mail & Guardian.

175 Head, T. (2021, October 26). 'Horrifying': Eskom fears for Koeberg, as skilled workers ditch nuclear plant. The South African.

176 Planting, S. (2022, July 11). Koeberg's skills exodus puts extension-of-life project further on the back foot. Daily Maverick.

177 Ntoyanto, S. (2016). Factors Causing Delay of Modification Projects at Koeberg. Department of Construction Economics and Management, Research Report, Master's Thesis

178 Payton, B. (2023, August 17). Nuclear 'fiasco' threatens to worsen South Africa's load-shedding - Overrunning maintenance work at the continent's only nuclear power station casts doubt on plans to expand nuclear electricity generation. African Business.

179 Illidge, M. (2022, October 3). Sabotage and spying bring Eskom to its knees and leaves South Africa in darkness. BizNews.

180 Creamer, T. (2022, October 19). Gas air heater fire could delay commercial operation at Kusile Unit 5 by up to a year. Mining Weekly, Creamer Media.

181 My Broadband. (2023, February 27). Eskom managers overruling engineers caused catastrophic Kusile chimney collapse.

Chapter 9 - References:

182 Ncana, N. (2023, August 27). Eskom accused of targeting whistleblowers who exposed their R500 million security contract. City Press.

183 Corruption Watch. (2020, April 17). CW Responds to Eskom's Statement on the COO.

184 Marrian, N. (2023, March 2). Milking the Eskom cow - The white-anting of Eskom isn't just a high-level problem. Unions estimate that 70%-80% of Eskom staff are corrupt — including their own members. The government, however, seems to have turned a blind eye. Financial Mail.

185 Moola, N. (2019, May 30). Why Eskom CEO Phakamani Hadebe resigned. Daily Maverick.

186 Leshoro, D. (2023, May 17). Eskom was 'not only a feeding trough for the ANC', but private companies as well - Gordhan. City Press.

187 Bloom, K. (2023, February 27). Introducing the four crime cartels that have brought Eskom and South Africa to their knees. Daily Maverick.

188 Nkanjeni, U. (24 March 2023). Ramokgopa on a mission to 'sanitise ANC corruption' at Eskom. TimesLive.

189 SA Labour News. (28 March 2023). NUM says Ramokgopa wrong to blame technical issues and not corruption. SA Labour News.

190 Eskom Media Desk. (2023, April 3). Eskom welcomes National Treasury's exemption on the annual reporting of irregular, fruitless and wasteful expenses, and assures South Africans of its commitment to complying with applicable legislation.

191 Vidojevic, I. C. (2020). Overcoming the Challenges of Governance - A New Way of Monitoring and Predicting Organisational Capacity. Government and Public Policy: GAPP Working Paper, Vol. 1, No. 3.

192 Tshisikhawe, F. L. (2019). The extent to which performance management system drives employee productivity at Eskom. North-West University, MBA Mini-thesis.

193 Energy News. (2019, November 19). Mixed reaction to Eskom's new CEO. Energy New South Africa.

194 Mahlaka, R. (2022, September 29). Reuel Khoza: Appoint bold people to Eskom board who'll resist government interference. Daily Maverick.

195 Engineering News. (2022, July 20). Gordhan sends SOS to trade union Solidarity, accepts offer to help Eskom with critical skills.

196 eNCA. (2023, January 27). Unions Reveal Culture of Fear at Eskom: Eskom managers do not listen to low-level workers, according to the National Union of Mineworkers. The union says this is contributing to the energy crisis.

197 Vermeulen, J. (2022, October 2). Truth about spying device found in Eskom CEO André de Ruyter's car. MyBroadband.

198 Department of Labour. (2010, January 20). Cancellation of Registration of a Trade Union: Eskom Employees Association (LR2/6/2176). Government Gazette, Notice 74 of 2010.

199 Ncana, N. (2023, December 3). Eskom 'hitman' allegedly offered R400 000 to kill former employee arrested after deadly heist. City Press.

200 Ramothwala, P. (2017, June 17). Murdered Eskom employee Thembisile Yende 'knew too much'. Times Live.

201 Lekabe, T. (2023, January 24). Tutuka plant manager continues to wear bulletproof vest, family protected by bodyguards – De Ruyter. The Citizen.

202 SA News. (2023, March 29). Eskom condemns employee abduction. South African Government News Agency.

203 Tech Central. (2023, January 7). Eskom CEO De Ruyter poisoned with cyanide: report.

204 South African Labour News. (2019, May 27). Eskom CEO Phakamani Hadebe twice 'collapsed' at work due to toll of the job.

205 Erasmus, D. (2023, June 7). Fearing his safety, top cop skips parliament hearing on Eskom graft. Mail & Guardian.

206 Corruption Watch. (2023, November 16). Eskom Functioning in a "Swamp of Organised Crime" - Retired Brigadier.

Chapter 10 - References:

207 Loayza, N. V. and R. Soto (2003). On the Measurement of Market-Oriented Reforms. Washington D.C., The World Bank.

208 Dollar, D., M. Hallward-Driemeier, et al. (2004). Investment Climate and International Integration. Policy Research Working Paper 3323. Washington D.C., The World Bank.

209 Jacobson, C. D. and J. A. Tarr (1995). Ownership and Financing of Infrastructure. Policy Research Working Paper 1466. Washington D.C., The World Bank.

210 PWC (2005). Under Pressure: Utilities Global Survey 2005, Price Waterhouse Coopers.

211 Tenenbaum, B. and A. K. Izaguirre (2007). Private Participation in Electricity: The Challenge of Achieving Commercial Viability and Improving Services. Gridlines, Public-Private Infrastructure Advisory Facility, The World Bank. Note 21.

212 Rigby, P. (2004). "Energy Merchant Debt Prospects: When —Worst-Case‖ Scenarios Become the —Base Case‖." The Electricity Journal 17(1): 37-50.

213 Vernon, R. (1971). Sovereignty at Bay: The Multinational Spread of U.S. Enterprises. New York, Basic Books.

214 Woodhouse, E. J. (2005). A Political Economy of International Infrastructure Contracting: Lessons from the IPP Experience. Working Paper #52, Program on Energy and Sustainable Development. Stanford, California, Center for Environmental Science and Policy, Stanford University.

215 Lamb, P. M. (2006). The Indian Electricity Market: Country Study and Investment Context. Working Paper # 48, Program on Energy and Sustainable Development. Stanford, California, Center for Environmental Science and Policy, Stanford University.

216 Irwin, T. C. (2007). Government Guarantees: Allocating and Valuing Risk in Privately Financed Infrastructure Projects. Washington, DC, The World Bank.

217 Ketkar, S. and D. Ratha (2001). Development Financing during a Crisis: Securitization of Future Receivables. Economic Policy and Prospects Group Working Paper Series 2582. Washington, D.C., The World Bank.

218 Gray, P. and T. Irwin (2003). Exchange Rate Risk: Allocating Exchange Rate Risk in Private Infrastructure Projects. Public Policy Journal for the Private Sector, The World Bank Group. Note 266.

219 Rector, J. (2005). The IPP Investment Experience in Malaysia. Working Paper #46, Program on Energy and Sustainable Development. Stanford, California, Center for Environmental Science and Policy, Stanford University.

220 Gray, P. and T. Irwin (2003). Exchange Rate Risk: Allocating Exchange Rate Risk in Private Infrastructure Projects. Public Policy Journal for the Private Sector, The World Bank Group. Note 266.

221 Woodhouse, E. J. (2005). The IPP Experience in the Philippines. Working Paper #37, Program on Energy and Sustainable Development. Stanford, California, Center for Environmental Science and Policy, Stanford University.

222 Eberhard, A. and K. Gratwick (2007). "From State to Market and back Again: Egypt's Experiment with Independent Power Projects." Journal of Energy 32(5): 724-738.

223 Jamison, M. A. and L. Holt (2005). "Measuring and Mitigating Regulatory Risk in Private Infrastructure Investment." The Electricity Journal 18(6): 36-45.

224 Lamech, R. and K. Saeed (2003). What International Investors Look for When Investing in Developing Countries: Results from a Survey of International Investors in the Power Sector, The Energy and Mining Sector Board, The World Bank.

225 Alexander, I. and A. Estache (1999). Infrastructure Restructuring and Regulation: Building a Base for Sustainable Growth. Growth and Investment in South Africa, Cape Town, South Africa, The World Bank.

226 Mwenechanya, J. M. (2005). Regulation of State-Owned Utilities. Frontiers in Managing Reform and Regulation of the Electricity Sector, Cape Town, South Africa, Graduate School of Business, University of Cape Town.

227 Gupta, P., R. Lamech, et al. (2002). Mitigating Regulatory Risk for Distribution Privatization – The World Bank Partial Risk Guarantee. Washington D.C., The Energy and Mining Sector Board, The World Bank.

228 Lovei, L. (2000). "The Single-Buyer Model: A Dangerous Path toward Competitive Electricity Markets." The World Bank Group, Private Sector and Infrastructure Network Note 225.

229 Woolf, F. and J. Halpern (2001). "Integrating Independent Power Producers into Emerging Wholesale Power Markets." The World Bank Group.

230 Harris, C., J. Hodges, et al. (2003). "Infrastructure Projects: A Review of Canceled Private Projects." The World Bank Group, Private Sector and Infrastructure Network Note No.252.

231 Dailami, M., I. Lipkovich, et al. (1999). INFRISK: A Computer Simulation Approach to Risk Management in Infrastructure Project Finance Transactions. Washington D.C., Regulatory Reform and Private Enterprise Division, Economic Development Institute of the World Bank.

232 Auffret, P. (2003). Catastrophe Insurance Market in the Caribbean Region: Market Failures and Recommendations for Public Sector Interventions. World Bank Policy Research Working Paper 2963. Washington D.C., The World Bank.

233 Sader, F. (2000). Attracting Foreign Direct Investment into Infrastructure: Why is it So Difficult? Washington, D.C., The World Bank Group.

234 Dailami, M. and R. Hauswald (2001). Contract Risks and Credit Spread Determinants in the International Project Bond Market. Policy Research Working Paper Series, No.2712. Washington D.C., The World Bank.

235 Bettignies, J.-E. d. and T. W. Ross (2004). "The Economics of Public-Private Partnerships." Canadian Public Policy Journal 30(2): 135-154.

236 Dailami, M. and M. Klein (1997). Government Support to Private Infrastructure Projects in Emerging Markets. Managing Government Exposure to Private Infrastructure Projects: Averting a New-style Debt Crisis, Cartagena, Colombia.

237 Klingebiel, D. and J. Ruster (2000). Why Infrastructure Financing Facilities Often Fall Short of Their Objectives. Policy Research Working Paper 2358. Washington D.C., The World Bank.

238 Klein, M. (1996). Risk, Taxpayers, and the Role of Government in Project Finance. Policy Research Working Paper 1688. Washington D.C., The World Bank.

239 Victor, D. G., T. C. Heller, et al. (2004). The Experience with Independent Power Projects (IPPs) in Developing Countries: Introduction and Case Study Methods. Program on Energy and Sustainable Development, Center for Environmental Science and Policy, Stanford Institute for International Studies. Stanford, California, Stanford University. Working Paper #23.

240 Woodhouse, E. J. (2005). A Political Economy of International Infrastructure Contracting: Lessons from the IPP Experience. Working Paper #52, Program on Energy and Sustainable Development. Stanford, California, Center for Environmental Science and Policy, Stanford University.

241 Eberhard, A. and K. N. Gratwick (2007). Take 4: the Contribution and Evolution of Independent Power Projects in Kenya. Cape Town, Management Programme in Infrastructure Reform and Regulation, Graduate School of Business, University of Cape Town.

242 Malgas, I, K.N. Gratwick, et.al. (2008). Moroccan independent power producers – African pioneers. The Journal of North African Studies 13(1):15-36.

243 Eberhard, A. and K. N. Gratwick (2007). Take 4: the Contribution and Evolution of Independent Power Projects in Kenya. Cape Town, Management Programme in Infrastructure Reform and Regulation, Graduate School of Business, University of Cape Town.

244 Gratwick, K. N. and A. Eberhard (2008). "An Analysis of Independent Power Projects in Africa: Understanding Development and Investment Outcomes." Development Policy Review 26(3): 309–338.

Chapter 11 - References:

245 Department of Minerals and Energy. (1998). White Paper on the Energy Policy of the Republic of South Africa. Pretoria.

246 Department of Energy. (2011, August 31). Fact Sheet for the Media Briefing Session on the Renewable Energy.

247 Engineering News. (2015, October 20). Molefe: Eskom budget can't support new IPPs. Creamer Media.

248 Centre for Environmental Rights. (2017, July 28). City of Cape Town v The National Energy Regulator of South Africa and the Minister of Energy.

249 City of Cape Town Media Office. (2020, January 21). Mayor Plato calls on Minister Mantashe to act now so that the City can proceed with buying independently produced power in future.

250 Global Energy Monitor. (n.d.). Boikarabelo power station (Resgen).

251 Fletcher, R. C. (2016). Boikarabelo coal project. Canberra: The Australia Institute.

252 Iannucci, E. (2021, July 6). ResGen goes into administration. Mining Weekly.

253 Global Energy Monitor. (n.d.). Khanyisa power station.

254 Theron, A. (2016, October 11). Thabametsi and Khanyisa take first in SA baseload IPP. ESI Africa.

255 Centre for Environmental Rights. (2021, June 3). Final nail in the coffin for proposed Khanyisa Coal Power Station.

256 Gobal Energy Monitor. (n.d.). Thabametsi power station.

257 Friends of the Earth International. (2015, May 13). African and French civil society challenge French funding of dirty energy.

258 Reuters. (202, November 11). Marubeni to pull out of South African coal-fired power plant project.

259 Global Energy Monitor. (n.d.). Musina-Makhado power station.

260 Centre for Environmental Rights. (2021, March 19). Activists relieved as Limpopo provice slams the brakes on Musina Makhado Mega-Project.

261 Organisation Undoing Tax Abuse. (2022, April). Karpowership: Not as simple as plug-and-play.

262 Nyathi, M. (2022, August 12). Creecy shoots down Karpowership appeal but extends a lifeline to the project. Mail & Guardian.

263 Moneyweb. (2022, January 30). DNG Energy's legal challenge to stop Karpowership IPP deal dismissed.

264 Engineering News. (2022, April 26). Eskom seeks indemnity from Karpowership in power-purchase pact. Creamer Media.

265 Steyn, et. al. (2022). Resolving the Power Crisis. Meridian Economics.

266 Development Bank of Southern Africa. (n.d.). Small IPP Programme.

267 Engineering News. (2022, July 13). Small IPPs consider legal action after programme is cancelled. Creamer Media.

268 Omarjee, L. (2022, July 8). Connect the watts: Officials hustle to speed up new power projects despite grid constraints. News24.

269 Bruce, P. (2022, August 10). Bid Window 5 is in big trouble and may need some degree of rescue. Business Day.

270 Barradas, S. (2023, June 2). Renewable Energy Independent Power Producer Procurement Programme – Bid Window 6 – South Africa – update. Engineering News, Creamer Media.

271 Paton, C. (2022, July 20). SA's renewable energy programme in trouble, many projects no longer financially. News24.

272 Smith, T. (2022, July 29). South Africa: refinancing REIPPPP projects for better electricity pricing. ESI Africa.

273 Choudhury, M. K. et. al. (2021, November 2). Can Banks Sustain the Growth in Renewable Energy Supply? An International Evidence. The European Journal of Development Research, Volume 35, pages 20–50.

274 Enerdata. (2022, December). South Africa's BW6 renewable tender shortlists only 5 solar projects (860 MW).

275 Creamer, T. (2023, June 27). Eskom's 'onerous' new grid access rules receive cool reception. Engineering News.

276 Slabbert, A. (2023, September 10). Eskom relaxes the rules for IPPs. City Press.

277 Vermeulen, J. (2023, April 2). Eskom fights to block town from using its own solar power. MyBroadband.

278 NERSA. (2022, April 6). Public hearing – Application by Greenstone Energy Ltd to distribute electricity to an area within Linbro Park from its exempted generator.

279 Business Tech. (2023, April 21). Eskom blocks private producer from cutting load shedding.

280 Laurence, S. (2023, April 21). 'A huge mess': Eskom court victory a setback for private power. Tech Central.

Chapter 12 – References:

281 Malgas, I., Eberhard, A. (2011). Hybrid power markets in Africa: Generation planning, procurement and contracting challenges. Energy Policy. Volume 39, Issue 6: 3191-3198.

282 Kagiannas, A. G., D. T. Askounis, et al. (2004). "Power Generation Planning: A Survey from Monopoly to Competition." International Journal of Electrical Power and Energy Systems 26(6): 413-421.

283 Awerbuch, S. (2006). "Portfolio-Based Electricity Generation Planning: Policy Implications for Renewables and Energy Security." Mitigation and Adaptation Strategies for Global Change 11(3): 693-710.

284 Harris, D. J. and B. C. L. Davies (1980). "Resource Allocation in the Nationalized Energy Sector of the United Kingdom." Journal of Managerial and Decision Economics 1(1): 28-36.

285 Anderson, D. (1972). "Models for Determining Least-Cost Investments in Electricity Supply." The Bell Journal of Economics and Management Science 3(1): 267-299.

286 De Oliveira, A. and J. Girod (1990). "Energy Diagnosis: Toward a Policy-Oriented Approach for Energy Planning in Developing Countries." World Development Journal 18(4): 529-538.

287 Dickel, R. (2003). Experience of Power Generation Investment in Liberalised Markets: In the Middle of the Stream. Joint IEA / NEA Workshop on Power Generation Investment in Liberalised Electricity Markets, Paris, Energy Diversification Division, International Energy Agency.

288 Eberhard, A. (1992). Integrated Energy Planning: A Methodology for Policy Analysis and Research. South African Energy Policy Research and Training Project, Paper No.2. Cape Town, Energy for Development Research Centre, University of Cape Town.

289 Michelfelder, R. A. (1993). "Evolving Electric Utility Regulatory Policy: Internalizing the Social Costs of Production." American Journal of Economics and Sociology 52(2): 227-239.

290 Spalding-Fecher, R. and D. K. Matibe (2003). "Electricity and Externalities in South Africa." Energy Policy Journal 31(8): 721-734.

291 Munasinghe, M. (1990). Energy Analysis and Policy, Butterworths Publishing.

292 Reddy, A. K. N. (2005). Integrated Electricity Planning: Some Personal Reflections. Bangalore, India, International Energy Initiative.

293 D'Sa, A. (2005). "Integrated Resource Planning (IRP) and Power Sector Reform in Developing Countries." Energy Policy 33(10): 1271-1285.

294 Andrews, C. J. (1995). "Evaluating Risk Management Strategies in Resource Planning." Power Systems 10(1): 420 - 426.

295 Lamb, P. M. (2006). The Indian Electricity Market: Country Study and Investment Context. Working Paper # 48, Program on Energy and Sustainable Development. Stanford, California, Center for Environmental Science and Policy, Stanford University.

296 Hill, L. (1999). Power to the People: Integrated Resource Planning in Developing Countries, Oak Ridge National Laboratory Review, US Department of Energy.

297 Malgas, I. (2008). Energy Stalemate: Independent Power Projects and Power Sector Reform in Ghana. MIR Working Paper, Graduate School of Business, University of Cape Town.

298 Marlow, E. (2008). Independent Power Producers: Some Thoughts. Namibia's Electricity Crisis: What to Expect and What to Do? Windhoek, Namibia, HSBC.

299 Huber, P. (1987). "Electricity and the Environment: In Search of Regulatory Authority." Harvard Law Review 100(5): 1002-1065.

300 Gardner, D. T. and J. S. Rogers (1999). "Planning Electric Power Systems under Demand Uncertainty with Different Technology Lead Times." Journal of Management Science 45(10): 1289-1306.

301 Arizu, B., D. Gencer, et al. (2006). "Centralized Purchasing Arrangements: International Practices and Lessons Learned on Variations to the Single Buyer Model." Energy and Mining Sector Board Discussion Paper, The World Bank Group(16).

302 Hoekman, B. (1998). "Using International Institutions to Improve Public Procurement." The World Bank Research Observer 13(2): 249-269.

303 Momodu, A. S., K. N. Gratwick, et al. (2006). Negotiations and Renegotiations: Nigeria's Independent Power Projects. Unpublished Draft Working Paper, Management Programme for Infrastructure Reform and Regulation, University of Cape Town, Graduate School of Business.

304 Bajari, P., R. McMillan, et al. (2003). Auctions versus Negotiations in Procurement: An Empirical Analysis. Stanford, California, National Science Foundation and the Stanford Institute for Economic Policy Research.

305 Albouy, Y. and R. Bousba (1998). "The Impact of IPPs in Developing Countries—Out of the Crisis and into the Future." Public Policy for the Private Sector, The World Bank.

306 Harris, C., J. Hodges, et al. (2003). "Infrastructure Projects: A Review of Canceled Private Projects." The World Bank Group, Private Sector and Infrastructure Network Note No.252.

307 Verma, R. (2007). Swiss Challenge System for Infrastructure Projects. Mumbai, India, Project Monitor.

308 Eberhard, A. and J. Kapika (2008). Plugging the Demand-Supply Gap: Challenges in Planning, Procurement and Contracting of New Power. Fifth

RERA Annual Conference, Arusha, Tanzania, Management Programme in Infrastructure Reform and Regulation.

Chapter 13 - References:

309 Creamer, T. (2023, September 21). Grid investment 'fully funded' for next three years, but scale-up requires alternative models. Engineering News.

310 Engineering News. (2023, June 19). SA can add 30GW of wind energy in 10 years, but grid challenges will be our undoing - expert. Creamer Media.

311 Tshitereke, S. L. (2023, March 6). Will coal's demise be the making of SA's Rust Belt? The economic prognosis for families, households and towns in Mpumalanga looks bleak due to the proposed decommissioning of six power stations. Business Day.

312 Global Energy Monitor. (n.d.). Medupi power station.

313 Brock, J. (2015, September 29). South Africa's opposition wants investigation into Hitachi payments. Reuters.

314 Sguazzin, A. (2022, June 2). Funder Says Eskom's $8.7 Billion Power Plant Won't Make Money. Bloomberg.

315 Global Energy Monitor. (n.d.). Kusile power station.

316 Goeller, R. (2008). SA Power Outlook. South African Financial Markets Journal.

317 World Nuclear Association. (2023, August). Nuclear Power in South Africa. Information Library, Country Profiles.

318 South African Government Archives. (2012, March 6). Address by the Minister of Energy, Minister Dipuo Peters at the Energy Month Launch.

319 IAEA. (2013). Mission Report on the Integrated Nuclear Infrastructure Review. Vienna: International Atomic Energy Agency.

320 Department of Energy. (22 September 2014). Russia and South Africa sign agreement on Strategic Partnership in Nuclear Energy. South African Government.

321 Areff, A. (2015, December 14). How South Africa got three finance ministers in four days. News24.

322 Gosling, M. (2017, April 26). Court finds nuclear deals unconstitutional: Agreements with Russia, Korea and US have been scrapped. GroundUp.

323 Department of Energy. (n.d.). Terms of Reference for the Appointment of a Service Provider to Develop a Procurement Framework for 2 500 MW Nuclear New Build Programme, for a Period of 12 Weeks.

324 MoneyWeb. (2023, March 7). Nersa's secret U-turn on Eskom gas generation.

325 Republic of South Africa. (August 2023). Energy Action Plan: One Year Progress Report. State of the Nation.

326 Business Day. (2023, January 9). Energy red tape on the chopping block.

327 Engineering News. (2023, February 9). Eskom air pollution puts almost 80 000 lives at risk, study says. Creamer Media.

328 Collins, J. (2022, March 18). Case No: 39724/2019. High Court of South Africa, Gauteng Division, Pretoria.

329 Paton, C. (2022, May 12). Eskom's grim warning: SA must more than double its generation capacity in just 13 years. News24.

330 World Nuclear News. (2014, September 8). Contract signed for Koeberg steam generators.

331 Faull, L. (18 September 2014). Koeberg documents show odd decisions. Mail & Guardian.

332 Clark, A. (2016, January 13). The story behind Eskom's 'unlawful' Koeberg contract. News24.

Chapter 14 - References:

333 My Broadband. (2023, July 2). Geyser controllers could cut five stages of load-shedding — Report.

334 Isibor, N. (2023, October 12). Geyser Control: A Key to Reducing Load Shedding in South Africa? Eskom News.

335 Allewell, M. (2023, June 14). Smart Geysers: The Loadshedding Solution That Empowers South Africans. Engineering News, Creamer Media.

336 Cannard, J. (2019, September 3). South Africa: Cancel Eskom's odious debt to the World Bank. Committee for the Abolition of Illegitimate Debt.

337 Moolman, S. (2022). 2022 Update: Eskom tariff increases vs inflation since 1988 (with projections to 2024). Power Optimal.

Chapter 15 - References:

338 Hunt, S. (2002). Making Competition Work in Electricity. New York, Wiley Finance.

339 BBC News. (27 June 2012). TEPCO shareholders agree to nationalization. British Broadcasting Corporation

340 Jenkinson, H. (10 February 2023). France moves to fully nationalise EDF and prevent break-up. Wind Power Monthly

341 More, R. (22 December 2022). Germany completes nationalization of Uniper – ministries. Reuters

342 Shirley, M. M. (1999). "Bureaucrats in Business: The Roles of Privatization versus Corporatization in State-owned Enterprise Reform." World Development Journal 27(1).

ABOUT THE AUTHOR

Isaac Malgas is an engineering graduate and a perennial scholar of power sector reforms in developing countries. He has worked at the South African national utility, Eskom, in various roles over a period of roughly 30 years. He holds a doctoral degree from the University of Cape Town and is an astute observer of power sector reforms on the African continent.

Made in United States
Orlando, FL
04 November 2026

90204187R00275